Gaia's Feasts

Gaia's Feasts

New vegetarian recipes for family and community

Julia Ponsonby & Friends at Schumacher College

Published by
Green Books,
an imprint of UIT Cambridge Ltd
www.greenbooks.co.uk
PO Box 145, Cambridge CB4 1GQ, England
+44 (0) 1223 302 041

In association with Schumacher College
www.schumachercollege.co.uk
Schumacher College is an initiative of the Dartington Hall Trust,
a charity registered in England (no. 279756).

First published 2014

Julia Ponsonby has asserted her moral rights under the
Copyright, Designs and Patents Act 1988

Front cover photograph © Joanna Brown
Back cover photographs: left panel © Joanna Brown
Interior photographs © Joanna Brown, with the exception
of those listed on page 259

Design by Jayne Jones

ISBN: 978 0 85784 052 3 (paperback)
ISBN: 978 0 85784 054 7 (ePub)
ISBN: 978 0 85784 053 0 (pdf)
Also available for Kindle

Printed by Cambrian, Aberystwyth, Wales

Disclaimer: The advice herein is believed to be correct at the
time of printing, but the author and publisher accept no liability
for actions inspired by this book.

10 9 8 7 6 5 4 3 2 1

For Frank Cook, who inspired many people at Schumacher College, in Totnes and all over the world, with his deep love of wild food, botany and fermentation.

Acknowledgements

This second cookbook for Schumacher College has taken a decade to put together. I therefore have a range of people to thank, who have helped at various stages of the book's journey to printhood. First, I would like to thank my most recent helpers, our wonderful team of cooks: Tara, Ruth, Sarah and Voirrey, for patiently testing these recipes over and over again. Next comes a big thanks to our photographer, Joanna Brown, for her careful portrayal of our food, always 'au naturel' – never put off by gale-force winds and often with her favourite robin angling for a bite of the action!

Going back to the mid-phase of this book's journey, a large thank you goes to Fran Bennatt, a local potter who lent her beautiful dishes to cradle our food. I would also like to thank my former colleagues Wayne Schroeder and Karen Blincoe, for the precious time given to our learning community. Thanks also to Jane Oddie for offering her time and skill as a food stylist; Minni Jain for working with me on an Indian food section; Tchenka Sunderland and Leslie Glassmire for sharing their recipes and (with Karen Butterworth and Inge Page) for cooking with us; Isla Burgess for sharing her botanical wisdom; Anne Phillips for early proofreading; Amanda Cuthbert, former Commissioning Editor of Green Books, for shaping this book – and Alethea Doran and Jayne Jones for skilfully continuing this painstaking work.

There are many more people at the College to thank – Jon Rae, Satish Kumar, William Thomas and Tim Crabtree, to name but a few. At home, I would like to thank my husband Stephan Harding and son Oscar, for putting up with a cooking habit that has sometimes left them feeling like 'baking orphans'. Thank you all.

Contents

For an explanation of special-diet notations see page 20. Please note: salads which include honey as an option in the dressing are listed here as vegan, and most breads showing 'V option' are vegan breads with an optional egg glaze.

*Although these recipes are V or GF, a dairy- or gluten-based serving option is suggested, and alternatives given. **Gluten-free pastry (see page 94) can be used for these recipes.

Foreword

Good food, to me, is not food that's merely well cooked and tasty. When I use that term, I'm thinking of food that has been produced in a sustainable way, harvested in season, and that has travelled as little as possible – food that has been cooked with care and enthusiasm and served with an understanding of its importance, not as mere sustenance, but as nourishment for body and soul.

By these criteria, there can't be many better places to eat than Schumacher College. Here, an understanding of the power of food to soothe and sustain is twinned with a strongly rooted belief in the importance of growing, cooking and eating together, as a community. This book is a vivid and delicious illustration of these principles.

Flick through these pages, take in the welcoming simplicity and cheeriness of the dishes, and you will be both comforted and inspired. As with Julia's first book, *Gaia's Kitchen*, the recipes are bold and unfussy, and they have a hearty generosity – in terms of both their abundant use of fresh produce and the suggested 'community sized' quantities listed against each one. This last feature creates an image, even as you read the recipe, of shared eating, and brings home just how enriching it can be to break bread with others.

Julia has been part of Schumacher College for 24 years and has been the chef there for 15 years. Such commitment and longevity in a professional cook is a rare thing these days,

and illustrates the integrity of her work – her cooking is inextricably linked to the principles of the college itself. This lends a real sense of authenticity to Julia's books – they're rooted in a place and a philosophy. The years at Schumacher have given her, and the talented cooks who work with her, the opportunity to develop recipes organically, as the College has prospered and grown. And of course all these dishes have been enjoyed and commented upon by the students and teachers who pass through – a reassuring endorsement if ever there was one!

Julia's food is beautifully simple, and it's honest – by which I mean it uses fresh, seasonal ingredients and does as little to them as possible. I love the fact that there's a slightly retro feel to the recipes: no concessions are made here to fashion. This is pleasingly no-frills vegetarian cooking that celebrates the abundance of vegetables and fruits, pulses and grains, herbs, spices and dairy products available to us. There's a wonderful array of sweet treats and cakes here too, and a very tempting chapter on baking – certainly something to please everyone.

With its emphasis on enjoying, sharing and appreciating food in the most profound sense, this book will not only make you want to cook but it will also make you want to cook for other people. It's that open-hearted spirit – the most important thing a cook can possess – that clinches it for me.

Hugh Fearnley-Whittingstall, June 2014

Introduction

From *Gaia's Kitchen* by name to Gaia's Kitchen by nature

In 2001, Schumacher College's *Gaia's Kitchen* became the winner of the Gourmand World Cookbook 'Best Vegetarian Cookbook' Award. At first, the fact that we were even being tempted with winning such an outrageously impossible and absurdly enormous category seemed like some kind of joke – akin to one of those random letters that come through the post, or emails that land in your inbox, telling you you've been selected to win a holiday, or a million pounds . . .

We called our first cookbook *Gaia's Kitchen* in honour of the inaugural course taught at the College by Professor James Lovelock on Gaia Theory. Inspired by author William Golding, Lovelock adopted the name of the Greek Earth-mother to label the evolving 'earth system science' he had been developing with evolutionary biologist Lynn Margulis. Calling the theory after Grandma Gaia seemed to honour the life-giving nature of our Earth – though Jim Lovelock may have wished many times that he'd stuck with some-thing plainer, as this might have avoided the cynicism of many hard-line scientists, for whom the mythological name seemed (unjustifiably) to create an 'unscientific' cloud around the theory.

Neither the name *Gaia's Kitchen* nor the Gourmand Award were intended as a joke – but the reality is that they could have been! We are now operating far more as a true Earth-system kitchen than we were 15 or 20 years ago. Then, much of our food was influenced by Californian 'fusion' cooking, and mixed together many 'out-of-sync' ingredients from all around the globe, in a way that is typical of people who cook from shops rather than from gardens. Now, with our own productive garden growing up around us in the grounds of the Old Postern, tended by our own horticulture students, we embed our kitchen and our cooking habits much more successfully in the environment we live in: our little patch of the living world; earth of the planet Earth, which some call Gaia.

The publication of *Gaia's Kitchen* quickly revealed a strong demand for the scaling up of quantities that we routinely practise when creating meals for a crowd at Schumacher College. It was with this in mind that we embarked on

and flow, and confront not just seasonal but also climatic change. Feasting has moved dangerously out of the sphere of special community activity and into the realm of normal everyday life. Baked-bean tins rub shoulders in our cupboards with chocolate bars, the two competing incongruously for first place in our diets, when neither should have any foothold. The challenges ahead seem unknown – and almost unendurable. Have we lost the opportunity to synchronize our lifestyles with Grandma Gaia? Will we ever again participate in her family's great seasonal dance? And, however did it come to pass that the dance turned into a toe-crushing brawl?

In this second cookbook, then, we will start in the same way we begin many of our courses at Schumacher College: by opening a route map for an ecological journey that charts how we got where we are – and where we are heading next. This is a journey out of the frying pan and into the salad bowl . . . It is a journey of hope, taste and revitalization.

We will chart our way forward by cooking up a modus operandi for a delicious gastronomy that is by necessity seasonally driven and ecologically friendly. The portfolio of recipes that have won a place in this book is as much a celebration of global diversity as of local speciality. Rooted in the place that gave birth to them, the recipes tell of people and their stories from around the world. At both a historical and a social level, the eclectic and experimental character which is the very essence of cooking is what prevents culinary stagnation. Meanwhile, fostering a more secure link with local soils and local microclimates allows traditional local variety to be renewed as part of our culinary renaissance – with the natural limitations of organic horticulture increasingly being overcome by the use of natural preserving techniques, not aeroplanes. To use E. F. Schumacher's time-honoured phrase, we need to *think global and act local*. When it comes to menu planning, this means holding a cherished global awareness and ecologically informed compassion in mind as we grow, buy, cook and eat local produce. This way, we can welcome everyone to our feasts.

producing another cookbook. It is, we hope, a timely and practical contribution at a moment in history when people in the West are rediscovering the potential of local community as an anchor for convivial survival, as society responds to the need for a more sustainable future. Once more, then, we have included both the 'family' and the 'community' scale for each recipe – although it is true that, for many people, even cooking for six is an event in itself!

But the number of mouths catered for is not the only way in which a kitchen needs to be 'elastic': a good cook's menu planning also needs to stretch and contract with the seasons. We need to develop a good relationship with the seasons and allow them to help us, not only with delicious cooking but also with embedding ourselves in the cycles of existence on this Earth. But have we, in fact, done this?

It seems we have done the contrary. The epitomization of seasonality as a struggle through which we have to pass each year has dogged us since the time of the Ancient Greeks, who related to the changing seasons as an expression of family separation in the realm of the gods. Theirs was not the first culture to dramatize the seasons with colourful stories of love, loss and feasting – yet it has only been since our twentieth-century attempts to bypass winter, and cherry-pick from summer using advanced technologies for growing and transporting produce, that we have come unstuck. We now live lifestyles dangerously at odds with Gaia's rhythmic ebb

Prologue

Sometimes it is difficult to appreciate that it is our very love of food that has led us astray and laid us open to the detours in culinary experience offered first by sail boats, then freezer ships and now aeroplanes. At every juncture, the degree of removal from an essential state of harmony between food and nurture has increased, often disguised as a benefit. When potatoes were first introduced to England, in Elizabethan times, people were enormously suspicious, but finally they became accepted and loved. In Ireland, the potato famines of Victorian times marked over-dependence on a commodity that did not reliably thrive in the local environment (as well as highlighting the enclosure of lands by the English aristocracy!). When the first freezer ships allowed us to import foreign fruit, our desire for these overwhelmed our habit of preparing and consuming an abundant harvest of local fruit. We have lost many seasonally and locally adapted varieties of fruit and vegetables this way, as well as the knowledge and practice of preserving foods – and the joy that comes with appreciating the way a food can morph into something slightly different as the seasons progress, showing its 'dried', 'bottled' or 'frozen' face.

And then there is the face of longing – which allows us to appreciate our fresh fruit in absence through imagination and to then love it even more when it returns. Losing touch with longing is another part of the 'getting lost' experience we encounter in modern society. Ours, it seems, is a culture that talks about boundaries in terms of personal psychological theory, but delights in entertaining the possibility of their removal. This happens via the medium of an all-powerful advertising industry – the means by which our modern society is reflected back to itself. This profane, fantastic, commercial voice speaks our dreams aloud to us and legitimizes their entry into reality – whether in the form of a flight to 'paradise' abroad or a rebranded packet of potato fries.

Transition and transformation begin at home

As I write, we are entering March – the 'hungry gap' for English and indeed European apples – the last refrigerated stores of late-blossoming, good-keeping apples are being used

up, and our suppliers are reaching to America, South Africa and New Zealand for new stocks. It will be a couple of months before the soft fruit is being harvested, but we have our stores of sweet dried apples to tide us part-way over.

However, nothing in nature is 100-per-cent reliable or given – even without the effects of climate change. In any year there may be a bumper crop of one thing, while another crop succumbs to harvest failure. Often, many crops will be affected by some weather phenomenon. For example, in 2011 we began to experience the squeeze of a particularly disastrous growing season. Excessive rain had led to apple harvests being down to only a third of their abundance in previous years, while large potatoes were also proving difficult to get hold of. Suddenly it was cheaper to buy shipped-in bananas than local apples, and the consequent price increases challenged our food policy and menu planning. Bananas reappeared in the fruit bowl.

In one year, when the English bee suffered a devastating decline and honey production almost ground to a halt, my colleague Wayne Schroeder kept the College supply of honey under lock and key. If people wanted honey, he argued, they could come and ask – and in the process they would learn more about the situation and be less inclined to take this amazing bee 'super food' for granted. At the heart of our food policy at Schumacher College is a cherished goal of

working with the seasons, and buying local wherever possible, even if it means a simpler diet, or working harder with our preserves. When we reach abroad for foods, it is with awareness that purchases must be fairly traded and organic, since this helps to protect the livelihood of producers as well as the health of the produce and its growing environment.

Schumacher College is a centre for learning which aims to deepen understanding of the Earth and our relationship with it, in a very concrete and transformative way. It is a practical as well as an academic place of education, and therefore every 'learning' includes a dimension of 'learning by doing'. Right from the beginning, students have cooked, washed up and swept leaves together, alongside staff and volunteers. They have rambled over Dartmoor and explored the Devon coastline together, and done countless practical exercises involving drawing, dancing, painting and music. Now, however, this practical side has begun a much more singular journey – a departure that reflects the urgency of what is happening on our planet in terms of climate change, and the need to develop resilience in the face of uncertainty and the shadow of potential economic collapse. Not surprisingly, Schumacher College's new practical thrust has a lot to do with sustainable food production (with ecological design and building now galloping up from the rear, offering a very complementary set of skills).

WHY ORGANIC?

It's healthy. On average, organic food contains higher levels of vitamin C, essential minerals and cancer-fighting antioxidants.

Organic foods contain no nasty additives. Among the additives banned by the Soil Association (the UK's largest organic certification body) are hydrogenated fat, aspartame (an artificial sweetener) and monosodium glutamate (MSG). Genetically modified (GM) ingredients are also banned.

It's pesticide-free. Over 400 chemical pesticides are routinely used in conventional farming, and residues are often found to be present on non-organic food.

It represents better care for animals. The benefits of the organic approach are recognized by animal welfare organizations and the UK government.

It's good for wildlife and the environment. Organic farming is better for wildlife, causes less pollution from sprays, and produces less carbon dioxide (the main global warming gas) and less dangerous waste.

(*Based on a restaurant handout from the Venus Beach Company, Blackpool Sands – now with a branch at Dartington.*)

The Dartington Hall Trust has a long history of experimentation with new ideas in the arts, social justice and land use. For almost three decades, Dartington was home to a nationally acclaimed diploma in horticulture, which spanned flower gardening, vegetables and garden design – guaranteeing its graduates the status of a true craftsperson. By the 1980s this had fallen by the wayside, but Marina O'Connell Brown continued to keep the horticulture tradition alive at the Old School Farm, converting the site to organic status and supplying Schumacher College with vegetables and fruit during its infancy. Indeed, it is the 'canker resistant' apple trees that Marina planted which now provide us with our annual apple harvest, principally for juicing.

Marina's experiment with growing selected dessert apple trees in a damp locality, conducive to mildew and normally considered suitable only for cider apples, might almost be considered a precursor to the Forest Garden model so successfully pioneered by Martin Crawford (see box overleaf) – especially with its 'understorey' of blackcurrants, of which the College has also been the beneficiary. For the last 20 years Martin's forest garden has been taking shape on a site adjacent to Schumacher College, and so inspiring has its evolution been that one of our Masters students, Justin West, worked with Martin and then applied the model to the College's own grounds. This has now become the outdoor learning environment for students and apprentices who come here to study sustainable horticulture for food production. Not only that, but the transformation in the College garden represents the first sustained move towards growing our own food that has been consistently maintained since the College began. A residential gardener, Jane Gleeson, has been employed, and it is now a daily practice for students to work in the garden. This activity includes engaging in the seasonal act of harvesting, which brings new meaning to the act of cooking – even though, as yet, the amount of produce our own garden supplies is relatively small. It is not the quantity that counts, but the direction – the embodiment of learning in a practical sense where previously the theoretical realm had been dominant.

With so much horticulture on the boil, it is perhaps not surprising that the next step in this direction has been to create a residential MSc in Sustainable Horticulture for Food Production. This is headed up by Jane Pickard, who teaches the course with Bethan Stagg and other visiting lecturers. This MSc joins the successful Holistic Science MSc, which started in 1998, and the MA in Economics for Transition, which had its first intake in 2011. Thus, students talking about botany and soil rub shoulders with students talking about Goethian observation, Gaia theory and steady-state economics, as they join together in washing-up and cooking groups. Though one group may spend a little more time in the garden than the other two, all three groups share teachers, and through their coexistence help to integrate the 'hand, head and heart' trinity of learning into the daily life of Schumacher College.

Still in its relative infancy, the MA in Economics for Transition was originally conceived and set up by Julie Richardson, with a critique of the economic growth economy at its heart. The faculty for this residential programme now includes Jonathan Dawson and Tim Crabtree, and continues to look at alternative economic models, many of which can be visited and experienced first-hand. The whole course has been greatly inspired and enriched by the power of the Transition movement, which was born in our own Totnes less than a decade ago. The Transition initiative is now replicated throughout the world, preparing and engaging people in the practical and psychological dimension of change, and building local resilience, as we move into a world where fossil fuels can no longer give flight to fantasy. With TTT (Transition Town Totnes) on our doorstep, Schumacher College students have been the beneficiaries of first-hand interaction with Transition groups in Totnes, and regular teaching sessions with Transition founders Rob Hopkins, Naresh Giangrande and Sophie Banks.

Looking outside the Schumacher Campus to the whole, beautiful, ancient, 800-acre Dartington Estate of which we are part, exciting developments are also afoot. When our neighbour, Ian Forbes, retires after 25 years running a dairy farm at Dartington, a new tenant committed to organic agriculture will begin to farm the land. Though we will miss Ian's consistent dedication to these pastures, not to mention his resonant serenading of the cows with bagpipes, it will be timely to move into a new phase. Perhaps, with Martin Crawford's ground-breaking work on forest garden food production literally around the corner, a very different concept

of food production will begin to be explored – in true keeping with the Elmhirst vision for Dartington as a place for discovery and experimentation for a better future.

NOTES FROM THE FOREST GARDEN, BY MARTIN CRAWFORD

It's not the gradually increasing global temperatures that will have a dramatic effect on what we grow, it's the increase in extreme weather events. Droughts, heatwaves, floods and extreme storms are all very destructive, especially to annual crops (on which, of course, the human population is largely dependent). We are likely to see yields from annual crops – including grains and most vegetables – fluctuate wildly: fantastic in one year and poor in another. This is where the Forest Garden model comes into its own. One way to reduce fluctuating yields is to grow more perennial crops, including trees and perennial vegetables. These will produce food year after year without the need for planting new seeds on an annual basis. Perennials have not been as highly bred and selected as annuals, so their annual yields are usually less. If, however, annuals are yielding less reliably, then the difference may not be significant. Increasing the diversity of plants in our diets, along with growing more diverse and long-lived plants, will help the health of both people and planet.

Local Food / Slow Food

As awareness of climate change moves into a new, more action-based phase, two food-based initiatives have spread across the world, linking food production with environmental and personal well-being. These are the Slow Food movement and the Local Food movement in its many guises.

The Slow Food movement was founded by Carlo Petrini in Italy in 1989. A defence of the sheer sensory pleasure of diverse and delicious food is its springboard into the pool of community and environmental politics, and building links between the two is a priority. In contrast, the Local Food movement begins with an ecological defence that is pitted against an international food system where 'food miles' become equated with the degradation of land, climate and food quality. Both movements view the local character of food as worthy of defending, not only because of the superior quality of local food but also because of the environmental impact associated with transporting food and engaging in large-scale industrialized farming.

However, it is perhaps because of the gastronomic beginnings of the Slow Food movement in Italy, a country renowned for its amazing cuisine, that this organization has developed a very particular character, which has led some critics to describe its ecological agenda as contradictory. On the one hand, Slow Food is a grassroots outfit, with supporters in 150 countries joining in local groups called 'convivia', and a network of some 2,000 food communities practising small-scale production of quality foods. On the other hand, Slow Food has a very international face in the form of its global network Terra Madre, which comprises over 7,000 food producers, cooks and university educators. Every two years, network delegates from all over the world come together to discuss global food sustainability issues – with air travel unrestricted. Furthermore, concurrent with its international Terra Madre meeting, Slow Food also runs the world's largest food and wine show, Salone del Gusto, in Turin.

Here, Terra Madre participants can showcase their products and hold taste workshops for thousands of people.

In 2004, Slow Food gave birth to the University of Gastronomic Sciences (UNISG), based in Pollenzo, aimed at giving academic strength to the field of food studies and pioneering a new definition of gastronomy. The programme, according to its website, "combines humanities, science and sensory training for a multi-experiential understanding of food production". As good fortune would have it, the Schumacher College kitchen was asked to host a group of UNISG students in 2012 – and cook lunch with them. Still in its early stages, the University did not yet have its own kitchen, so it was a great pleasure to provide this practical dimension for a very enthusiastic international group of foodie undergraduates – and to learn more about their studies. This was not the first contact Schumacher College had had with the Slow Food movement, as Carlo Petrini has taught at the College, and Schumacher Fellow Vandana Shiva represents the organization in India. In 2006-7, the former Head of Food, Wayne Schroeder, and former Short Course coordinator, Inge Page, represented the College at a Terra Madre gathering in Italy and came back deeply inspired.

The Local Food movement, it seems, is represented by a slightly more horticultural and local-economic range of activities and concerns: still all about real, quality food, but with the edge of gastronomy slightly less dominant. It is for this reason, I believe, that the two organizations are complementary, with an overlap among their supporters. The high profile of the Slow Food movement lends credence to the Local Food agenda at the gourmet level and provides an international reference point and support system for those 'Local Foodists' who particularly love their food. The downside of the association with Slow Food is that it provides fuel to the critics of Local Food, who say it too is 'elitist' – which is hardly fair when you consider that a diet of local food, if consumed by an indigenous group with a non-Western lifestyle, is about as natural and low-impact as you can get.

The Local Food movement has gathered pace rapidly in the last two decades, regaining a local territory for supply and demand that was almost eroded in the industrialized world by a post-war economy that increasingly promoted imported food and national, centralized food distribution networks. Since the 1980s in the USA and the late 1990s in the UK, however, outlets for farmers to sell directly to consumers have been returning apace. There are now around 750 farmers' markets in the UK, and 80 Community Supported Agriculture initiatives (CSAs), with 150 more in development. The benefits of local food have become so well accepted that the movement has gained the support of government and lottery funding in the UK, as well as European funding.

The benefits of Local Food initiatives have been recognized as going beyond the realms of environment and nutrition. Not only are local farms which sell products to local people more climate-friendly, because less energy is needed to refrigerate during storage and transportation, but also they feed into farmers' markets which have been shown to inspire more social behaviour. For example, 75 per cent of shoppers at a farmers' market arrive in groups, as opposed to 16 per cent in supermarkets – and, similarly, far more shoppers at a farmers' market interact with other customers. They also interact with the farmers, and learn more about how food

is grown. Thus, the grant-distributing body the Local Food Fund had as its mission statement: "*Local food builds community vibrancy and retains local traditions while establishing a local identity through a unique sense of community*." This Fund was part of the UK Big Lottery Fund's £59.8-million programme to distribute grants to a variety of food-related projects in order to make locally grown food more accessible to local communities. Sadly, the Local Food Fund and the Making Food Work programme closed in 2012. Schumacher teacher and community food expert Tim Crabtree writes: "With the closure of these funds, the future for the local food sector looks uncertain. This is compounded by the ongoing 'austerity' in the UK, which has impacted on sales of local and organic produce, and reduced the availability of grant funding for local food initiatives."

Over in the USA (which has more Slow Food members than any other country outside Italy), the term 'locavore' has been coined to describe anyone who is dedicated to eating only local food. This was inspired by the book *Coming Home to Eat* by ecologist Gary Paul Nabham, and has led to a 16-point public 'Food Declaration' being made via the San Francisco-based non-profit organization Roots of Change. High-profile signatories to this include Michael Pollan (author of *The Botany of Desire*), Alice Waters and Wendell Berry. With 17,000 signatories, the Declaration was launched at a Slow Food Nation event and aims "to promote food and agricultural policies that benefit all Americans".

When the economic multiplier effect that occurs within a community when people buy local, and the social multiplier effect that occurs when seeds are swapped, gardens shared, and community orchards established, are added up with the environmental and gastronomic benefits of local food, it is difficult to imagine how anyone could find fault with the Local Food movement. But they do. Studies such as Christopher Weber and H. Scott Matthews's report on food miles[1] suggest that the total amount of greenhouse gas emissions in the production phase of organic eggs, free-range chicken and cattle raised on open pastures far outweighs emissions in the transportation phase of factory-farmed animals and eggs, etc. Similarly, Steve Sexton[2] argues that the technological advances made by farming over the last 70 years risk being lost if Local Foodists get their way. The efficiencies of production that could feed a world with an exponentially growing population will be lost, he says, at the expense of the less privileged. Such are the arguments that have led to 'locavores' in the West being termed 'elitist'.

But such a label, so often a criticism made by vested interests in the agri-food industry, should not be allowed to goad anyone away from this bountiful course. Just return to the 'whole' picture – and think not just of the people but also of the animals who are being put in service to the international factory-farming method of world food production. If the fact that they produce 14 per cent more greenhouse gases (according to Weber and Matthews) when allowed to live a more natural lifestyle means that their well-being, as well as the well-being of people and environment, is greatly enriched, then this is something that must be built into and not cut out of the food-production equation. And it is another argument for eating less meat and dairy products – not an argument for continuing with global factory farming and the global transportation of food. The Local Food movement and its counterparts (such as the Food Sovereignty movement[3]) mark a positive departure in the direction of rural revitalization and the return of the right to define food systems in a more equitable way, with the people who grow, distribute and consume local food put back at the centre of decision-making. Even without continued government funding, the Local Food movement is now so imperative that it will surely continue to grow hand in hand with the Transition movement. And it will continue to nurture ecologically and socially fulfilling lifestyles. However, policy change and action, at both national and international levels, also need to happen – and keeping the pressure on to achieve these changes must be one of the continued goals of community food enterprises, NGOs and anyone who cares about good food for all.

Seasons and celebrations

The age-old role of feasting (and fasting) has been to mark rites of passage in our lives, our culture and in the year. The orbit of our Earth on its tilted axis around the sun results in changing lengths of day and night, and of sunlight intensity, in the northern and southern hemispheres, and hence the seasons of summer, autumn, winter and spring are born. It is not such an emotionally charged story as the Ancient Greek myth relating to the kidnap of a goddess's daughter – but, whether winter reflects personal loss or the logic of science, the result is the same. It is this reality of diverse growing seasons that we must engage with, and this that makes our experience of food over the year so rich and varied, involving times for planting, harvesting and storing; for praying, feasting and fasting.

This rhythmic ebb and flow of abundance underpins many of the religious festivals, and has done for thousands of years. In the traditional Christian liturgy of feasts and fasting,

1 Christopher L. Weber and H. Scott Matthews (2008). 'Food-Miles and the Relative Climate Impacts of Food Choices in the United States'. *Environ. Sci. Technol.*, 42(10): 3508-13. (See also Vasile Stănescu (2010). 'Green Eggs and Ham? The Myth of Sustainable Meat and the Danger of the Local'. *Journal for Critical Animal Studies*, 8(1/2).

2 Steve Sexton (2011). 'The Inefficiency of Local Food'. wwww.freakonomics.com

3 Food sovereignty proposes an alternative food system that creates sustainable and democratic solutions to the industrialized food model. 'Food sovereignty' is defined as the right of peoples to healthy and culturally appropriate food, produced through ecologically sound and sustainable methods, and their right to define their own food and agriculture systems.

auspicious days were often grafted over festivals from an older time, taking advantage of what may be a generic human need to mark the underlying natural staging posts with which these coincided. Christmas Day (in the northern hemisphere) falls in the middle of the coldest time of year – the time most in need of brightening with convivial, indoor activity and feasting. It is perhaps not surprising, then, that the celebration of the birthday of Christ comes on the same day that the birthday of Osiris was celebrated by the Ancient Egyptians, the birthday of Dionysus by the Ancient Greeks and the birthday of the goddess Freya by the Norse people of Scandinavia.

Also during the November/December period falls the Jewish celebration of the re-dedication of the temple in Jerusalem, Hanukkah, also known as the 'Festival of Lights'. At this time the candles of the menorah are ceremonially lit, and feasting on fried foods such as latkes (potato fritters) takes place, to commemorate the miraculous way that a small amount of oil kept alight for eight days. In India, December marks the beginning of the Tamil new year, which means offering gifts of rice and milk to the gods, then to the garlanded cattle, and finally to the people. Also at roughly this time (a little earlier) the Hindu festival of Diwali – also called the 'Festival of Lights' – like our Bonfire night, culminates in an explosion of fireworks. All these festivals are in some sense not just religious

festivals but also festivals of light, occurring around the time of the winter solstice, when, in the places where these cultures originated, the longest night of the year occurs. They are associated with the joy of welcoming light back into the world, as the sun passes its nadir and starts to regain strength.

In addition to these cyclic reasons for celebration, there are also, in everyone's lives, personal landmarks that cut across the seasonal boundaries – birthdays, weddings, graduations, great achievements, etc. At Schumacher College, our food policy states that 'celebration' should always be an important part of what we do. Not that every meal should be a sumptuous feast running into many courses, but that every meal should be well prepared and abundantly enjoyed – enjoyed both in the preparing and in the eating together.

> "The dining table must return to our lives, our homes, our inner and outer spaces. To enjoy a meal we should sit down, leave our watches and our mobile phones elsewhere, for the convivial enjoyment of food and companionship."
> Wendy Cook, *The Biodynamic Food and Cookbook*

So, we have simple feasts most days of the week, and slightly more lavish feasts to celebrate the end of a course (which has often been a transformative journey and so marks a rite of passage within the Schumacher College context).

More and more I notice how the traditional feast days that make up an essential part of the 'food biographies' students bring with them begin to creep into what we cook. "Can we make pancakes? It's Shrove Tuesday." "Let's bake pumpkin pie – it's Thanksgiving." "Hurrah, Christmas is coming and it's time for mince pies!" "It's Hanukkah, I want to make latkes for everyone." This provides a comfortable point of learning and understanding about the deeply symbolic aspect of feasting and being 'feasted'. Often, people don't know why different foods are associated with different festivals – they are shy to ask if they feel they should already know since it's part of their own culture, but bold to ask if it is another culture and they are not the only ones discovering about it. Because Schumacher College attracts such a very international group of students, unfamiliar dishes are created and introduced as the year progresses, always with great excitement and enthusiastic sharing.

Sometimes, of course, the focus on food is more to do with abstaining than indulgence – as, for example, when individuals decide to give up chocolate for Lent, or 'risen' ('chametz') food during the Jewish Passover festival. Ostensibly, these abstinences are to do with commemorating or 're-living' a historical event, such as, for example, the deprivations of Jesus during his time in the desert, or the liberation of the Israelites from slavery in Ancient Egypt, when the flight from Egypt to Mount Sinai became so hurried that the provisions of bread did not have time to rise. But, in addition to the historical framework, I also sense that the need for engaging in regular periods of self-limitation is pretty universal, and particularly likely to occur in a place where food is offered freely – a relatively new phenomenon in evolutionary terms, and one to which we are still adapting.

Because the kitchen is so central to what Schumacher College does, in terms of both team building and nurturing a residential community experience, it gives us the means (and the excuse!) to create frequent feasts and to build up

a stash of well-tested recipes. These come from our whole community – our vegetarian chefs, our staff and our students, and also from a few brilliant contemporary cookery writers, to whom we are greatly indebted for their inspiration and generous sharing of recipes and culinary ideas as we develop our own house style (see Bibliography for some favourite cookbooks). I believe it is because everyone here comes fresh to cooking and enjoys what they do, without it being a chore, that the food tastes so good – it has lots of love stirred into it. Not that cooking is always an entirely ego-free task – the love that goes into it may sometimes be conditional on well-appreciated results . . . But that doesn't matter, and it acts as a motivator when it comes to improving food: false praise is seldom given twice where the stomach is concerned.

So, please enjoy creating feasts with these 'twice baked and thrice praised' recipes. They are the ones that people have asked for over and over again, and can be trusted when it comes to cooking for yourself, your friends, your family and your community.

How to use this book

Quantities, scaling up and units of measurement

For every recipe in this book, ingredients are listed in two columns: 'family sized' (usually 6 people) and 'large group sized' (usually about 50 people, although this varies in the cake section). In general, the amounts given for the larger quantity cater for an average male/female mixed-age group such as we usually have for meals at Schumacher College. Of course, large groups will always vary in demand, and it is therefore difficult to give a foolproof guide to quantities that will suit all appetites, but you should find that the amounts in these recipes are generous and suitable for most occasions.

It is important to bear in mind that the amounts for the large quantity may not always be an exact scaling up of the small quantity – for two reasons. First, amounts have been rounded up or down for ease of measurement, where this is judged to make no difference to the success of the recipe. In some cases, this results in the metric measurements making a different quantity from the imperial, because the rounded amounts (e.g. 500g compared with 1lb) are different (usually larger). Where this occurs to any significant degree it is noted in the text. Because of this, and as a general rule, it is advisable to stick to one set of measurement units: metric, imperial or cups. The second reason that scaling up may not always appear proportional is that some ingredients do not need to be scaled up to the same extent as others. Timescale needs to be increased when cooking for large numbers, not only for preparation time but for actual cooking time, which may double or even triple. Herbs and spices should be added cautiously, little by little, as longer cooking times mean greater time for flavour development.

Special diets

Special diets are very much a feature of large-scale cooking today, and we have used abbreviations on the Contents pages to indicate the most common requests. These are as follows:

GF: gluten-free. Avoids wheat, rye, couscous, bulgur and most oats (unless guaranteed gluten-free), e.g. someone with coeliac disease.

WF: wheat-free. Specifically avoids wheat but should be fine with rye, oats and other grains containing gluten.

DF: dairy-free. Avoids milk, and all milk products – cheese, butter, cream, yoghurt, etc. (but will eat eggs).

V: vegan. Avoids dairy and eggs, and other animal products, sometimes including honey for strict vegans.

A note for American readers

There are a number of differences between British imperial and American measurements – though some of these differences are masked by a common terminology. Although this book was written from the standpoint of a British cook, and the amounts lead with metric measures, we have also included the equivalent cup, pint and quart volume measures with the American cook in mind. However, for larger amounts of dry ingredients, we are assuming that weighing scales will be available.

Unless otherwise indicated, the word 'pint' refers to the imperial pint (20fl oz) as opposed to the US pint (16fl oz). By contrast, all 'quarts' refer to US measurements (and are marked as such). When it comes to cup measures, either metric or US cups can be used, because the difference is so small – the US cup measure is 8fl oz (237ml) whereas the metric cup is 9fl oz (250ml). For baking, you should, if possible, take the precaution of 'calibrating' your cup – a cup of flour should weigh 5oz (140g) – and adjust your cup-filling technique if necessary. Some other volume/weight equivalents for common ingredients are given on the right. Below are some translations of UK ingredient names which may be unfamiliar to the American or Canadian reader.

UK	US
almonds, flaked	sliced almonds
almonds, ground	almond meal
aubergine	eggplant
beetroot	beets
bicarbonate of soda	baking soda
butter beans	use lima beans
cherries, glacé	candied cherries
coriander leaves	cilantro
cornflour	cornstarch
courgette	zucchini
double cream	use heavy or whipping cream
flour, plain	all-purpose flour (white)
flour, strong	use bread flour
ginger, crystallized	candied ginger
golden syrup	cane sugar syrup - use rice syrup, honey, etc.
oats, rolled	porridge oats (not quick-cook)
sugar, caster	use superfine or granulated sugar
sugar, icing	confectioner's (powdered) sugar
sugar, muscovado	use brown sugar
sultanas	white (or golden) raisins
tomato purée	tomato paste

And a quick note for Australian readers

An Australian tablespoon is 20ml, as opposed to the standard 15ml. Australian cooks using Australian measures should therefore use 3 x 5ml teaspoons to obtain one tablespoon as indicated in these recipes.

A few approximate equivalents

1 teaspoon (tsp) = 5 millilitres (ml)
1 tablespoon (tbsp) = 15ml
2 tbsp = 1 fluid ounce (fl oz) / 30ml
1 pound (lb) = 450 grams (g). (1lb = 16oz)
1 kilogram (kg) = 2lb 3oz. (1kg = 1000g)
1 cup = 237ml / 8fl oz (US) or 250ml / 9fl oz (metric)
1 pint (UK) = 20fl oz / 560ml. 1 pint (US) = 16fl oz / 450ml
1 US quart (2 US pints) = 32fl oz / 900ml
1 tbsp butter or fresh yeast = 10g / $^{1}/_{2}$ oz
1 US 'stick' of butter = 110g / 4oz
3 level / 2 heaped tbsp sugar = 25g / 1oz
1 cup sugar (granulated or packed soft brown) = 200g / 7oz
1 cup icing/powdered sugar = 125g / 4$^{1}/_{2}$ oz
1 cup flour = 140g / 5oz
1 cup rolled oats = 85g / 3oz
1 cup tahini or peanut butter = 225g / 8oz
1 cup nuts = 110-140g / 4-5oz
1 cup dried fruit = 140g / 5oz
1 cup rice / lentils (dry) = 170g / 6oz
1 cup grated Cheddar cheese = 110g / 4oz
1 cup chopped fresh herbs = 70g / 2$^{1}/_{2}$ oz
1 cup diced onion, potato or carrot = about 140g / 5oz

Oven temperatures

Variations between ovens often occur. These can be checked with an oven thermometer. General values and conversions are as follows:

	°C	°F	Gas Mark
Very low	110-130	225-250	$^{1}/_{4}$ – $^{1}/_{2}$ or 1
Low	140	275	1
Lowish	150	300	2
Warm	170	325	3
Moderate	180	350	4
Fairly hot	190	375	5
Fairly hot	200	400	6
Hot	220	425	7
Very hot	230	450	8
Very hot	240	475	9

Meet the cooks

Many people have contributed recipes and ideas to *Gaia's Feasts*. Here is a little bit about some of the cooks whom you will find mentioned more than once in these pages. They are our enduring kitchen enthusiasts – the ones who have cooked at Schumacher College the most in recent years, really loving the opportunity to share and grow their culinary skills.

Tara Vaughan-Hughes

Current job: Vegetarian Chef at Schumacher College.

Other activities: Mother of three – with private catering business. Loves literature and also dabbles in home sewing projects (with, she says, varying success).

Previous foodie incarnations: After on-the-hoof cookery training in restaurants in London and the USA, Tara became owner/manager/cook at her own two award-winning concept restaurants in Vermont: 'Eat Good Food' 1&2.

Favourite food to cook: "Anything that all three kids will eat happily!"

Favourite cooking activity: "I find peeling carrots to be meditative and very satisfying."

Recipes contributed: Mushroom sformato (page 72); Brutti ma buoni (page 230).

Ruth Rae

Current job: Vegetarian Chef at Schumacher College.

Other activities: Mother of one medium-sized boy. DIY, gardening, cycling and co-organizing art workshops for children. Member of the Dartington Print workshop.

Previous foodie incarnations: Before training as a physiotherapist, Ruth spent a few years mixing cocktails and serving as a croupier aboard a cruise ship. She also worked in a vegan restaurant in London.

Favourite food to cook: "Bread, plain and simple – or fancy and beautiful!"

Favourite cooking activity: "Inventing new meals using abandoned ingredients!"

Recipes contributed: Courgette 'conkers' (page 65); Walnut & fig bread (page 238).

Sarah Bayley

Current job: Vegetarian Chef at Schumacher College.

Other activities: Mother of one smallish boy and 'mother' of one accident-prone greyhound!

Previous foodie incarnations: Ran own catering business 'Veggie Heaven' with husband Dan and was a catering focalizer at the Grimstone Manor Community. Worked on the British festival scene with Veggie Heaven; now enjoys festivals without having to work.

Favourite food to cook: "Anything bready or chocolatey."

Favourite food to eat: "Egg sandwiches."

Favourite cooking activity: "Tasting!"

Recipes contributed: Moorish squash soup with coconut (page 37); Wild golden oaties (page 223); Squidgy choc-chip cookies (page 232).

Julia Ponsonby

Current job: Catering Manager / Head of Food / Vegetarian Chef at Schumacher College.

Other activities: Mother of one biggish boy. Writing. Doing the washing! Guinea pigs!

Previous foodie incarnations: Used to run own catering business for special events and on arrival in Totnes sold cakes for 'acorns' – a currency of the local exchange trading system (LETS)

Favourite food to cook: "I really like variety – but baking bread and chocolate cake have to be at the top of the list!"

Favourite food to eat: "Fresh spicy winter salad – scintillating! Hot buttered brown toast."

Favourite cooking activity: "Dicing a stack of carrots with a sharp knife. Kneading dough. Whipping egg whites into snowy peaks – what a meditation!"

Voirrey Watterson

Current occupation:
Volunteer at Schumacher College – the longest-serving helper ever!

Other activities: Baking speciality bread, often at midnight, usually listening to the radio. Informally teaching preserving skills, sauerkraut- and bread-making at Schumacher College and in Burma. Coordinating the harvesting and juicing of School Farm apples!

Previous foodie incarnations: Worked for a wholefood collective in Oxford called Uhuro (which means freedom in Swahili) – back in the days when wholefoods were 'political'.

Favourite food to cook: "Bread."

Favourite cooking activity: "Anything with a crowd cooking a meal together!"

Recipes contributed: Luxury fruit Borodinsky (page 244).

Tchenka Sunderland

Current occupation:
Astrologer, natural philosopher and grandmother.

Other activities: Writing, labyrinth designing, gardening. Teaching philosophy of nature to the MSc Holistic Science students.

Previous foodie incarnations: Ran a B&B and was tempted back into cooking at Schumacher, where she would be in charge of cooking when Wayne or Julia were away.

Favourite food to cook: "Chocolate brownies! I think they call to my Scorpionic soul . . ."

Favourite cooking activity: "Soup-making – so simple and yet so satisfying."

Recipes contributed: Roast red pepper & tomato soup (page 46); Lime, lentil & coconut whizz (page 29); Puy lentil & fennel salad (page 120); Marinated mushroom salad (page 114).

Wayne Schroeder

Current occupation:
Self-employed change agent and idea monkey; runs a business called Holistic Healthy Options.

Other activities: Husband, teacher, photographer . . .

Previous foodie incarnations: Food technologist, baker and cheese maker at the Findhorn Community and Head of Food with Julia for 11 years at Schumacher College.

Favourite food to cook: "Healthy, simple and elegant – Italian hits the mark pretty well."

Favourite food to eat: "I just love eating: if you look really close you'll see how fat I am!"

Favourite cooking activity: "Being touched by the creative genius of vegetables."

Recipes contributed: Grape & almond coleslaw (page 103); Warm parsnip & hazelnut salad (page 128); Portuguese marinated carrots (page 127).

Minni Jain

Current occupation:
Director & trustee of the charity Earthlinks UK; Research and Design editor on the *Holistic Science Journal*.

Other activities: Collaborated with Satish Kumar in setting up the first Tagore Festival at Dartington in 2011 – so successful that it has now become an annual event.

Previous foodie incarnations: Learned to cook pickles at her mother's knee; has led the cooking of many Indian meals at the College.

Favourite food to cook: "Dal, rice and seasonal vegetables."

Favourite food to eat: "Khichdi (made with dal and rice cooked together)."

Favourite cooking activity: "Harvesting fresh produce from my own garden."

Recipes contributed: Onion pakoras (page 64); Potato parathas (page 248).

Soups

English onion soup with cider & croutons

Minestrone

Lime, lentil & coconut whizz

Bobbing broccoli & cauliflower soup with blue cheese

Herbed yoghurt & bulgur soup with turmeric

Greek lentil soup

Ratatouille soup

Chestnut & artichoke soup

Moorish squash soup with coconut

Squash & corn chowder

White Hart parsnip & apple soup

Wild green soup with nettles

Cream of nasturtium (or watercress) soup

Roast red pepper & tomato soup

Carrot, leek & butter-bean soup

Tomato & black-eyed-bean soup

English onion soup with cider & croutons

This variation of the classic French onion soup uses our local apple cider, which has been the traditional drink in Devon for centuries. If you don't have access to cider, just revert to the time-honoured French style and use a medium white wine for an equally delicious result. The croutons that typically accompany onion soup are fun to make and will help use up leftover bread. Once dunked, they absorb liquid like a sponge, wrapping themselves in the goo of melting cheese and developing an almost melt-in-your-mouth consistency that is both soft and crunchy.

Whenever I think of croutons, a memory comes to mind of the remote mountain cabin of philosopher Arne Naess, the founder of the Deep Ecology movement. Some 15 years ago, Stephan and I climbed across the Norwegian bogs and up the rocky outcrops with Arne and his wife Kit-Fai to reach Tvergastein. After three hours of squelching and clambering we arrived. The door of the cabin was unlocked and we were ushered into a sitting room that embraced panoramic views and old Norwegian folk-style-painted wooden furniture. Next to the large window was Arne's hand-crafted writer's chair, complete with mug flaps and bookstand, and his dining table. It was an orderly, harmonious scene – but what were all those dull white nuggets doing strewn across the bed in the corner? It emerged that these were croutons, cut from the remaining bread at the end of Arne's last visit and left to dry. Our first job was to scoop them into tins. They were served with soup at every meal – and tasted very good and filling.

For 6	For 45-50
1.25kg (2lb 12oz) white onions	10kg (22lb)
2 tsp garlic, minced	6 tbsp
3 heaped tbsp parsley, finely chopped	150g (5oz / 2 cups)
1 tsp dried sage	2-3 tbsp
approx. 1.4l (2½ pints / 3 US pints) vegetable stock	approx. 11l (20 pints / 12 US quarts)
250ml (9fl oz / 1 cup) medium-sweet cider (or white wine)	2l (3½ pints / 4¼ US pints)
2 tsp grainy mustard	6 tbsp / ⅓ cup
1-2 tsp salt	3-4 tbsp
½ tsp black pepper	1-1½ tbsp
A little butter and/or olive oil to sauté	approx. 125g (4½ oz) butter and/or 100ml (4-5fl oz / ½ cup) olive oil

To serve

50-85g (2-3oz / 1-1½ cups) Cheddar or Parmesan-style* cheese, grated	400-700g (12oz-1½lb / 8-12 cups)
croutons: 250g (9 oz) bread (stale is OK) – see method	2kg (4½lb)

*True Parmesan contains rennet and so is not vegetarian – hence 'Parmesan-style'. You can buy a vegetarian substitute: it won't be called Parmesan, though it may look similar and be indicated as a pasta cheese. Alternatively, use a hard goat's cheese or other local hard cheese that has been made with a vegetarian rennet.

1. Prepare the croutons. Slice up the bread into 1cm (½") cubes, discarding any crusts or mouldy bits. White or brown bread may be used, depending on your preference. Bear in mind that it is better to avoid bread with 'bits' in (e.g. seeds, nuts and whole grains), which can become tooth-breakingly hard when dried out. Leave the bread cubes in a warm cupboard or the lower oven of an Aga overnight to dry out. If you need to fast-track this process, leave them in a low oven or for an hour or two. Once dried (or dry-ish), fry the cubes in a mixture of olive oil and butter, turning them frequently, until they are browned at the edges. If you need to mop up any excess oil, leave them to stand on kitchen paper. (It is also possible to serve them completely plain and unfried, as Arne Naess did.)

2. Slice the onions in half, from shoot to root. Peel back the skin, then, using it as a handle, slice the onions into fine half-moon slices, discarding the root and skin when you get to it. (Leaving the root on until the end of the process will help to reduce the 'crying effect'.) Now sauté the onions in olive oil and/or butter with half the salt for a long time, until golden-brown. It is advisable to do this in two pans if you are making the larger quantity.

3. Add the garlic, dried sage and half the parsley, and sauté for a little longer.

4. Add the stock and cider (or white wine) and continue to simmer for a further hour.

5. Stir in the mustard, then season to taste with more salt and pepper.

6. Stir in the rest of the parsley just before serving. The croutons (preferably re-warmed in the oven) and the grated cheese should be presented in separate bowls, to be heaped on top of the soup as desired.

Minestrone

Minestrone soup is a wonderfully hearty Italian soup that easily adapts to the fluctuating abundances of a summer and autumn vegetable garden. So long as you include a little pasta, a lot of tomato and some kind of bean, you can call it minestrone. Never blended, and served with a sprinkling of Parmesan-style cheese and a hunk of bread, this soup is a meal in itself, and verges lavishly on the side of an elegantly chopped vegetable stew. When in Rome you may also find your minestrone includes bacon – but never at Schumacher College!

For 6-8	For 45-50
1 medium onion, diced small	6-7 (1.5kg / 3lb 5oz)
approx. 2 stalks celery, diced small	approx. 1½ heads
150g (5oz / ⅔ cup) carrots, finely sliced	1kg (2lb 3oz)
4 medium tomatoes, chopped	24 (2kg / 4lb 6oz)
2-3 cloves garlic, crushed	approx. 1 large head or 3 tbsp, crushed
1.5l (2¾ pints / 1½ US pints) water / vegetable stock	approx. 9l (16 pints / 10 US quarts)
150g (5oz / 1 cup) leeks, finely chopped	1kg (2lb 3oz)
150g (5oz / 1 cup) cabbage, finely shredded	1kg (2lb 3oz)
1 small/medium courgette, diced or half-moons	6 courgettes (approx. 750g / 1½lb)
3-4 green beans, in 2cm (¾") lengths (if available)	24-36 (400g / 14oz)
85g (3oz / ½ cup) fusilli / mini conchiglie, etc.	500g (1lb 2oz)
2-3 tbsp tomato purée	150-180ml (5-6fl oz / ⅔ cup)
2 tbsp basil, chopped, or 1 tsp dried	70g (2½oz / 1 cup) or 3 tbsp dried
2 tbsp parsley, finely chopped	70g (2½oz / 1 cup)
Salt, pepper and vegetable stock powder to taste	2-4 tbsp salt or stock powder & 2-3 tsp pepper
1-2 tbsp olive oil to sauté	approx. 100ml (4-5fl oz / ½ cup)
100g (4oz / 1½ cups) Parmesan-style cheese	approx. 600 (1½lb / 4 packs)

1. Begin by sautéing the onion, celery and carrots in the olive oil. Shortly afterwards, add the tomatoes and crushed garlic, with a little salt, and dried basil if using. Cover with a lid and allow the vegetables to sweat, stirring occasionally to prevent them sticking.

2. Add the stock or water and bring to the boil. Add the leeks, cabbage, courgettes and/or green beans and pasta. Reduce to a simmer and continue to cook for another 20-30 minutes.

3. Stir in the tomato purée. Season to taste with salt and pepper, stock powder, etc., as required. When you are happy with the taste and consistency of the soup, make sure it's at the required serving temperature, then add the fresh herbs and you're ready to serve!

4. Accompany with a small bowl of finely grated Parmesan-style cheese to sprinkle on the minestrone, and some rustic bread to dunk.

Lime, lentil & coconut whizz

This smooth, creamy and 'sophisticated' soup was a great favourite of the College's former director Anne Phillips. It is entirely the invention of Tchenka Sunderland and has the great advantage of being "very, very easy" to make. The method of whizzing the oil into the soup at the end is one Tchenka loves, and is probably one of the healthiest ways you can add oils to a cooked food mixture, since it minimizes the chance of the oil getting too hot and spoiling. This approach is in keeping with much traditional Mediterranean cooking, where olive oil is added to food at a later stage.

For 6+	For 45-50
325g (12 oz / 2 cups) red lentils	2.3kg (5lb)
1½l (2½ pints / 5-6 cups) water	approx. 7l (12 pints / 7½ US quarts)
5 cloves garlic, chopped	35 cloves (approx. 3 good heads)
1 organic lime, juice and grated zest	7-8
1 x 400ml (15fl oz / 1¾ cups) can coconut milk	2.5-3l / 6-7 cans (6 pints / 7½ US pints)
60ml (2fl oz / ¼ cup) olive oil	400ml (15fl oz / 2 cups)
1-1½ tsp salt	1½-3 tbsp
1-2 pinches black pepper	1-3 tsp
25g (1oz / ½ cup) fresh coriander, chopped	200g (6-7oz / 3 cups)

1. Simmer the red lentils in the water until mushy.

2. Add the finely chopped garlic, lime juice, zest and coconut milk.

3. Return to the boil, reduce the heat and simmer for a while.

4. In a steady stream, pour in the olive oil, whizzing with a hand rod blender all the time.

5. Season well. Taste and garnish lavishly with lots of coriander before serving.

Bobbing broccoli & cauliflower soup with blue cheese

Cauliflower and broccoli are both members of the brassica family and both have generously floretted, bouquet-like heads. While there is a tendency to favour the florets when serving as a side vegetable, the tender stalk is easily blended when it comes to soup. The result is a mellow, creamy texture – and a taste that beautifully complements the bitter bite of blue cheese. At Schumacher College we use a Devon blue, but you could equally use Stilton or another local blue cheese.

For 6	For 45-50
1 small/medium cauliflower (500g / 1lb)	8 small/medium (3.6kg / 8lb)
1 head broccoli (350g / 12oz)	8 heads (2.7kg / 6lb)
1 large onion	1.4kg (3lb)
2 stalks celery, finely chopped	1 head
2-4 cloves garlic, chopped	1 head
1 tsp rosemary, chopped	approx. 3 tbsp
approx. 500ml (1 pint / 2 cups) vegetable stock or water	approx. 4l (7 pints / 9 US pints)
100g (3½oz / 1 cup) blue cheese, crumbled	800g (2lb)
150ml (5fl oz / ⅔ cup) whole milk	1.2l (2 pints / 2½ US pints)
2 tbsp cream	600ml (1 pint / 2½ cups)
4 tbsp parsley, chopped	150g (5oz / 2 cups)
approx. 1 tsp salt and 1-2 pinches black pepper	2-3 tbsp salt and 1-2 tsp black pepper
¼-½ tsp English mustard	2-3 tsp to taste
2-3 tbsp olive oil to sauté	approx. 150ml (7fl oz / ¾ cup)

1. Begin by removing the outer leaves of the cauliflower and donating them to your goat, compost heap or guinea pig. Carefully cut about one-third of the white cauliflower heads into neat florets, no bigger than the size of a walnut. The stalks and the remainder of the heads can be rough-chopped, which is quicker. Keep the florets and rough-chopped cauliflower in two separate piles.

2. Likewise, prepare the broccoli into a pile of florets and a pile of rough-chopped green vegetable. However, as the stalk of the broccoli is tougher than that of the cauliflower, you will have to not only cut off the ends but also pare away the fibrous outer skin of the trunk before chopping.

3. Chop the onion, celery, garlic and rosemary and begin to sauté them in the olive oil with a little salt and pepper. Cook for about 5 minutes until the onion is soft, then add the rough-chopped cauliflower and broccoli. Continue to cook for a further 5 to 10 minutes, stirring regularly – add a little water to prevent burning if necessary.

4. Meanwhile, measure out the stock (or water that will become your stock) and bring it to the boil in a separate pan. Add the florets of broccoli and cauliflower and return to the boil. Simmer briefly until the florets are just tender. Strain the liquid into the pan containing the other cooked vegetables. Put the florets back in the empty pan with a lid on to keep them warm.

5. Add the crumbled blue cheese to the cooking chopped vegetables and stock. Blend this with a rod blender, then add the reserved florets.

6. Lastly, warm the cream and milk and add it just before serving. (If you are serving your guests with individual bowls, the cream can be used unheated and swirled on top of each helping.)

7. Season to taste with salt, pepper, mustard and plenty of chopped parsley, holding back some for garnish. To serve, bring the soup to the desired temperature very gently, remembering not to let it boil once the milk and cream have been added, as this may cause it to curdle. Garnish with the remaining freshly chopped parsley.

Herbed yoghurt & bulgur soup with turmeric

Maya Walters was a student on the MSc in Holistic Science in 2004–5 and was quickly recognized for her culinary skills. Her interest in food goes beyond cooking: she wrote her dissertation on 'Rethinking the Place of Food'. This scintillating soup, the most popular recipe Maya left behind when she returned to Vancouver, simply ripples with the goodness of herbs and yoghurt.

For 6	For 45-50
1½ large onions, coarsely chopped	12 large (2.5kg / 5½lb)
2-3 cloves garlic, chopped	20 cloves
75g (2½oz / ½ cup) mung beans	600g (1lb 4oz / 4 cups)
1l (2 pints / 5 cups) vegetable stock or water	10l (16 pints / 10 US quarts)
100g (3½oz / 1 heaped ½ cup) bulgur wheat	700g (1lb 12oz / 4½ cups)
¾ tsp ground turmeric	2 tbsp
1½ tsp dried mint	4 tbsp
1½ tsp salt	34 tbsp
¾ tsp black pepper	2 tbsp
100g (4oz / 1½ cups) fresh spinach, chopped	800g (1lb 12oz)
50g (2oz / ¾ cup) fresh parsley, chopped	400g (14 oz / 6 cups)
50g (2oz / ¾ cup) fresh coriander, chopped	400g (14 oz / 6 cups)
50g (2oz / ¾ cup) fresh dill, chopped	400g (14 oz / 6 cups)
350ml / 100g (12fl oz / 1½ cups) plain yoghurt	3l (5 pints / 3 US quarts)
2-3 tsp fresh lime juice	100ml (3fl oz / 6 tbsp)
approx. 1-2 tbsp olive oil to sauté	approx. 100ml (4-5fl oz / ½ cup)
Fresh herbs for garnishing (reserve 1-2 tbsp from the above)	a handful (4 tbsp) reserved from above

1. Sauté the onions in the olive oil until soft. Add the garlic during last few minutes of cooking, then scrape onions and garlic from the pan and set aside. Do not wash the pan, but add the mung beans and water or stock to it and bring to the boil. Reduce the heat to medium-low and simmer, covered, until the beans are nearly soft. This will take 20-30 minutes, depending on the quantity you are making. Stir occasionally.

2. Add the bulgur wheat, turmeric, mint, salt and pepper. Simmer, covered, over a medium-low heat for 5-10 minutes, or until the beans and bulgur wheat are tender.

3. Remove from the heat. Add the reserved onion/garlic mixture and the chopped spinach. Put aside 2-4 tbsp (½-¾ cup) of the fresh herbs for garnishing and add the rest to the soup, stirring until the greens are just wilted.

4. Beat the yoghurt for five minutes to prevent curdling, then add to the soup, stirring constantly (again to prevent curdling). Add the lime juice. Adjust the seasonings to taste, adding more salt or lime juice if needed. Keep warm over a very low heat. Serve garnished with fresh herbs.

Greek lentil soup

Throughout her time as an Msc student at Schumacher College, Beatrice Yannacopoulos cooked herself a hearty Greek-style lentil soup and was sustained by it. By the time she left, everyone was cooking it and everyone was eating it.

This recipe comes with thanks to Bee, Brenda, Alex, Adam, Clive, Anna and the whole crew of MSc 2006-7, who invited me, five-year-old Oscar and Stephan to a delightful lunch they'd cooked specially – and who listened with genuine enthusiasm to all of Oscar's jokes, and shared some of their own. So, where does a soldier keep his armies? Up his sleevies!

For 6	For 45-50
1 large (225g / 8oz) onion	1.8-2kg (4lb)
250g (9oz / 1½ cups) carrots	2kg (4½lb)
250g (9oz / 2 cups) mushrooms	2kg (4½lb)
2-3 cloves garlic, crushed	1-2 heads
approx. 2l (3½ pints / 2 US quarts) vegetable stock or water	approx. 14-16l (25-28 pints / 15 US quarts)
½ tsp dried thyme	1-2 tbsp
1 bay leaf	3-4
1 tbsp balsamic vinegar	100ml (4fl oz / ½ cup)
1 cinnamon quill (or 1 tsp ground cinnamon)	4 quills or 2½ tbsp
250g (9oz / 1 rounded cup) brown or green lentils	2kg (4½lb)
1 large handful parsley, chopped	150g (5oz / 2 cups)
1 tsp salt, ¼ tsp black pepper and	1-2 tbsp salt, 1-2 tsp pepper
1 tbsp tamari, to taste	100-150ml (5fl oz / ½ cup)
approx. 50ml (2fl oz / ¼ cup) olive oil to sauté	approx. 200ml (9fl oz / 1 cup)

1. Peel and chop the onions finely. Cut the carrots into small chunky pieces or disks. The mushrooms can be quartered if smallish, otherwise rough-chopped.

2. Begin sautéing the onion and carrot with a little olive oil in the bottom of your soup pan. After about 5 minutes, when the onions are beginning to go pearly, add the thyme, garlic and mushrooms. After a further couple of minutes' cooking, add the stock or water along with the bay leaf, balsamic vinegar and whole cinnamon quill (or powder).

3. Carefully sort through the lentils on a plate and remove any stones (hopefully there won't be any). Add the lentils to the brew and bring to the boil. Turn down the heat and simmer gently for half an hour until the lentils and veggies are tender.

4. Dilute with more stock/water until you judge this stew-soup to be thick enough for your liking. Season with salt, pepper and tamari to taste. Add plenty of chopped parsley if available. Finally, drizzle with a little more olive oil just before serving.

Ratatouille soup

Ratatouille may have originated in the Mediterranean as a peasant dish, but, speaking as someone who grew up under much cooler growing conditions, there's something deliciously luxurious about this juicy combination of nightshades. I was certainly very excited to meet ratatouille for the first time as a teenager – when, unbothered by the concepts of food miles or eating local, the tastes of this tomatoey stew were much more appealing that the plain boiled carrots, potatoes and cabbage I was used to. With hindsight, the temperate growing season for aubergine and red pepper is so short (and, in the UK, almost exclusively achieved in greenhouses) that those of us who live in cooler climes should rightly go on regarding ratatouille as an exotic summer treat… not that you can't freeze or bottle it and bring it out later to brighten up your winter repertoire!

This recipe is a simple adjustment of a normal ratatouille, with the pieces of vegetable being cut slightly smaller and the liquid levels upped to soup proportions. It is delicious served with grated cheese, and will be even better the next day. A real favourite for many people.

For 6	For 45-50
300g (11oz / 2 cups) aubergines	2kg (4lb 4oz)
400g (15oz / 2 cups) tomatoes, chopped (fresh or tinned)	2.5kg (5½lb)
225g (8oz / 1½ cups) onions, chopped	1.5kg (3½lb)
1-1½ peppers (preferably red)	8-10, depending on size (1.6kg / 3½lb)
170g (6oz / 3 medium) whole tomatoes for blending	1.2kg (2½lb) (skinned or tinned)
1 tbsp tomato purée or 3-4 sun-dried tomatoes (optional)	100ml (5fl oz / ½ cup) purée or 24 (1 cup) sun-dried (optional)
2 cloves garlic, crushed or finely sliced	14 cloves / 1 head
1l (2 pints / 4-5 cups) vegetable stock or water	approx. 7-8l (12-14 pints / 7 US quarts)
300g (11oz / 2 cups) courgettes, rings/chunks	2kg (4lb 4oz)
50g (2oz / ⅓ cup) black olives, de-stoned	400g (14oz / 2-3 cups)
2 tsp dried oregano	3-4 tbsp
10g (½oz / a few leaves) fresh basil, chopped or torn	100g (4oz / 1½-2 cups)
1 tsp salt, 1-2 pinches black pepper and 1 tsp Dijon mustard	2-4 tbsp salt, 1-2 tsp pepper and 3 tbsp mustard
approx. 4 tbsp olive oil to sauté	approx. 100ml (4-5fl oz / ½ cup)
100g (4oz / 1 cup) grated Cheddar	approx. 750g (1lb 12oz)

1. Begin by considering the size you are going to cut all your vegetables to. As a guide, imagine fitting 2-3 vegetable pieces on to your soup spoon. First, prepare the aubergines. Slice them lengthways, then cut into medium-small chunky pieces, perhaps 1½-2cm (½-¾") square. Sprinkle with salt and leave in a colander over a bowl for half an hour to sweat.

2. Set aside the whole tomatoes for blending, then continue by preparing the rest of the vegetables to roughly the same size as the aubergines – though the onions and chopped tomatoes should be smaller, allowing them to meld into the background.

3. Take the whole tomatoes and place in boiling water to soften them, then either peel them (see tip on page 105) and blend in a liquidizer or blend them unskinned in the liquidizer and then sieve – this will remove the seeds and skins. The latter method is probably more time-efficient when making the larger quantity of soup, but you will still need to soften the tomatoes in boiling water. Alternatively, blend tinned chopped tomatoes. Tomato purée will also add a little extra richness, if required. This can be substituted with some quickly soaked sun-dried tomatoes whizzed up with some of the liquid – useful when you are making the large quantity but do not want to open a large tin of purée.

4. Once the tomato liquid has been created, turn to sautéing the onions with the red peppers. Add the aubergines after rinsing and draining. Continue to cook until these are soft, adding the garlic, oregano and more oil as required.

5. Add the water or vegetable stock and the courgettes. Bring to the boil and simmer until all the vegetables are soft.

6. Prepare the black olives if they are not already pitted: halve them and remove the stones.

7. Finally, add the tomato liquid, freshly chopped or torn basil and olives. Taste and complete the seasoning with salt, pepper and mustard as required. Serve hot with grated cheese to sprinkle on – and crusty bread to dunk.

Chestnut & artichoke soup

The smoky drift of boiling chestnuts draws people to the kitchen with the question "What's that you're brewing up?" Jerusalem artichokes, a healthy but much-berated cousin of the sunflower, had as far as I was concerned been off-menu for several years, due to the explosive effect they were having on some staff members.

One of those responsible for putting artichokes back in the pot was Alex Laird, a professional herbalist, who attended Brian Goodwin's Health workshop in 2007. Via the magic flying network of Schumacher, she soon found herself welcoming our Australian Holistic Science MSc student Sophia Van Ruth to her London home – and improvising a deliciously soupy supper for her. Sophia eagerly helped us to recreate the brew at the College, where it has met with *almost* the same enthusiasm.

For 6	For 45-50
100g (4oz / ¾ cup) dried chestnuts (or double for fresh)	900g (2lb / 6 cups)
200g (7oz / 1½ cups) onions	1.3kg (3lb)
1-2 stalks celery	1 head (approx. 500g)
300g (11oz / 2 cups) Jerusalem artichokes	2.25kg (5lb)
200g (7oz / 1½ cups) leeks	1.5kg (3lb 4oz)
approx. 750ml (1½ pints / 2 US pints) water or veg stock	approx. 6-7l (10-12 pints / 6-7 US quarts)
1-2 tsp rosemary or thyme, finely chopped	3-4 tbsp
2-3 tbsp parsley, finely chopped	85g (3oz / 1 heaped cup)
60-90ml (3-4fl oz / ½ cup) single cream	600ml-1l (1-1½ pints / 2½-3 cups)
1-2 tsp each of salt, pepper and Dijon mustard	2-3 tbsp salt and mustard, 2-3 tsp pepper
A little olive oil to sauté	approx. 100ml (4-5fl oz / ½ cup)

1. Soak the chestnuts in twice their depth of cold water for several hours, preferably overnight. Bring to the boil, then simmer until tender (30-40 minutes). If using fresh chestnuts, slit the skins with a knife and boil until tender before skinning – watch out for your nails!

2. Sauté the chopped onions and celery with olive oil until beginning to soften. Add the scrubbed, chopped Jerusalem artichokes, the chopped, washed leeks and the rosemary or thyme. Sauté together briefly and then cover the vegetables with water or stock and bring to the boil. Simmer gently until tender.

3. Drain the cooked chestnuts. Pick over, removing any obviously large woody bits.

4. Blend the soup. Add more stock or water until you have the consistency of a still fairly thick soup. Add salt and pepper to taste and a little mustard if desired. Warm up the cream and add this shortly before serving – be careful not to boil the soup once you've added it. Also toss in the finely chopped fresh parsley, reserving a little to use as a garnish.

Variation: If you're badly affected by the inulin in Jerusalem artichokes, try making this soup with squash instead.

Moorish squash soup with coconut

This glorious coral-coloured soup, created especially with vegans in mind, evolved while Sarah Bayley was cooking at the Grimstone Manor Community. The coconut milk makes it wonderfully smooth and creamy, and when whizzed up with Sarah's special blend of spices this becomes a real history-soup. The combination of coconut, cumin, chilli and paprika reflects the intermingling of North Africa's Moorish traditions with a Spanish culture that had assimilated the invigorating nip of chilli into its cuisine from South America. Any of the orange-fleshed winter squashes are suitable, as is the yellower butternut squash.

For 6	For 45-50
1kg (2lb 4oz / 7 cups) orange-fleshed squash	8kg (15lb)
1 smallish potato	7 medium (1kg / 1½lb)
1-2 tbsp ginger root, grated	80-100g (3-4oz / ⅔ cup)
1-2 cloves garlic, chopped	5-8 cloves or 2-3 tbsp
3-4 tbsp olive oil for sautéing and blending	approx. 250ml (9fl oz / 1 cup)
1 largeish onion, finely chopped	1.6kg (3½lb)
1-2 stalks celery, finely chopped	1 head (approx. 500g / 1lb 2oz)
⅛-¼ tsp sweet chilli powder	1-1½ tsp
¼-½ tsp smoked paprika	2-3 tsp
1 rounded tsp ground cumin	3 tbsp
approx. 600ml (1 pint / 2½ cups) water or vegetable stock	4-5l (8-10 pints / 5-6 US quarts)
Just over ½ tin (250ml / 9fl oz) coconut milk	5 tins (2l / 3½ pints / 2 US quarts)
2 tsp coriander leaf, rough-chopped	70g (2½oz / 1 cup)
1-2 tsp salt	2-3 tbsp

1. To give yourself a better grip on the squash, divide it into sections first, then remove the skin with your knife or peeler. De-seed and cut into large chunky pieces. Scrub and dice the potato, peeling it if not organic.

2. Grate the ginger root coarsely. Peel and rough-chop the garlic. Whizz these up with some olive oil in a liquidizer until smooth.

3. Sauté the onion and celery at the bottom of a large saucepan, using olive oil. Add a little salt together with the sweet chilli, smoked paprika, cumin and blended ginger/garlic mix. Continue to stir until the onions begin to soften.

4. Add the prepared squash and potato. Stir to coat with the oily juices, then add water or stock until the vegetables are well covered. Bring to the boil, turn down the heat and simmer for 30-40 minutes, until the squash is soft. Stir occasionally.

5. Blend until smooth, using a rod blender. Add the coconut milk and enough additional water/stock to achieve the desired consistency. Taste and adjust the seasoning. Gently bring to simmering point to serve. Just before serving, stir in about three-quarters of the chopped coriander leaf – and garnish with the rest. (If presenting bowls of soup individually, stir in less and use more to garnish.)

Squash & corn chowder

This squash and corn soup was always a great hit with the regulars at Leslie and Bill Glassmire's café-bakery in Oregon, long before they came to Schumacher College and decided to experiment with settling in England. It was "a real bowl-scraper", Leslie says, "perfect in the fall when butternut squash and corn are plentiful". In Devon too, autumn is the time for scraping corn off the cob and marrying it with squash in hearty soups and stews. Although the addition of sweet potato isn't quite so local (for us it comes from Spain at the closest), it completes Leslie's recipe beautifully, and can be replaced with a more ordinary spud if need be.

The term 'chowder' is particularly used in North America, and probably dates back to the eighteenth century, when some Native American people began to cook their traditional clam soups in the heavy iron pans brought by the French. These were called 'chaudières'. Although still often associated with seafood soups, 'chowder' has also come to refer to other hearty soups containing milk.

For 6-8	For 45-50
1 medium butternut squash (about 675g / 1½lb)	approx. 5kg (10½lb)
150g (6oz / 1 heaped cup) onions, chopped	1.1kg (2½lb)
1 stalk celery, diced	7 stalks
1 large sweet potato, peeled and diced	7 large (approx. 2kg / 4½lb)
2 tbsp sunflower oil, margarine or butter	approx. 100g (4oz / ½ cup)
2 bay leaves	4-6
½ tsp dried thyme	1 heaped tbsp
approx. 1l (1½ pints / 4 cups) vegetable stock or water	approx. 7l (10-11 pints / 6-7 US quarts)
300g (10oz / 2½-3 cups) sweetcorn kernels	approx. 2kg (4½lb)
250ml (½ pint / 1 cup) milk	approx. 1.75l (3 pints / 2 US quarts)
approx. 1 tsp salt and ½ tsp pepper	2-3 tbsp salt and 1-3 tsp pepper

1. Cut the squash into rings. Remove the seeds and fibrous interior, then peel off the skin. Cut the squash into smallish pieces.

2. Prepare the onions, celery and sweet potato.

3. Now place all the prepared vegetables (except the sweetcorn) into a large soup pot and cover with enough water or stock to immerse all but the top 2cm (1") or so of the veggies. Bring to the boil, then add margarine, butter and/or oil, bay leaves, thyme and seasoning. Cover with a lid and simmer over a low heat, stirring occasionally, until the squash and sweet potato are tender (25-30 minutes).

4. Scoop out about 500ml (2 cups / 1 pint) of the vegetables if making the small quantity; 3-4l (7-8 pints / 4 US quarts) if making the large quantity. Mash these well and stir back into the soup.

5. Prepare the sweetcorn kernels. If fresh corn on the cob is not available, use frozen corn cooked briefly as per the instructions on the packet, or tinned corn with its juice. The fresh cobs will need to be stripped of their leaves and boiled for 20-30 minutes in salted water. Then, holding the cobs upright, slice off the kernels with a sharp knife and separate them with your fingers. Expect approximately 100g (3½oz / 1 cup) of kernels per (average-sized) cob. Once your corn is ready, stir it into the soup with the milk. Taste and adjust the seasoning as needed. Warm the soup gently, being careful not to boil it, as this may cause the milk to curdle, creating a more grainy appearance.

Leslie's tip: This soup may be served at once, but if time allows, let the chowder stand for an hour or so before re-heating gently. Enjoy!

White Hart parsnip & apple soup

On entering the busy kitchen that serves Dartington Hall's magnificent medieval White Hart bar and dining room, you know that you have entered the realm of professional Cordon-Bleu-trained chefs – a whole pecking order of them, from head chefs to sous chefs to dessert chefs. It is here, as in so many of the best hotel restaurants, that stress and perfectionism are hyped to the max to keep a wide range of clients happy. These include conference guests, wedding parties, music school attendees and random visitors seeking a relaxing evening out with friends. It is to the White Hart that we send course participants who arrive at the College saying they can't survive without meat, and to the White Hart that we go for a glass of wine after viewing a film in Dartington's Barn Cinema.

The White Hart kitchen will serve you beautifully presented (yet generous!), locally sourced dishes complete with fancy names. Included in the choices will be some wholesome 'comfort food' in the shape not only of Vera's puddings but also of soups, local cheeses and crusty bread. Here is one of my favourite autumn soups from the White Hart collection, with thanks to Archie (former Head Chef) for his invaluable cooking tips. I have cooked this soup most successfully with pleasantly sweet yet tasty dessert apples such as Cox's Orange Pippins, Granny Smiths, Braeburns and Russets.

For 6	For 45-50
500g (1lb 2oz / 4 cups) parsnips	3.5kg (7½lb)
225g (8oz / 1½ cups) onion	1.5kg (3½lb)
1 large stalk celery	1 good head
4-5 (1lb 2oz / 4 cups) dessert apples	3.5kg (7½lb)
Splash of olive oil and/or butter to sauté	approx. 200ml (7fl oz / ½-1 cup)
approx. 1l (1¾ pints) water or vegetable stock	approx. 7l (12 pints / 7 US quarts)
1 pinch nutmeg, grated (optional)	½ tsp (optional)
4-6 tbsp single cream	600ml (1 pint / 2 cups)
2 tbsp parsley or chervil, freshly chopped	70g (2½oz / 1 cup)
Salt, pepper and stock powder to taste	3-4 tbsp salt or stock powder and 1-3 tsp pepper
A quarter of a nice dessert apple for garnishing	A half

1. Peel the parsnips if they're not organic, or if the skins are blemished and tough. Remove tough, stalky ends, then rough-chop. Wash and chop the celery and peel and dice the onions. This is a blended soup and therefore doesn't require much attention to be paid to the size of the pieces, though they should not exceed 2cm (1").

2. Peel the apples to ensure a smooth blend, then slice, core and chop them roughly.

3. Sauté the chopped onion and celery in the bottom of your soup pot with the olive oil or butter. Once the onions begin to soften and look a little translucent, add the parsnip and cook for another 5-10 minutes, stirring regularly. Next stir in the apples, before covering with the stock or water. Bring to the boil. Turn down and simmer with lid ajar for 20-40 minutes, depending on the quantity.

4. Once the vegetables are tender, the soup is ready to be blended and seasoned, with salt, pepper, stock powder and nutmeg if desired. Blend until smooth using a rod blender. Warm the cream and add this just before serving. Taste and adjust seasoning and liquid levels as required, but be careful to avoid boiling once the cream is added.

5. The soup may be served with a sprinkling of fresh parsley or chervil, and thin half-moon slices of unpeeled dessert apple floating on top. If preparing the garnishing apple in advance, squeeze a little lemon over it to stop it discolouring. Leaving the bright red-green skin on provides a nice contrast with the muted pastel shade of this soup.

Wild green soup with nettles

Lap up the vibrant energy of the new growing season as wild garlic (ransoms; *Allium ursinum*) and nettles (*Urtica dioica*) begin to curl out of the hard winter's soil, transforming the landscape into its spring mode. Within a few weeks all the uncultivated spaces around the College and in the adjacent woodland glades become carpeted with an abundance of fresh, tender greenery, concentrated with antioxidants, vitamins and minerals – ours to harvest modestly and with respect for the other creatures who may also benefit from the nutritional bonanza. Wild garlic is best gathered before the white pom-pom-like flowers emerge, heralding the plant's need to re-seed itself. After flowering, the plant appears to die back almost completely, and is overtaken by brambles and other taller plants.

Nettles, however, may continue to be gathered in summer's twilight weeks. As ever, the darker, tougher, lower leaves of the nettles should be avoided – and also the stringy flowers. The plants may also be cut back to encourage tender new leaves to come again. However, it is worth bearing in mind the recommendation of our Holistic Science MSc graduate and clinical herbalist Isla Burgess. She advises that for optimum benefit, nettles should be harvested "before flowering, after two moon cycles of growth".

Nettles are cooked widely in Europe and Asia – indeed, the Tibetan Saint Milarepa was reputed to have lived solely off *satuk* (nettle soup) for years, until he turned green! For ordinary mortals, however, pure nettles and wild garlic can be very intense and are best mixed with leeks, onions and potatoes. (Alternatively, oats or barley can replace the potato as a starch.) Later in the summer, wild garlic may be substituted with hedge garlic (garlic mustard), followed by spinach or chard and a few garlic cloves.

With the wide variety of people coming to Schumacher College bringing different levels of exposure to wild food, I prefer to cook the nettles and blend them separately to remove any possibility of irritation. That said, many nettle-eating aficionados are quite happy to rough-chop their nettles and eat whole pieces cooked in with the rest of the vegetables. Whether you choose to eat your nettles whole or blended, however, they do need to be cooked to destroy the formic acid that gives them their sting – never be tempted to use raw nettles as a garnish.

For 6	For 45-50
200g (7oz) tender nettles, de-stalked	1.6kg (3½lb) after de-stalking
100g (4oz) wild garlic leaves	800g (1lb 12oz)
2 medium (300g / 10oz) onions	2.4kg (2lb)
2 stalks celery	1-2 heads
400g (9oz / 1½ cups) potatoes	2kg (5lb)
200g (7oz / 1½ cups) leeks	1.6kg (3lb 4oz)
1.4l (2½ pints) vegetable stock or water	10l (16 pints / 10 US quarts)
200ml (7fl oz / 1 cup) semi-skimmed milk	1.6l (3 pints / 2 US quarts)
100ml (4fl oz / ½ cup) cream	800ml (1½ pints / 3 cups)
1 pinch salt and black pepper to taste	2-3 tbsp salt and 1-2 tsp pepper
1 tsp mustard	2 tbsp
½-1 tsp stock powder to taste (if required)	2-3 tbsp to taste (if required)
A little olive oil or butter to sauté	approx. 100ml (4-5fl oz / ½ cup)
2 tbsp parsley, chopped, when in season (optional)	70g (2½oz / 1 cup) (optional)

1. Prepare the nettles. It is best to wear rubber gloves when picking and preparing the early spring shoots or nettle tops. Strip the nettle leaves from the stalks and rinse the leaves briskly in cold water. Leave to drain in a colander, while you prepare the other vegetables.

2. Rinse, drain and rough-chop the wild garlic, then leave on one side. Peel and chop the onions, quite finely. Rinse and chop the celery. Scrub and dice the potato. Chop the tough end off the leeks, slice them lengthways down the middle, chop and rinse in cold water to remove any grit.

3. Begin sautéing the onions and celery in the olive oil until they become soft and pearly. Stir in the potatoes and leeks and cover with water or stock. Bring to the boil and reduce heat. Simmer gently with lid ajar until the vegetables are tender.

4. Meanwhile, in a separate saucepan, cover the nettles minimally with some water and simmer until tender but still strong in colour. Blend to a purée, along with about a quarter of the main soup mixture.

5. Return all ingredients to the main soup pan and add most of the chopped wild garlic, reserving some for a final garnish.

6. Heat up the milk and cream ready to add to the soup shortly before serving. Reserve a little unheated cream to streak on the top of the soup when serving, if you like.

7. Season the soup with salt, pepper, mustard and stock powder.

8. Just before serving, add the heated cream/milk to the soup. Do not allow the soup to boil once the cream has been added, as it may curdle, causing a slightly grainy appearance (which most people won't notice – though you will!). Finally, streak the wild green surface of your soup with cream (if reserved), and scatter with the reserved chopped wild garlic (and parsley if using) before serving.

Wayne's tip: Try scattering individual bowls of soup with crumbled white goat's cheese — the flavour complements the wild greens deliciously.

Cream of nasturtium (or watercress) soup

This vibrant cream–green soup is a delicious way to use up a surplus of nasturtium leaves and stalks. Because the pepperiness of nasturtium mellows considerably with cooking, you need feel no nervousness about using this unusual ingredient. Nasturtium leaves really do make a delectable soup, with the piquancy reduced to little more than a muted glow by the time it arrives in your bowl. Outside the summer season, watercress can be substituted for the nasturtium to make another delicious soup, or you can combine the two. The leaves and stalks of both plants are high in antioxidants and rich in minerals. (For more about nasturtium see Creamy risotto with nasturtium & squash, page 86.)

For 6	For 45-50
1 medium onion, rough-chopped	1.3kg (3lb)
1 stalk celery, chopped	1 head
1 medium potato, rough-chopped	1.3kg (3lb)
¾l (1¼ pints / 3 cups) vegetable stock or water	approx. 5l (10 pints / 6 US quarts)
250g (9oz / 2 cups) leeks, rough-chopped	2kg (4½lb)
125g (5oz / 1 bunch) nasturtium or watercress	1kg (2lb 4oz / 8 bunches)
125g (5oz / 1 cup) frozen 'petit pois' peas	1kg (2lb 4oz)
1 tsp dried tarragon or 2 tsp fresh, finely chopped	3 tbsp dried or 25g (1oz / ⅓ cup) fresh
1-2 tsp fresh parsley, finely chopped (x 2 if no fresh tarragon available)	3 tbsp (x 2 if no fresh tarragon available)
3-5 tbsp single cream	600-800ml (1-1½ pints / approx. 3 cups)
approx. 1 tbsp olive oil to sauté	approx. 100ml (4-5fl oz / ½ cup)
½-1 tsp salt, ¼ tsp black pepper and 1 tsp stock powder	2-4 tbsp salt and/or stock powder and 2-3 tsp pepper
2-3 nasturtium flowers to garnish (if available)	5-6

1. Sauté the chopped onions and celery in olive oil until soft and pearly. Add a pinch of salt as you go. Also add the dried tarragon if using.

2. Add the potato and vegetable stock or water and bring to the boil.

3. Prepare the leeks, discarding the root tip and tougher-looking dark green outer leaves. Chop and rinse in cold water to remove any grit. Also rinse the nasturtium or watercress leaves in cold water and drain. Put aside a few perfect smaller nasturtium leaves or watercress sprigs for garnishing, before rough-chopping the rest, including quite a bit of the stalk.

4. When the onion, celery and potato have been simmering for about 10 minutes, add the chopped leeks and cook for a further 5-10 minutes. When the leeks are just softening and still bright green, toss in the peas and return to a simmer.

5. Preferably just 5-10 minutes before serving, add the rough-chopped nasturtium or watercress to the pan.

6. Warm the cream in a separate saucepan, holding back about 3-4 tbsp (⅓ cup) for drizzling over the top later.

7. Blend the soup just a few minutes after you have added the watercress or nasturtium – they will soften very quickly. Season to taste with salt, pepper and stock powder.

8. Stir in the hot cream and adjust the seasoning if necessary. Be careful not to let the soup boil once you've added the cream. Add the finely chopped fresh herbs.

9. Just before serving, swirl the remaining cream over the hot soup and garnish with either the water-lily-like nasturtium leaves or some sprigs of watercress. Float a few bright orange nasturtium flowers on the surface, if you have them. (This can also be done to decorate individual servings, in which case allow more leaves for garnishing – one flower per portion is ideal.)

Roast red pepper & tomato soup

Tchenka Sunderland introduced this cheering recipe to the College during her time as a visiting chef. Now, putting her astrologer's headscarf on, she invites you to cook it especially on Tuesdays, since Tuesdays are ruled by Mars, the red planet!

From an ecological perspective, there really is something a bit 'Martian' about our national obsession with (as Guy Watson* puts it) "that overpriced cousin of the deadly nightshade" – the colourful bell pepper. Perhaps it harks back to the days when Elizabeth David revitalized the post-war diet with her Mediterranean cookbooks, providing a welcome antidote to the monotony of British fodder that had been held in place by rationing, nutritious though it undoubtedly was. Capsicums demand the prolonged warmth of a Mediterranean or tropical climate, and it is at great cost to the environment that those of us who live in more temperate regions must simulate this in heated greenhouses. It is nice, therefore, to think of this recipe being cooked more regularly by our many warm-weather visitors and friends.

For 6	For 45-50
3 medium red peppers	24 (approx. 4kg / 9lb)
1 large onion, finely chopped	8 large (1.8kg / 4lb)
4 cloves garlic, thinly sliced	approx. 2 heads
1 stalk celery	1 head
400g (14oz / 2 cups) tomatoes	3.2kg (7lb) fresh or tinned
approx. 800ml (1½ pints / 3½-4 cups) veg stock	approx. 6½l (10 pints / 6 US quarts)
2 tbsp tomato purée or 4 sun-dried tomatoes	200ml (8fl oz / 1 scant cup) purée or sun-dried
50ml (2fl oz / ¼ cup) white wine	400ml (¾ pint / 1½ cups)
1 handful fresh basil, chopped	50-100g (2-4oz)
Knob of butter (optional)	approx. 50g (2oz / ½ stick) (optional)
approx. 1 tsp salt, ¼ tsp pepper and 1 tsp stock powder	1-3 tbsp salt and/or stock powder and 1-3 tsp pepper
4-6 tbsp olive oil to roast and sauté	approx. 500ml (¾ pint / 1-2 cups)

*Riverford Farm Cookbook, *page 273*

1. Begin with the red peppers – whose flavour you will be enhancing with a gentle roasting. Pre-heat the oven to 200°C (400°F / Gas Mark 6). Slice the peppers into thin strips, removing seeds and stalk. Tip the strips on to baking/roasting trays and drizzle liberally with olive oil. Sprinkle with salt, stir and spread out in a one-piece-thick layer. Roast in the hot oven for 20-30 minutes, checking and stirring a couple of times on the way. Remove when the pepper is becoming tender – the tips may be slightly charred in places. (Alternatively, if you have no oven, sweat them with the onions for a good 30 minutes until tender.)

2. Meanwhile prepare and sauté the onions, garlic and celery with a little olive oil in the bottom of your soup pan, stirring regularly.

3. Chop the tomatoes and add them, along with the tomato purée or sun-dried tomatoes, white wine and stock to the sautéd onion mixture and cook for a further 15-20 minutes. As soon as the red peppers are ready, add these too. Cook for a further 5 minutes and then whizz up with a rod blender until smooth-ish.

4. Optional: If you have anyone with a sensitive digestion at your meal table, you can rub the whole soup through a coarse sieve with a large spoon. Tchenka never bothers with this, but it will remove all the skins of the red pepper, which is the part of the vegetable some people find difficult to digest. It will also make for a smoother soup.

5. Finally, return the soup to the heat as you season with salt, pepper and stock powder. Stir in most of the chopped basil and the knob of butter (which Tchenka says will enrich it no end – though it can be left out for vegan diets). Serve with a garnish of the remaining fresh basil.

Carrot, leek & butter-bean soup

This hearty soup brings together chunky vegetable pieces and large beans in a simple soupy ensemble. All the vegetables are cut quite generously in rings or half-moons, to match the ample proportions of the butter beans, which will be known to American readers as lima beans.

For 6	For 45-50
100g (4oz / ½ cup) dried butter (lima) beans	800g (1lb 12oz)
1 bay leaf	4-5
200g (7oz / 1½ cups) onions	1.6kg (3½lb)
2 stalks celery	1 head
300g (11oz / 2 cups) carrots	2.5kg (5½lb)
250g (9oz / 2 cups) leeks	2kg (4½lb)
approx. 1l (1¾ pints / 2¼ US pints) veg stock or water	approx. 7l (12 pints / 7 US quarts)
1 tsp dried mixed herbs	3 tbsp
2-3 tbsp parsley, chopped	70-100g (3oz / 1-1½ cups)
1 tsp stock powder (if required)	3 tbsp (if required)
approx. 1 tsp salt, ¼ tsp pepper and 1 tsp mustard	2-3 tbsp salt and mustard, 1-3 tsp pepper
1-2 tbsp olive oil to sauté	150-200ml (5-7fl oz / ½-¾ cup)

1. The evening before making your soup, soak the dried beans in 2-3 times their depth of cold water.

2. Next day, get the beans cooking gently on the hob with a bay leaf as you prepare the rest of the vegetables. Once they are tender (but still holding together well), remove from the heat. Add a few spoonfuls of stock powder to help them keep their shape (alternatively, use a pinch or 1 tsp of salt).

3. Prepare the vegetables. None of them need be chopped too finely for this chunky soup. The carrots and leeks should be about as thick as the cooked butter beans. If the carrots are huge, halve or quarter the rings.

4. Sauté the onions and celery together with the olive oil. Add a pinch of salt and some mixed herbs. After 5 or 10 minutes, add the carrots and continue to sauté briefly, before covering with water or stock. Bring to a simmer and continue to cook for 20-30 minutes, until the carrots are tender. If you like, whizz up a little (½ cup / 4 cups) of this until smooth and return it to the pot.

5. Add the leeks and continue to cook until they are ready. Meanwhile, re-heat the beans and add these, with their cooking water.

6. Adjust the liquid levels as required, and season with salt, pepper and mustard to taste. Stir in the chopped parsley just before serving.

7. If your guests are helping themselves, remind them to delve deeply – so they find all the treasures that are buried at the bottom of the pot!

Tomato & black-eyed-bean soup

This soup embraces a colourful medley of summer-to-early-autumn vegetables, mixed in with some 'perennials' – mushrooms, black-eyed beans and onions. To make it even more substantial, serve with grated cheese – and vary the dried beans as you feel inspired. Fine florets of broccoli may be used instead of green beans, or let courgette lead the dance of the greens on its own.

For 6	For 45-50
125g (4½oz / ¾ cup) black-eyed beans	1kg (2lb 4oz)
4-6 sun-dried tomatoes (if available)	24-30 (200g / 7oz / 2 cups)
1 medium onion (approx. 170g / 6oz)	9-10 medium onions (1.5kg / 3½lb)
1-2 cloves garlic, crushed	8-12 cloves
1 smallish red pepper (100g / 4oz)	6-8 (approx. 800g / 2lb)
Half a medium aubergine	4 (800g / 2lb)
100g (4oz / 1 cup) mushrooms	800g (2lb)
1-2 medium-small courgettes	8-10, depending on size (1.4kg / 3lb)
4 young runner beans, or other green beans	20 (approx. 500g / 1lb)
6 tomatoes (300g / 12oz)	2.4kg (5lb) tinned chopped tomatoes
approx. 1.5l (2½ pints / 3 US pints) veg stock or water	approx. 10l (16 pints / 10 US quarts)
2-3 tbsp tomato purée	200 ml (7 oz / ⅔ cup)
2 tsp dried oregano	3-4 tbsp
1 tbsp stock powder (if required)	4-6 tbsp (if required)
A few leaves fresh basil, chopped/torn (or parsley/chives)	40g (1½oz / ¾-1 cup)
½-1 tsp salt, ¼ tsp pepper and 1 tsp Dijon mustard	1 tbsp salt, 1-2 tsp pepper and 3-4 tbsp mustard
1-2 tbsp olive oil to sauté	150-200ml (5-7fl oz / ½-¾ cup)

1. The evening before, soak the beans in three times their depth of cold water with a strip of kombu seaweed, if available. The sun-dried tomatoes may also be put to soak in a separate bowl of cold water. Next day, cook the beans for approximately 1 hour, until tender but definitely not mushy. Drain and spread out so they do not continue to cook in their own steam. Chop the sun-dried tomatoes small, and reserve their soaking liquid.

2. Skin the tomatoes (see tip on page 105), then cut them and all the other vegetables into roughly equal 1cm (½") pieces.

3. Begin sautéeing the onion, garlic, red pepper, aubergine and oregano in some olive oil, stirring gently. You can add a few pinches of salt at this stage. When the vegetables are beginning to soften, add the mushrooms and cook for a few more minutes. Then cover the vegetables with stock or water, to about a hand's width above the veg. Add the green beans, courgettes and tomatoes (both kinds) and bring to the boil. Turn down the heat and simmer until the vegetables are all tender.

4. Add the cooked beans and season with the tomato purée, stock powder, mustard, salt and pepper. Check the seasoning and adjust the water volume as required. Finally, add the chopped basil just before serving. (Substitute with parsley or chives when basil is not available.)

Main courses

Sweetcorn & beansprout fritters
Cherry tomato tarte tatin
Stuffed squash boat
Mushroom & tofu stroganoff
Courgette carbonara
Aubergine parmigiana
Onion pakoras
Courgette 'conkers'
Humble homity pie
Savoury stuffed pancakes
Three Kings' pie
Mushroom sformato
Arancini & arancioni (Little and large rice balls)
Chick-pea tagine with apricots & cashews
Twice-baked potatoes
Monkey-nut stew
Quinoa goulash with blue cheese & leeks
Whole mushroom & wild garlic (or spinach) quiche
Creamy risotto with nasturtium & squash
Red kidney-bean burgers – with Red onion, rosemary & cranberry marmalade
Old Postern pasties
Gluten-free pastry
Sprouting seeds & pulses: a quick guide

Sweetcorn & beansprout fritters

There is something terribly more-ish about fried food, served fresh and hot straight from the frying pan. But where does this irresistibility come from? Perhaps it's the combining of oils with food at a high temperature that does it, because it brings out the smells, the crunch and the flavour of food all in one go. The oil acts as a carrier for the flavour molecules, while the heat launches the smell into the room . . . Unhealthy though frying is as a routine way of cooking (especially when old oil is reused), it is nice to succumb to its temptation once in a while.

There are advantages to frying too: the frittering-way of cooking provides a means of serving all sorts of vegetables in a form that is acceptable to fussy young vegetable-resisting children. A bit like hiding a cat's pill in a piece of cheese! Indeed, I have successfully 'hidden' freshly grated mushroom, carrot, courgette and shredded spinach in my mixtures on occasion, and would encourage everyone to try out their own combinations.

As the reference to 'more corn' in the ingredients list for the larger quantity suggests, this is one of those elastic recipes that can include more canned or frozen corn in the winter months and 'hungry gap', and more courgette in the summer and early autumn. All these sit alongside the mung-beansprouts – which can be grown indoors at any time of year (see page 95 for sprouting instructions), and bear in mind that you'll need to begin with at least a quarter of the volume given in the recipe when measuring the dry weight of beans: that's ¼ cup (small quantity) and 2 cups (large quantity).

For 6 (approx. 12 fritters)	For 45-50
175g (6oz / 1 cup) sweetcorn (pre-cooked)	1.3kg (3lb)
125g (5oz / 1 cup) mung-beansprouts, etc.	1kg (2lb 4oz / 8 cups)
50g (2oz / ⅓ cup) carrot (or more corn)	450g (1lb / 3 cups – or more corn)
50g (2oz / ⅓ cup) courgette (or more corn)	450g (1lb / 3 cups – or more corn)
40g (1½oz / ½ cup) Cheddar, grated (optional)	350g (12oz / 4 cups) (optional)
2 eggs, separated	16-17
50ml (2fl oz / 4 tbsp) milk and/or corn juice	400ml (14fl oz / 1¾ cups)
125g (4½oz / 1 level cup) white flour or gram flour	1kg (2lb 4oz / 8 level cups)
1½ tsp baking powder (or use self-raising flour)	4 tbsp
¼ tsp salt	2 tsp
¼ tsp / 1 pinch black pepper or paprika	1-2 tsp
½ tsp Dijon mustard	4 tsp
1-2 tbsp olive or sunflower oil (plus more for frying)	approx. 200ml (½ pint / 1 cup)

1. Drain the corn and reserve the liquid. If using fresh corn, carve it off the cob before or after cooking in boiling salted water (see page 39: Step 5 of Squash & corn chowder recipe).

2. Combine the corn and beansprouts in a bowl. If using grated carrots, courgettes or cheese, add these too. Stir in the egg yolks, mustard, salt, pepper/paprika and oil, reserved corn liquid and/or milk. Fold in the flour and baking powder.

3. Whisk the egg whites into snowy peaks and fold these gently and minimally into the fritter mix.

4. Now get a couple of millimetres of sunflower oil hot in your frying pan and use a large, deep serving spoon (or ⅓ cup measure) to place dollops of the fritter mixture on the sizzling oil. Fill the pan with several such fritter-heaps, usually oval-shaped and at least 1cm (½") deep in the centre. If possible, keep the fritters from touching each other. Turn the heat down and cook gently for 5-7 minutes, then turn them over and cook the other side. The point at which the fritter is ready to turn can be judged by the way the batter is setting – it will be losing the wet, uncooked shine and turning matt or dull around the edges and on top. Little holes may appear, signifying air bubbles rising to the surface and bursting. Using a lid can help to focus heat on the upper surface of the fritters. When the fritters are ready, keep them warm in a low oven until the whole batch is ready to eat.

Serving suggestions: These fritters are very nice accompanied by sour cream as well as with chutneys – whether a home-made green tomato chutney or a shop-bought mango chutney. We often serve them with leafy green salads, red cabbage, baked mushrooms and baked tomatoes, and sometimes even baked potatoes, depending on how hungry everyone is.

Cherry tomato tarte tatin

This upside-down style of tart was originally popularized by the Tatin sisters, who were renowned for serving the classic apple version at their restaurant near Orleans in France. Upside-down cooking suits my retrograde gas oven perfectly, and is a welcome technique for anyone who finds, as I do, that the bases of tarts and quiches tend to remain undercooked despite all efforts.

Creating a *tarte tatin* provides an opportunity to think back-to-front, as you construct a wonderfully light and flavoursome 'pie' that you will later flip over and turn into a 'tart' that has had no need of being blind-baked. Once inverted, a delightful sight awaits you: in this case, a clutch of whole baked cherry tomatoes sparkling in a pastry nest, ready to spurt the sweet yet tangy juice of summer on to your plate and into your mouth.

For 6-8 (1 x 20cm / 8" tart)	**For 45-50** (7 x 25cm / 10" tarts)
700g (1½lb) cherry tomatoes	7kg (12½lb)
1 large onion (150g / 6oz), cut into fine half-moon slivers	8 large (1.2kg / 3lb)
85g (3oz / ½ cup) Cheddar, grated, or other hard cheese	650g (1½lb)
1 tsp balsamic (or cider) vinegar	7 x 1½ tsp (approx. 50ml / 2fl oz)
1 tsp tamari	7 x 1½ tsp (approx. 50ml / 2fl oz)
1 pinch dried thyme or other herbs	2-3 tsp
A little basil, chopped, or other fresh herb (optional)	50g (2oz / ½ cup)
1 pinch salt	1-2 tsp
1 pinch black pepper (optional)	1½ tsp (optional)
2 tbsp olive oil	7 x 2½ tbsp (approx. 250ml / 9fl oz)

Pastry

110g (4oz / 1 scant cup) flour	900g (2lb)
60g (2oz / ½ stick) butter	450g (1lb)
1 egg yolk (for extra stretchiness)	2 whole eggs or 7 yolks
1 tbsp cold water	250ml (9fl oz / 1 cup)
½ tsp dried oregano (optional)	1 heaped tbsp (optional)
1 pinch salt	2 tsp
1 tsp olive oil	3 tbsp

Garnish

1 sprig fresh basil and approx. 1 tbsp pine nuts (optional)	7 sprigs and 7 tbsp (optional)

1. Begin by making the shortcrust pastry in the usual way (see Step 1 on page 85 – Whole mushroom & wild garlic quiche recipe – though the ingredients here are slightly different and include a little oregano). Once you've rubbed the butter into the dry ingredients, bind them together with the egg, olive oil and water. Divide into as many pieces as you have tins, shape into balls and pat down to the thickness of a couple of fingers. Cover these patties with a plastic bag/lid or baking parchment and leave to stand in a cool place while you prepare the filling and tin.

2. If using a tin with a detachable bottom, line it with a circle of baking parchment that is about 1cm (½") larger than the base, so it will go up the sides and prevent juices oozing out through the join. A smear of butter around the edge will help hold this in place.

3. Having prepared your tin(s), you will need to create a pool of juices at the bottom of each that the tomatoes will roast in. Begin by depositing the olive oil (2-2½ tbsp per tin). Spread this around with a pastry brush or your fingers to create a layer of olive oil that is perhaps a millimetre thick. Next add a sprinkling of tamari and vinegar, a pinch of dried herbs and a tiny pinch of salt.

4. Place the washed and drained cherry tomatoes on top of this, preferably with the stalk end uppermost or to the side, completely covering the surface with a single layer of crammed together tomatoes. Pre-heat the oven to 180°C (350°F / Gas Mark 4).

5. Sauté the finely sliced onion in a little olive oil, with a sprinkling of salt. You can also add some freshly chopped basil or marjoram and a little freshly ground black pepper. When the onions are soft and opalescent, spread them over the tomatoes.

6. Sprinkle a layer of grated cheese over the onions. The onions help to hold the cheese more or less in place and prevent it from dribbling down and obscuring the underside of the tomatoes (the top-to-be).

7. Roll out the pastry until it forms a large thin ring, 1-2cm (½-1") wider than your tin. Place this over the cheese and tuck it in around the sides of the tomatoes, folding it back on itself if necessary. Gently press it down on top of the filling so it makes a good contact, piercing it in one or two places to let warming air escape.

8. Bake in the oven for about 30-40 minutes, until the pastry is golden-brown. Double-check for readiness by gently poking a small knife or skewer into the middle of the tart to check that the tomatoes beneath are nice and soft. Allow to cool for 5 minutes or so.

Turning out and serving: Check that the pastry hasn't stuck to the edge of the tin – go around it with a knife if necessary. Cover with a suitable plate (its centre should match the size and curve of the pastry, and it should have a good rim to contain the juices). Gripping both the plate and tin edges with a tea towel, swiftly turn the *tarte tatin* upside-down. Remove the tin. Hey presto – let's hope it's perfect! Rearrange any straying tomatoes and garnish with a sprig of fresh basil and a scattering of pine nuts, if you have any to spare.

Stuffed squash boat

Throughout the 1990s the College was the grateful recipient of huge marrows for stuffing at harvest time, provided by our then local vicar, Paul Wimsett. The church marrows were often huge: bigger than any other vegetable in our food store, measuring in at some 40cm (1½') long. They were proper marrows, not overgrown courgettes, and as such had distinctive wide stripes of yellow and green along their backs – well coordinated with our aprons!

Nowadays, marrows grow in the College's own vegetable patch from late August to October, and, as fortune would have it, Mel Risebrow arrived on the staff team with a particular penchant for cooking them. He said it was their very hugeness he loved – the way they would sit in a vegetable patch getting bigger and bigger, a bit like James's Giant Peach.

In this recipe, 'boats' of marrow or squash are stuffed with a wholesome cargo of vegetables, nuts and cheese, and served with a fresh tomato–pepper sauce. The intense tastiness of sauce and filling acts as a foil for the mild flavour of the marrow. Outside the marrow season, the more flavoursome butternut squash also lends itself deliciously to being cooked in this glorious way.

For 6+	For 45-50
1 medium marrow or large butternut squash (1.5kg / 3lb 5oz)	10 kg (4-5 larger marrows or 8-10 butternut squash)

Stuffing

For 6+	For 45-50
50g (2oz / ½ cup) dried chestnuts or buckwheat	400g (14oz)
50g (2oz / ½ cup) breadcrumbs (or use GF oat or buckwheat flakes)	400g (14oz)
1 large onion	1.5kg (3lb 4oz)
2 cloves garlic, crushed	1-2 heads
1 stalk celery	1 head
200g (7oz / 1½ cups) open mushrooms	1.6kg (3lb 4oz)
200g (7oz / 1½ cups) carrot	1.6kg (3lb 4oz)
Any surplus good squash flesh not used in the sauce	(see left)
85g (3oz / ⅔ cup) walnuts or cashews, quite finely chopped	600g (1lb 4oz)
140g (5oz / 2 cups) Cheddar, grated	1.1kg (2½lb)
2 eggs	16
1 bay leaf	1 only
1-2 tsp dried thyme	3 tbsp
2 tbsp fresh parsley, finely chopped	70g (2½oz / 1 cup)
1 tsp Dijon mustard	3 tbsp
2-3 pinches salt and 1 pinch black pepper to taste	2-4 tsp salt and 1-2 tsp pepper
2-3 tsp olive oil to sauté	approx. 100ml (4-5fl oz / ½ cup)

Tomato-pepper sauce

1 small red onion	4 medium
2 cloves garlic, crushed	2-3 tbsp, crushed
1 small or half a large red pepper	3 red peppers
1 small or half a large green pepper	3 green peppers
6 medium red tomatoes	2kg (4½lb)
80g (2-3oz / ⅓ cup) squash/marrow flesh	450-600g (1-1½lb / 2-3 cups)
150ml (5fl oz / ½ cup) vegetable stock or water	approx. 1-1½l (2-3 pints / 2½-3½ US pints)
¼ tsp dried basil or oregano	2 tsp
4-5 leaves fresh basil, chopped or torn (if available)	25g (1oz / ½ cup)
Dash of red wine / sherry / lemon juice (optional)	100ml (4fl oz / ½ cup) (optional)
½ tsp salt and 1 pinch black pepper to taste	2-3 tsp and ½ tsp pepper to taste
½ tsp Dijon mustard	2-3 tsp
A little olive or sunflower oil to sauté	approx. 100ml (4-5fl oz / ½ cup)

1. Soak the dried chestnuts in twice their depth of cold water for several hours or overnight. Once rehydrated, simmer them with a bay leaf until soft. Drain and pick out any large woody bits, then mash or chop quite roughly. If using buckwheat grain, cook in three times its volume of water until the grain is soft. Drain.

2. *Preparing the squash/marrow:* If you don't have a large enough steamer for a marrow or squash (see below), pre-heat the oven now to 180°C (350°F / Gas Mark 4). Wash the squash/marrow, remove the stalk and cut lengthways through the middle. Scoop out the seeds, and also some of the flesh – reserve this for later. The flesh wall should now be about 2-3cm (¾-1") thick. If using butternut squash, remove the seeds and steam or bake before scooping out any flesh, as it will be easier to scoop away when softened. At the College we steam the boat-shaped squash/marrows in huge bamboo steamers until just beginning to soften but still holding their shape (see page 88) – they don't need to be completely cooked, as they will cook further in the oven when stuffed. On a domestic scale, the same effect can be achieved by baking the squash halves in the oven, although you can get domestic-sized bamboo steamers to fit butternut squash, which are a bit smaller than marrows. In the absence of one of these, place the squash/marrow in an ovenproof dish with a little water, cover with foil, and bake for 30-45 minutes until just tender. When ready, set aside.

3. *Breadcrumbs:* Weigh out the bread for the breadcrumbs and tear up roughly. Place the bread pieces in your food processor until half-full and whizz up with the knife attachment – they don't have to be very fine. (The nuts may also be chopped in the food processor, or by hand.)

4. *Stuffing:* Sauté the finely diced onion and celery in a little olive oil. After a few minutes add the dried herbs, garlic and finely chopped mushrooms, and continue to stir over the heat until all are soft and cooked.

5. When the cooked vegetables have cooled a little, drain off any surplus liquid and reserve this for the sauce. Tip the veg into a large mixing bowl and combine with the other ingredients: grated carrots, fresh herbs, mashed chestnuts or cooked buckwheat, breadcrumbs / buckwheat flakes / GF oat flakes and eggs, as well as any squash/marrow flesh not needed in the sauce. Also add about three-quarters of the grated cheese and chopped nuts, setting the rest aside for the topping. Season the stuffing mixture to taste with salt, pepper and Dijon mustard.

6. *Stuffing the squash/marrow:* Place the 'boat' in a lightly oiled baking dish. Spoon in the stuffing mixture, patting it down and heaping it up as you go. Build your cargo up so that it rests on the edges of the squash/marrow and forms a mound of some 2-3 cm (¾-1") high. Bake in the oven at the same temperature as before for 30 minutes, then sprinkle with the reserved grated cheese and nuts and cook for another 15-20 minutes. When ready, the stuffing should be 'set' – firm but spongy, not wobbly – when a knife is inserted it should come out moist but relatively clean, because the eggs are cooked. Remove the boat from the oven and let stand for 10 minutes before serving in generous thick slices.

7. *Sauce:* While your boat is baking, prepare the tomato-pepper sauce. Sauté the chopped red onion, garlic, finely diced peppers and dried herbs in a little oil (use a large saucepan, which will eventually hold the whole volume of the sauce). Add the blanched and peeled (see tip on page 105) chopped tomatoes and the finely chopped squash/marrow flesh. Add the stock or water and continue to cook until all the vegetables are soft. Season to taste with salt, pepper and mustard. A dash of red wine, sherry or lemon juice may be added to improve the taste. Adjust the liquid volume until you have a thick but pourable sauce. Blend all or part of the sauce and remix. Stir in the freshly chopped or torn basil at the end, if using. We usually serve the sauce separately from the stuffed squash using a jug, or a pan with a ladle, so people can help themselves.

Mushroom & tofu stroganoff

It is amazing how tofu can be transformed into something deeply flavoursome and interesting, just through using the technique of an overnight marinade followed by a spell of baking in the oven to toughen the outside (while keeping the inside as soft as a marshmallow.) The mushroom, considered by Jain monks to be too meat-like in texture to eat, also helps enormously with this 'meat–amorphosis'.

For 6

500g (1lb 2oz) tofu, pressed, cubed and marinated
Orange / cider vinegar marinade (see page 108 – quantities as there)
4-5 dried porcini mushrooms
1 large onion, diced medium-small
2 tsp garlic, minced
½ tsp paprika and 1 tsp nutritional yeast flakes (if available)
1 tbsp tamari
500g (1lb 2oz) mushrooms, thick-sliced
125ml (4fl oz / ½ cup) red wine
200ml (7fl oz / ¾ cup) mushroom or vegetable stock
300ml (10fl oz / 1¼ cups) sour cream or crème fraîche
1-2 tbsp parsley, chopped
100g (4oz / 1½ cups) Parmesan-style cheese, grated (optional)
3-4 tbsp olive oil to sauté

For 50

4kg (9lb)
As shown on page 108
100g (4oz / 3 cups)
1.5kg (3lb 4oz)
1 head (5 tbsp / ⅓ cup)
2 tbsp and 3 tbsp
150ml (5fl oz / ½ cup+)
4kg (10lb)
1l (1¾ pints / 2 US pints)
1l (2 pints / 2½ US pints)
2.25l (4 pints / 5 US pints)
approx. 40g (1oz / ½ cup)
approx. 800g (2lb)
approx. 150ml (7fl oz / ¾ cup)

1. Slice the tofu into 1.25-2cm (½-¾") cubes. Marinate the cubes overnight in orange / cider vinegar marinade (see Orange-marinated tofu recipe, page 108, but use porcini mushrooms instead of shiitake).

2. Next day, drain the marinated tofu. Skim off the porcini mushrooms and set them aside. Spread the tofu out on baking trays, one layer thick. Bake at 180°C (350°F / Gas Mark 4) for 20 minutes, until plumped up and tougher to touch.

3. Fry the diced onion in olive oil until soft, then add the garlic, paprika and nutritional yeast, followed by the tamari and mushrooms.

4. As the mushrooms begin to show signs of cooking, add the wine and half the stock. Simmer for 10 minutes, then add the baked marinated tofu and the dried porcini mushrooms. Continue to simmer and reduce for a further 5-10 minutes.

5. Warm the remaining stock and whisk it into the sour cream or crème fraîche. Once the mushrooms are cooked, add the sour cream mixture to the pan. Cook gently until the sauce is hot and thick, but do not boil vigorously or cook for too long, as it will curdle.

6. Taste and season if you wish – although the tamari should make the dish salty enough. Garnish with freshly chopped parsley and serve with rice, noodles or pasta – plus freshly grated cheese if you like! A crisp green salad studded with tomatoes is very nice on the side.

Courgette carbonara

Nowadays it's difficult to imagine a week going by without the convenient pasta meal, but it wasn't until after the Second World War that Italian noodles of all shapes and sizes arrived at the English table. Long, long before this, the Italian charcoal burners (*carbonari*) in the woods around Rome knew all about the convenience of dried pasta: they were cooking up simple meals from just a few ingredients that could easily be carried to work without spoiling. Thus, in a typical dish of *spaghetti carbonara* you will find salted or smoked pork such as bacon or pancetta, alongside hard cheese (Parmesan) and egg.

I've added a little cream to the basic recipe, as it helps to prevent the egg from scrambling. The bacon is replaced with smoked tofu – and to remind us of the Mediterranean roots of the dish, some sun-dried tomatoes and courgettes have been included.

For 6	For 45-50
500g (1lb 2oz) spaghetti, fettucini or tagliatelli	3.5kg (7½lb)
30g (1oz / ⅓ cup) sun-dried tomatoes	250g (10oz / 2½ cups)
250g (9oz / 1 pack) smoked tofu	2kg (4½lb / 8 packs)
1-2 tbsp tamari or soy sauce	approx. 100ml (4fl oz / ½ cup)
3 plump cloves garlic, 'bruised'	2 large heads
4 medium courgettes (approx. 80g / 1lb 1oz)	28 (approx. 6kg / 13lb)
100g (4oz / 2 cups) Parmesan-style cheese, grated	700g (1½lb)
50g (2oz / ½ cup) smoked Cheddar, grated	350g (12oz)
4 eggs + 1 extra yolk	30 eggs
3 tbsp cream	300 ml (10fl oz / 1¼ cups)
1-3 pinches salt and black pepper to taste	1-2 tbsp salt and 1-3 tsp pepper
A little butter and olive oil to sauté	approx. 100ml (4-5fl oz / ½ cup)

1. A few hours before cooking, cover the sun-dried tomatoes in water. When they are rehydrated, drain and slice into strips then set aside.

2. Slice the smoked tofu into thinnish (½cm / ¼") slices. Cut each slice into three smaller rectangles – not too big or they'll break up when tossed into the pasta. Layer these loosely in a dish, sprinkling with tamari or soy sauce as you go.

3. If making the large quantity, pre-heat the oven to 200°C (400°F / Gas Mark 6). Peel the garlic and 'bruise' each clove by crushing *slightly* with the back of a knife (the clove should remain whole).

4. Wash and cut the courgettes into narrow half-moons, similar in thickness to the tofu. Toss with olive oil and a sprinkling of salt. Spread out on a baking tray and roast in the oven for about 15-20 minutes, until cooked to taste and perhaps lightly browned in places. Then reduce the oven temperature to a minimum, just to keep the courgette warm. (If making the smaller size, you may prefer to sauté the courgettes on the hob.)

5. In a large frying pan, melt some butter with a little olive oil, then gently fry the tofu with the bruised garlic until lightly browned. Decant into an oven dish and keep warm in the oven. The garlic may be kept as part of the dish (either chopped small or kept whole), as you prefer.

6. While the courgettes and tofu are cooking, put a large saucepan (or two) of water, no more than two-thirds full, on to boil. Add a few pinches of salt and a dash of oil to the water.

7. Meanwhile, grate the 'Parmesan' finely and put about a quarter of it aside to sprinkle on the pasta later. Also grate the smoked Cheddar.

8. Crack the eggs into a bowl with the cream and whisk. Season with a little salt and pepper. Stir three-quarters of the grated 'Parmesan' and all the grated smoked Cheddar into this.

9. 15-20 minutes before serving time, put the pasta into the boiling water and return to the boil, stirring occasionally so it does not stick. Once boiling, reduce the heat to a simmer and cook for 10 minutes, until the pasta is 'al dente' – still slightly chewy. When ready, a strand of spaghetti chucked against a wall will stick to it! Drain, but save a small jug of the pasta water to moisten the pasta with later.

10. Return the pasta to the hot pan and *immediately* pour over the egg, cheese and cream mixture. Lift up the pasta with a large fork to ensure the sauce covers it all. The mixture should not scramble, but rather coat the pasta smoothly (turn the burner very low – or off – while you do this).

11. Gently mix or layer in the tofu, courgette and sun-dried tomato pieces, holding back a small amount of each to decorate the top with later. Add a bit of the pasta water if you think the mixture needs moistening.

12. Plate-up the pasta individually or serve in a large dish. Toss some of the reserved grated 'Parmesan' on top, together with the reserved vegetables and tofu, and put the remaining cheese in a small bowl to be added to taste at the table. Serve straight away.

Aubergine parmigiana

Waverlie Neuberger was a participant on Schumacher College's Certificate of Education for Sustainability programme. This unique programme was the creation of Toni Spencer, based on an idea that came into the mind of Karen Blincoe during her brief spell as the College's director. The programme gathered together students interested in setting up their own ecological education centres at home. Waverlie, for example, was involved in setting up a project that aimed to establish a sustainability axis at the Methodist university of São Paulo, Brazil. The Schumacher-Brazil connection remains very much alive with a regular flow of Brazilian students coming to the College, often occupying key volunteer roles when their studies are complete, and Schumacher staff making return visits to Brazil.

Returning to the recipe, Waverlie remembers her grandmother, Nona Anna Matarazzo, with great love. Nona Anna came to Brazil as a young woman of 25, escaping Mussolini's Italy. She loved to cook, and in her new country she found herself confronted with a whole new culinary culture and strange ingredients. When she first encountered cassava, for example, she thought it was timber and used it as wood for the fire — until someone put her right and showed her how to cook the tuber. She also had some of her own traditional recipes to share, including this delicious aubergine-Parmesan dish from Naples, which she taught her little granddaughter Waverlie to make.

For approx. 8
(1 medium baking dish, 6-7cm / 2½" deep)

1.5kg (3lb 4oz) aubergines
approx. 4 tbsp flour to coat (optional)
100ml (4-5fl oz / ½ cup) olive oil (double for deep-frying)

Tomato sauce
2-3 large onions (450g / 1lb), finely chopped
2-4 cloves garlic, finely chopped or crushed
1 tsp dried basil or oregano
1.25kg (2lb 12oz) fresh tomatoes (use tinned out of season)
2-3 tbsp tomato purée
55g (2oz / ½-¾ cup) black olives, chopped
20g (1oz / ¼ cup) fresh basil, chopped or torn
2-3 tsp brown sugar (or malt extract), if using tinned tomatoes
approx. 1 tsp salt and ¼ tsp pepper
A little olive oil to sauté

For 45-50
4 large (4-litre / 7-pint) dishes

8kg (17lb)
approx. 30g (10oz / 2 cups) (optional)
Up to 400ml (¾ pint / 2 cups)

2.8kg (6lb)
1 large head
2 tbsp
7.5kg (16lb)
250-300ml (10fl oz / 1 cup)
225-300g (8-12oz / 2-3 cups)
100g (4oz / 1½ cups)
4-6 tbsp
2 tbsp salt and 1-2 tsp pepper
approx. 100ml (4-5fl oz / ½ cup)

Cheese topping

250g (9oz / 2-3 cups) Cheddar, sliced or grated	1.5kg (3lb 4oz)
150g (5-6oz) buffalo mozzarella or goat's cheese, sliced	1kg (2lb)
30g (1oz / ¼-⅓ cup) Parmesan-style cheese, grated	200g (7oz / 1½-2 cups)
2 eggs	14
1-2 pinches salt and pepper	2-3 pinches

1. Pre-heat the oven to 200°C (400°F / Gas Mark 6). Begin by preparing the aubergine, slicing lengthways into thin (0.5cm / ¼") slabs. Press these in flour and, according to Nona Anna, deep-fry in either sunflower or olive oil. Alternatively, miss out the flour, paint with olive oil on both sides and lay out in one layer on metal baking trays. Bake in the oven for 20-30 minutes, turning over halfway through – the aubergine should be tender and lightly browned in places (this oven-baking method is what we favour at the College as it frees up the hob for other things). When ready, reduce the oven temperature to 180°C (350°F / Gas Mark 4).

2. Next prepare the tomato sauce. Sauté the onions in olive oil with the garlic and basil or oregano. Once the onions are softening well and beginning to look pearly, add the chopped tomato and continue to cook. Add the tomato purée and season with salt and pepper. A few teaspoonsful of sugar (or malt extract if not catering for gluten-free diets) will help mellow the sharp taste tinned tomato can give. Finally, add the black olives and fresh basil.

3. Grate or thinly slice the Cheddar cheese and slice the mozzarella or goat's cheese ready for use. Keep separate.

4. *Layering the parmigiana:* First, make a thin layer of tomato sauce in the bottom of your baking dish. Next, arrange a wall-to-wall layer of aubergines, two slices thick. Waverlie says it is most important that this layer is complete and substantial, so that the meal will be easy to slice. Follow the aubergine layer with another layer of tomato sauce, then a layer of Cheddar cheese, then more aubergines (this layer does not have to be two slices thick, but can be!). Then comes more tomato sauce and – if you have any left – more Cheddar, more aubergine and another layer of sauce. (We found ourselves stopping at two layers of aubergine.) Follow the top layer of tomato with a layer of mozzarella or goat's cheese slices.

5. *Topping:* Beat the egg and season with a little salt and pepper. Pour this over the mozzarella / goat's cheese, then sprinkle the grated 'Parmesan' over this.

6. Bake in the moderate oven for 45-60 minutes until the top is golden-brown, bubbling gently and smelling delicious! Allow to stand for 5 or 10 minutes before serving, as you would a lasagne – this will help with slicing.

7. Serve with a crisp green salad and warm crusty bread.

Onion pakoras

For me, pakoras and bhajees, golden-brown and sizzling as they are lifted from dangerously hot oil, typify the tempting little morsels of the wayside food sellers in the big cities of India. At home they can be served warm as a 'gut teaser' before a meal. This formula from Minni (who normally cooks by eye) works well and is especially useful for the uninitiated!

For approx. 6	For 45-50
2 large or 4 small onions (400g / 1lb), red or white	16 large (3.5-4kg / 7-8lb)
250-300g (9-11oz / 2 cups) gram flour	2kg (4½lb)
1 finely chopped green chilli (optional)	6-8 (optional)
½ tsp garam masala	1½ tbsp
1 tsp ground coriander	2-3 tbsp
1 pinch turmeric	2-3 tsp
1 pinch asafoetida (if available)	1 tsp
1 tsp salt to taste	2 tbsp
approx. 250ml (9fl oz / 1 cup) water	approx. 2l (3½ pints / 4¼ US pints)
A little oil to fry (e.g. sunflower or corn oil)	approx. 100ml (4-5fl oz / ½ cup)

1. Peel the onions and slice across into disks of concentric circles 3-4mm (⅛-¼") thick. Divide the pile in half, leave one half in circles and cut the rest into half circles. Mix all the onions together into a sort of tangled bird's nest, separating the rings with your fingers if they insist on sticking together. Set aside.

2. In a bowl, combine all the dry ingredients: gram flour, spices, chilli (if using), etc. Add a little water and mix until you have a creamy batter that will adhere to the onions. Minni says the consistency should resemble that of 'a thick smoothie'. Stir well until smooth.

3. Take a wok or saucepan and fill with oil to a depth of about 4-5cm (2"). Bring to a gently rolling simmer.

4. Test the heat of the oil by dropping some of the batter into it. If the batter sizzles and swims to the top, the oil is hot enough to begin cooking.

5. Mix a handful of the chopped onions into the batter (only a portion or two at a time, so the onions don't sit there producing liquid, which makes the batter too runny). Or, if making the large quantity, separate a couple of cups of batter into breakfast bowls and mix a small amount of onions into this, to avoid losing sight of the onions in the batter-swamp. Using a dessertspoon and/or fork to lift, put small spidery clumps of coated onions into the hot oil. Fry each portion until golden-brown, turning as required. Keep the cooked pakoras warm in the oven while you fry the rest.

Variations: Use other vegetables, such as cauliflower florets, round disks of aubergine and potato, and shredded spinach. A maximum width of 0.5-1cm (¼-½") is recommended for all vegetables, to ensure even and thorough cooking without burning.

Courgette 'conkers'

These tasty courgette mouthfuls have been evolved by our Vegetarian Chef Ruth Rae, who says she loves the recipe because it's "hard to get wrong". If the mixture is too runny, you need only add more breadcrumbs; if too dry, a little more grated courgette. This is an excellent recipe for using up surpluses of overgrown marrow too. Serve with potato wedges and some home-made chutney, fresh tomato sauce or sour cream.

The courgette balls should be made about the same size as a green conker — before it comes out of its shell. In fact, at the suggestion of our gardener Jane Gleeson, we've named them 'conkers' in honour of the great horse-chestnut tree that stands on the front lawn — still an inspiration to many, despite age and recent visits from tree surgeons.

For 6	For 45-50
500g (1lb 2oz / 3 cups) courgette or marrow, grated	4kg (9lb)
1 medium onion, diced finely	8 medium (1.5kg/ 3½lb)
2 cloves garlic, minced or crushed	2-3 tbsp
2 sprigs rosemary, finely chopped	10-16
10 sage leaves, finely chopped	85g (3oz / 1 cup)
150g (5½oz / 1¼ cups) Cheddar (preferably smoked), grated	1.2kg (2lb 12oz)
150g (5½oz / 1½ cups) breadcrumbs, brown or white (see Step 2)	1.2kg (2lb 12oz)
1 egg	8
1-3 pinches each of salt and pepper to season	1-2 tbsp salt and ½-1 tsp pepper
approx. 100ml (4-5fl oz / ½ cup) olive oil to sauté	approx. 600ml (1 pint / 3 cups)

1. Wash the courgettes or marrow. If the marrow is old and tough-skinned, peel it before grating. Collect the grated vegetable in a bowl and salt well before tipping into a colander and leaving to drain for 20 minutes (put another bowl under the colander to catch the drips).

2. To make the breadcrumbs, tear up stale bread and quickly whizz it up in your food processor. (See also Ruth's tip below.)

3. Pre-heat the oven to 190°C (375°F / Gas Mark 5). Sauté the onion and garlic in olive oil until tender. Rinse the courgette in cold water, then wring it out by pressing it against the walls of the colander to remove surplus liquid.

4. Combine all the ingredients in a large bowl, season well and form into snooker-ball-sized balls or sausages. Place your courgette 'conkers' a little apart on a baking tray lined with non-stick baking parchment and bake in the oven for 20 minutes or until golden-brown and set.

Ruth's tip: Whenever you have old bits of bread, cut or tear them up and whizz them into crumbs in your food processor using the knife attachment. Put them in a plastic bag in the freezer until needed for a recipe like this, which does not require bone-dry crumbs.

Humble homity pie

Homity pie is a traditional open-topped British pie that was probably invented back in the 1940s by the Land Girls to make the best of wartime food rationing. Just such belly-filling, inexpensive comfort foods were among Helen Chaloner's favourite everyday meals at Schumacher College when she started to plan the five-week-long course menus back in the early 1990s. With only a few fairly basic ingredients, which are available all year around, this potato, cheese and onion-based pie makes an excellent accompaniment for whichever greens (or reds) are growing in your garden – chard, courgettes, beans. . . carrots, tomatoes, squash. . .

At home, you can make individual homity pies in 10cm (4") tins or foil dishes: a bit fiddly, but great for picnics or packed lunches. For supper at the College we make larger round or rectangular pies that get sliced up at mealtimes.

For 6
(6 individual pies or 1 x 25cm (10") round pie)

For 45-50
(6 round 25cm (10") or 4-5 rectangular 30cm x 25cm (12" x 10") roasting tins)

Shortcrust pastry

For 6	For 45-50
75g (3oz / ¾ stick) butter	600g (1lb 4oz)
75g (3oz / rounded ½ cup) wholewheat flour	600g (1lb 4oz)
75g (3oz / rounded ½ cup) plain white flour	600g (1lb 4oz)
2 tsp sunflower seeds (optional)	50g (2oz / ½ cup) (optional)
¼ tsp salt	2 tsp
2-3 tbsp water	300-400ml (12-15fl oz / 1½-2 cups)

Filling

For 6	For 45-50
500g (1lb 2oz) potatoes	4kg (9lb)
500g (1lb 2oz) onions	4kg (9lb)
2-3 cloves garlic, crushed	1-2 large bulbs
200g (7oz / 1½ cups) celery, fennel or leek	1.6kg (3½lb)
160g (6oz / 1½ cups) Cheddar, grated	1.3kg (3lb)
25g (1oz / ¼ stick) butter	225g (8oz / 2 sticks)
1-2 tbsp milk	100ml (4fl oz / ½ cup)
3-4 tbsp parsley / other garden herbs, or 2 tsp dried mixed herbs	100g (3-4oz / 2-3 cups) or 3-4 tbsp dried
1-2 tsp Dijon mustard	3 tbsp
2 pinches salt	approx. 2 tsp
1 pinch black pepper	approx. 1 tsp
3-4 tbsp olive oil to sauté	100ml (4-5fl oz / ½ cup)

1. Begin by making the shortcrust pastry and leaving it to rest in a cool place (see page 85, Step 1, using the ingredients given here).

2. Scrub and chop the potatoes into 1cm (½") cubes and boil until just tender. Drain through a colander.

3. While the potatoes are cooking, get out the rested pastry, roll it out fairly thinly (about 3mm / ⅛" thick), and use it to line 6 small (10cm / 4") tins or 1 round flan tin, for the small quantity; or 48 small tins, 6 round flan tins or 4-5 large roasting tins for the large quantity. If you have used up all the pastry and built a 3cm (1½")-high wall with it at the edge of each dish, you will have the right amount of containers to hold the filling!

4. Peel and chop the onions and celery (or leeks or fennel instead of celery). Sauté these in olive oil with the crushed garlic until soft.

5. Pre-heat the oven to 180°C (350°F / Gas Mark 4). Chop the parsley finely, adding a little rosemary, thyme or marjoram from your garden if available. (Dried mixed herbs can be used if you do not have fresh ones.)

6. Combine and mix the cooked potatoes, onion mixture, butter, milk, parsley, mustard and half the cheese. Season well to taste. Usually, stirring the mixture breaks up the potato enough for it to stick together while maintaining some of its distinct cubed-potato form, but you can also mash the potato a bit if you want.

7. After the mixture has cooled a little more, fill the pastry cases with it and sprinkle the remaining cheese on top. Bake in the oven for 20-25 minutes for the small pies and 40-50 minutes for the larger ones. The top should be golden-brown when ready. Leave the small pies to cool for at least 15 minutes before attempting to remove from the tins – longer if you are going to eat them cold.

Savoury stuffed pancakes

We had never served stuffed pancakes at Schumacher College until Ed Brown, Zen Abbot and author of the Tassajara recipe books, came to teach a mixture of meditation and cooking at the College in 2001. We ordered in several small frying pans – and opened the door to a decade of pancake-making. First in line to inherit the tossing pans were Ralph and Tchenka, who teamed up to produce many delicious pancake meals, the inspiration for this recipe. Ralph Freelink was an MSc student in 2003 and will always be remembered for tossing frisbees in the garden, as well as for tossing pancakes for breakfast every weekend. These morsels are delicious served with a selection of hearty salads – or on their own as an appetizer.

For 5-6 (makes 8-10 medium pancake rolls)	For 45-50 (72-80 rolls)
Filling	
400g (14oz / 4 cups) open or chestnut mushrooms	3.6kg (7lb)
300g leeks, giving 200g (7oz / 1½ cups) when prepared	2.7kg (6lb), giving 1.8kg (4lb)
2 medium cloves garlic, crushed	10-15
2 tbsp olive oil	100ml (4-5fl oz / ½ cup)
200g (7oz / 1 cup) cottage cheese or cream cheese	1.8kg (4lb)
50g (2oz / ½ cup) walnuts, chopped	300-450g (12oz-1lb)
1 tsp Dijon mustard	3 tbsp
1-2 tbsp parsley, finely chopped	approx. 200g (7oz / 1½ cups)
1-2 pinches salt and black pepper to taste	2-3 tsp salt and 1-2 tsp pepper
Pancake batter	
2 eggs	18
50g (2oz / scant ½ cup) plain wheat flour	450g (1lb)
50g (2oz / scant ½ cup) buckwheat flour	450g (1lb)
(or use all plain wheat flour – 100g / 4oz / 1 scant cup)	(900g / 2lb)
300ml (10fl oz / 1¼ cups) whole milk	2.7l (4¾ pints / 3 US quarts)
2 pinches salt	2 tsp
A little sunflower oil to fry	approx. 100ml (4-5fl oz / ½ cup)

Topping

approx. 85g (3oz / ¾ cup) Cheddar, grated (for variety, use a mix of red Leicester and Cheddar)	700g (1½lb)
50g (2oz / ½ cup) walnuts, chopped	300-450g (12oz-1lb)
A meagre drizzle of olive oil	1-2 tbsp

1. *Preparing the batter:* For the small quantity, all the ingredients can be mixed and blended in a measuring jug for ease of pouring. If you don't have a rod blender or rotary whisk, first blend the egg, salt and flour into a smooth paste using a fork, then mix in the milk bit by bit, so the mixture remains smooth. If using a rod blender / rotary whisk, mix all the ingredients together in one go and blend until smooth. The resulting mixture should have the consistency of unwhipped cream. Ideally, allow the batter to stand for half an hour (this is especially important when including buckwheat in the mix).

2. *Frying the pancakes:* Heat a teaspoonful of sunflower oil in a medium-sized frying pan (about 23cm / 9" diameter). Get it hot but not smoking, and use a metal spatula to make sure the oil is spread around the whole base of the pan and slightly up the edges. Pour in your batter (about half a cup per pancake) and swill the frying pan around to spread the mixture evenly. Keep the heat moderate-to-low. As soon as the batter is no longer runny but has gone dull and set, the pancake will usually be lightly browned on the underside and ready to toss or flip with a spatula. Cook the other side until also light brown. Keep pancakes stacked on a plate with a butter paper or foil over the top to prevent drying out. Keep warm in a low oven or on the hob. No need to add more oil with every pancake you cook – a little with every third or fourth pancake will be enough. Add this when you start to feel them sticking.

3. *Filling:* The mushrooms and leeks should both be chopped quite small – 1cm / ½" pieces. For the small quantity, they can be sautéd together in the olive oil. Add the garlic and a pinch of salt halfway through. When cooked, remove from the heat and tip into a bowl. Complete the filling by adding the chopped walnuts, soft cheese, mustard and parsley, plus salt and pepper to taste. If making the large quantity, you may wish to soften the leeks first in a little boiling water to ease the cooking process.

4. Pre-heat the oven to 200°C (400°F / Gas Mark 6).

5. *Rolling and stuffing:* Take one pancake at a time on a plate or chopping board and spoon a sausage-sized portion of the filling on to the pancake in a line, just off-centre from the middle. Do not spread it out. Fold the shorter exposed side of pancake neatly over the filling and then continue to roll the whole thing over to complete the cigar-shaped parcel.

6. *Baking:* Arrange the pancakes in a lightly oiled baking dish, so they are almost touching, but not quite. Sprinkle over with grated cheese and walnuts – ideally going from cheese to walnuts and back again to cheese, so the walnuts are slightly trapped by the cheese and won't fall off. Drizzle sparsely with olive oil and a few dried herbs if you like. Twenty minutes before serving time, finish the pancakes in the hot oven. The cheese will be melting and light brown in places when ready.

For gluten-free diets: Use all buckwheat flour in the mix and allow to stand for an hour before using to make pancakes.

Three Kings' pie

This is a hybridized version of a shepherd's pie, such as might be concocted by three latter-day wise men from the Orient, their pockets filled with Eastern spices. Inspired by Simon Rimmer's Oriental Pie recipe, it has been adapted by Melanie Stewart, our Postgraduate Course Manager, who happily includes shiitakes from our garden in the chunky mushroom brew.

Melanie is a multi-talented lady who seasons her life with astrology, reflexology and music, as well as having a great flair for administration. Schumacher College attracts polymaths of all varieties – and these delightful people often stay at the College longer than originally intended, enjoying its wealth of ideas, teamwork and 'gold' measured in moments, not money. As Melanie herself said, "Where else could you find a job that involves cooking with interesting people from all over the world one moment, and performing Schubert's Impromptu No 1 on a grand piano that's built like a top racehorse the next?"

For 6	For 45-50
Filling	
375g (13oz) large open mushrooms, halved (preferably field mushrooms or portabellos)	3.4kg (7½lb)
100g (4oz) shiitakes, or more of the above	1kg (2lb), or more of the above
8 spring onions (1 bunch) or 2 small leeks	6-8 bunches or 1.5kg (3lb) leeks
1-2 cloves garlic, crushed	1 good head
2 tbsp root ginger 'matchsticks', freshly sliced	200g (7oz / 1 cup)
1 cinnamon quill	4-6
2 star anise, crushed seeds only	14-16 stars, crushed seeds only
75ml (2½fl oz / ⅓ cup) tamari or soy sauce	675ml (22fl oz / 2½ cups)
100ml (3½fl oz / ½ cup) vegetable stock	800ml (1½ pints / 3¼ cups)
80g (3oz / ½ cup) dried cannellini (or other) beans or 200g (7oz / 1 cup) cooked	750g (1lb 12oz / 4 ½ cups) dried or 1.8kg (4lb) cooked
A little olive or sunflower oil to sauté	approx. 100ml (4-5fl oz / ½ cup)
Mash	
375g (13oz) potatoes	3kg (6½lb)
375g (13oz) celeriac or sweet potatoes	3kg (6½lb)
50g (2oz / ½ stick) butter (or margarine for dairy-free diets)	350g (12oz / 3 sticks)
approx. 50ml (2fl oz / ¼ cup) milk (or soya milk or water)	approx. 300ml (10fl oz / 1¼ cups)
2 tbsp cream (or soya cream)	approx. 200ml (7fl oz / ¾ cup)
1 tsp Dijon mustard	3 tbsp
2-3 pinches salt and black pepper to taste	approx. 1-2 tbsp salt and 1-2 tsp pepper

1. If using dried cannellini beans, they should be soaked in three times their depth of cold water overnight. Next day, drain and refresh the water so that it covers the beans by three fingers' width. Bring to the boil and simmer until just tender but not mushy (45-60 minutes).

2. Scrub the potatoes and celeriac or sweet potatoes. Cut into large chunks and cook together in salted boiling water, until soft.

3. Prepare the mushrooms and spices. If using shiitakes alongside the open mushrooms, quarter or cut into thick strips – they are a bit tougher than the ordinary mushrooms, so need to be cut smaller.

4. Trim the roots of the spring onions (or leeks) and remove any dry or tatty-looking leaves. Fry them whole in a little oil until they wilt. (If using leeks, divide into 8cm / 3"-long 'logs' and quarter these lengthways before frying.) All the mushrooms can then be added to the pan and cooked for a further 5 minutes. Add the garlic, ginger, cinnamon and star anise, and cook for another 5 (small quantity) or 15 (large quantity) minutes.

5. Add the soy sauce or tamari, drained beans and stock. Bring to the boil, then simmer for about 10 minutes to reduce by half. For large groups, I prefer to remove the cinnamon quills after this. Pre-heat the oven to 180°C (350°F / Gas Mark 4).

6. Drain the potato / celeriac / sweet potato once tender, and mash up with butter/margarine, milk and cream. Season with mustard, salt and pepper.

7. Pour the mushroom/bean mixture into a baking dish, leaving a good 3cm (1") clear for the mash. Spoon the mash on top and bake in the oven for 20-30 minutes. Grill the top to brown the peaks (or simply place the pie at the top of the oven). Serve with greens of the season.

Variations: Leave out the oriental spices for a plainer pie and experiment with using other pulses.

Mushroom sformato

Before coming to live in Devon, Tara Vaughan-Hughes ran her own award-winning restaurants in Vermont. They were called, appropriately, Eat Good Food! True to their name, Tara's restaurants waved the flag for real 'from-scratch' cooking against the tidal wave of fast-food outlets selling factory-born meals that sometimes seem to be taking over the world.

Now, as one of Schumacher College's chefs, we are lucky to have Tara sharing many of her mouthwatering recipes with us, as well as her great breadth of experience. So far, this mushroom *sformato* is streaking ahead in the popularity stakes, and we are frequently asked for the recipe. If you've never encountered *sformato* before, it is (yet another) Italian classic that you will want to make again and again – a bit like a soufflé, but not quite as airy (or as nerve-racking!), because the egg whites are not whipped up and the béchamel gives it stability. It is nonetheless a deliciously light creation that can be used as a starter or a main course, accompanied by fresh green leaves and perhaps a juicy tomato salad.

For 6 (1 x 3-litre / 6 pint baking dish)	**For 45-50** (4-6 medium [max. 4l (7 pint / 4½ US quarts)] dishes)
30g (1oz / ¼ cup) ground walnuts or hazelnuts	225g (8oz / 2 cups)
1 medium onion (180g / 6oz), diced	1.3kg (3lb)
40g (1½oz / 3 tbsp) butter (for the onion béchamel)	340g (12oz / 3 sticks)
40g (1½oz / 3 tbsp) white flour or rice flour	340g (12oz / 2½ cups)
4 tbsp white wine	400ml (14fl oz / 2 cups)
350ml (12fl oz / 1½ cups) milk	2.7l (4¾ pints / 6 US pints)
1 bay leaf (if available)	2-3
650g (1½lb / 8 cups) mushrooms, sliced	5.3kg (12lb)
1 tsp fresh thyme leaves (optional)	approx. 2-3 tbsp (optional)
80g (3oz / ¾ cup) cheese, grated*	650g (1½lb)
5 eggs, lightly beaten	40
1 pinch nutmeg, grated	1-2 tsp
¼ tsp salt to taste	2-3 tsp
1 pinch black pepper to taste	½-1 tsp
Knob of butter and 2-3 tbsp olive oil (to sauté the mushrooms)	approx. 100g (4oz / 1 stick) and 100ml (4-5fl oz / ½ cup)

*Tara's number-one favourite cheese for this dish is pecorino, an Italian hard sheep's-milk cheese. This translates into a vegetarian Parmesan in the Schumacher kitchen (see footnote on page 26 re Parmesan). Tara has also used Cheddar with great success, as well as a firm local goat's cheese, so take your pick.

1. Get together your baking dishes, avoiding any really huge ones, as this will lead to the outside edges of the *sformato* becoming overcooked before the middle is ready. Rub the dishes generously with butter, whizz up your nuts and coat the inside of the dishes with them. Set aside.

2. In a good-sized saucepan, sauté the onions in the larger amount of butter with a bit of salt and pepper until translucent. Sprinkle the flour over them and cook, stirring, for about a minute.

3. Next, stir in the wine and the milk, and stir constantly until thickened. If available, a bay leaf makes a nice addition to the milk at this stage. Reduce the heat and continue cooking – the béchamel should be quite thick. (Alternatively, this can be made ahead of time and refrigerated.)

4. In a wide frying pan, sauté the mushrooms in the butter / olive oil combination, adding a sprinkling of salt and pepper as you go. A few leaves of fresh thyme can also be added. When the mushrooms have released their liquid, continue cooking until most of the liquid has evaporated. Take off the heat and whizz up in a food processor until they are the size of puy lentils – or wait until they are cool and chop by hand.

5. Remove the bay leaves (if used) from the béchamel. Then, by hand, combine the mushrooms with the béchamel, cheese, lightly beaten eggs and grated nutmeg. Pour the mixture into the prepared dish(es) and bake at 180°C (350°F / Gas Mark 4) for about 45-60 minutes, depending on your oven. The *sformato* is done when it has risen, is slightly browned on top, and the centre does not wobble when you pat it. Allow to cool for a few minutes, then serve.

Arancini & arancioni (Little & large rice balls)

Originally a Sicilian street food, *arancini* and *arancioni* take their names from oranges – little ones and large ones! With their tender mozzarella centre and breadcrumbed exterior, these risotto balls are also reminiscent of Scotch eggs. Unlike Scotch eggs, however, they are vegetarian and best served warm – allowing the cheese to melt into a state of seductive gooeyness in the middle. When first lovingly prepared at the College for a Christmas tea party by Italian volunteers Anthony Pacitto and Tanja Mancinelli, *arancioni* acquired almost mythical status. Overjoyed and overwhelmed by the pile of a hundred rather large rice balls, some guests were seen wrapping them in napkins and popping them in their pockets to take home! Back at the ranch, we continued to dine off them for days.

Try making smaller, golf-ball-sized *arancini* to serve as canapés. Or serve the larger, tennis-ball-sized *arancioni* as a main course entrée, and let them carry the meal to triumph unhindered by any sweet competition (from mince pies, brownies, etc.). If porcini mushrooms are not available, try substituting with other dried mushrooms such as shiitake – or use four times as much weight in fresh mushrooms, chopped small and fried with the onions.

For 15-20 small / 6-8 large balls	For 100 small / 50+ large balls
50g (2oz / 2 cups) dried porcini mushrooms	300g (10oz / 10 cups / 2½ US quarts)
2 small onions	1.4kg (3lb)
2 cloves garlic, crushed	12
1 tsp dried thyme	2 tbsp
200g (8oz / 1⅓ cups) Arborio/risotto rice	1.2kg (2lb 10oz)
100ml (4fl oz / ½ cup) white wine	600ml (1 pint / 2½ cups)
700ml (1¼ pints / 3 cups) vegetable stock	4l (7 pints / 9 US pints)
40g (1½oz / ¾ cup) Parmesan-style cheese, grated	250g (9oz / 4½ cups) to taste
Knob of butter (optional)	50g (2oz / ½ stick)
1 tsp Dijon mustard	2-3 tbsp
½ tsp salt to taste	2-3 tsp
¼ tsp black pepper to taste	1½ tsp
200g (8oz) buffalo mozzarella	1.2kg (2½lb)
2 eggs, beaten	8-10
200g (8oz / 2 cups) dried fine breadcrumbs (use 350g / 12oz bread to make)	1.2kg (2½lb) (use 2kg / 4½lb bread to make)
120ml (8 tbsp / ½ cup) olive oil	approx. 600ml (1 pint / 2½ cups)

1. Soak the porcini mushrooms in boiling water that just covers them. After about 30 minutes, drain the liquid off and use it to make up the volume of vegetable stock required. Chop the porcini finely and set aside.

2. *Preparing the risotto*: Heat a little of the total amount of olive oil (e.g. 1 tbsp; 6 tbsp for the larger quantity) in a large shallow pan and cook the finely chopped onions for a few minutes until soft. Add the mushrooms, garlic, thyme and rice and cook for a further few minutes. Pour in the white wine and cook until the liquid has reduced. Add the stock gradually, a couple of ladlefuls at a time, stirring well and simmering between each addition. By the time all the stock has been absorbed, the rice should be cooked. Turn off the heat and stir in the Parmesan, butter and mustard. Season to taste with salt and pepper, and tip into a ceramic dish to cool. The risotto can be made up to two days in advance and stored in the fridge.

3. *Shaping the arancini*: For the larger-sized balls, cut the mozzarella into 6-8 (small quantity) or 50-60 (large quantity) pieces. For the smaller, canapé-sized balls, cut it into 15-20 (small quantity) or 100 or so (large quantity) pieces. For the smaller balls, you'll need to scoop out a portion of risotto the size of a large walnut or a small clementine. For the larger balls, as mentioned, you are aiming for a portion the size of a medium orange. Press a piece of mozzarella into the middle of the rice and mould the risotto over it so that the cheese is completely encased. Roll gently with your hands, then dip in beaten egg and roll in fine breadcrumbs. The prepared balls can be amassed and kept in the fridge for several hours or even a day before frying.

4. *Cooking the arancini:* Heat the remaining olive oil in a large frying pan and sizzle the balls for 4-5 minutes at a low temperature until golden-brown. They should be turned regularly and a careful eye kept on them to ensure that the temperature does not get too hot, or they will burn: there is no need to risk this, as all the ingredients except the egg have already been cooked, so the objective is simply to serve them warm and crisped on the outside. The larger balls may require more oil to fry, and can also be deep-fried in a saucepan using 2-3cm (1") of oil: drain them on to kitchen paper to absorb surplus oil.

5. Keep the *arancini* temptingly warm in the oven until ready to serve – or re-heat on a baking tray: allow 8-10 minutes for the small balls and 15-20 minutes for the large ones at 150°C (300°F / Gas Mark 2).

For gluten-free diets: Make breadcrumbs using gluten-free bread (see page 245) or cornflakes (ones that don't contain malt as a flavouring).

Tip: You can use any risotto to make these. For example, tomato risotto or squash risotto will also make delicious rice balls – in fact, making *arancini* is a great way to expand any leftover risotto into a feast!

Chick-pea tagine with apricots & cashews

This savoury-sweet Moroccan stew takes its name from the thick earthernware pot known as a *tagine slaoui* that it is tradition-ally cooked in, simmering slowly over an open fire or on hot charcoal. The influence of Arab cuisine is also present in the combination of sweet and savoury ingredients that typically go into a tagine. Medieval European cookery absorbed the same influences and continued to express them in much Elizabethan fayre – food that would have been typical for many Totnesians in the 1600s, as demonstrated in the kitchen of the town's Elizabethan museum.

At Schumacher College, we avoid the Moroccan tendency to include lamb or chicken in the dish, and instead use another typically Arab ingredient, the wholesome chick pea. Combined with dried apricots, apple, cashew nuts and many other 'saucy' ingredients, this makes an extremely tasty and satisfying tagine – very popular at suppertime. Serve with couscous and greens; cooked or raw.

For 6	For 45-50
175g (6oz / 1 cup) dried chick peas	1.4kg (3lb)
1 large onion, finely chopped	8 large (1.5-2kg / 4lb)
4 cloves garlic, minced	2 large heads
500g (1lb / 3 cups) tomatoes, chopped	4kg (9lb)
75g (2½oz / ½ cup) sultanas	500g (1lb 4oz / 4 cups)
75g (2½oz / ½ cup) dried apricots, chopped	500g (1lb 4oz / 4 cups)
1 apple, peeled and grated	8
1 tbsp peanut butter	200ml (4fl oz / ½ cup)
1 tsp garam masala	3 tbsp
1 tsp medium curry powder	3 tbsp
1 small glass apple juice (if available) to taste	approx. 1l (1¾ pints / 2 US pints)
75g (2½oz / ½ cup) cashew nuts/pieces	500g (1lb 4oz / 4 cups)
Sprinkling of tamari or soy sauce	A little more
Half an organic lemon – juice and zest	4
A little honey and/or vinegar (if required)	3-4 tbsp (if required)
2-3 pinches salt and black pepper to taste	1-2 tbsp salt and 1-2 tsp pepper to taste
250g (9oz / 1½ cups) couscous*	2kg (4½lb)
600ml (1 pint / 1¼ US pints) vegetable stock or water	4.5l (8 pints / 5 US quarts)
2-3 tbsp fresh coriander, finely chopped (optional)	70g (2½oz / 1 cup) (optional)
3-4 tbsp olive oil to sauté	approx. 100ml (4-5fl oz / ½ cup)

*For gluten-free diets use rice.

1. Soak the dried chick peas overnight in three times their depth of cold water. Rinse and cover with fresh water. Boil for one hour or until cooked. Reserve the cooking water to use as stock, adding in some apple juice (in the abundant juicing season!).

2. Fry the onion and garlic in a little olive oil until soft and pearly.

3. Now add the tomatoes, dried fruit, grated apple, peanut butter, spices and a little chick pea stock. Mix as you go to form a sauce. Simmer for about 20 minutes, adding more stock (or apple juice) if necessary. Pre-heat the oven to 200°C (400°F / Gas Mark 6).

4. Spread the cashews out on a baking tray and roast in the hot oven for 10 minutes or so until they start to turn light brown. Remove from the oven and sprinkle tamari or soy sauce over them *immediately* while they are still hot, so that they absorb the flavour, steam off the moisture and remain crunchy!

5. Now combine the chick peas with the sauce in a big pot. Gently bring the sauce to the boil. Season to taste with salt, freshly ground black pepper, and lemon juice and zest. The tagine mixture should be mildly spicy with an appealing sweet-and-sour aspect to it. Adjust with tamari, honey, apple juice, lemon juice or vinegar to taste. Mix in the toasted cashews just before serving, saving a few to sprinkle on the top.

6. Measure the dry couscous into a big pan that allows plenty of room for the grain to expand. Bring the stock or water to the boil. If you haven't any stock to hand, add stock powder or cubes to the water to flavour it. Pour the boiling stock or water over the couscous, stir and leave to stand for 5 minutes with a lid on. During this time it will absorb the moisture and soften. Stir in some finely chopped coriander at the last moment, if you like, and garnish with the rest. The couscous is now ready to serve with the tagine.

Twice-baked potatoes

Although the potato has been cultivated in Peru for some 2,000 years, it was only introduced to Europe in the sixteenth century, and despite its initial (unfounded) reputation as an aphrodisiac, it took a couple of centuries to win popularity. Before that, potatoes were regarded with deep religious suspicion, stemming from the fact that they were not mentioned in the Bible and (like all the Solanaceae family) they grow during those 'devilish' dark hours of night.

Today, potatoes have become the staple of the snack food industry, with many forms of crisps being made from potato flour, as well as potato slices. They have been bred into all sizes, are used in many different dishes and are available all year around.

But despite the great variety of ways of eating potato, a plain baked King Edward potato remains one of the most popular easy meals, served simply with butter and grated cheese. The following recipe is an easy way to make this old favourite just a little bit fancier. Baked, stuffed and baked again, these scrumptious potato halves provide a satisfying meal that can be served with salads or whatever greens the season offers.

For 6	For 45-50
6 medium baking potatoes (approx. 1.5kg / 3lb 4oz)	50 (approx. 1.2kg / 26lb)
4 eggs	32
1 onion or leek (200g / 1½ cups), finely chopped	8 good-sized onions (1.5kg / 3½lb)
1 small courgette (approx. 150g / 5oz), grated	8 small or equivalent (1.2kg / 2lb 10oz)
1 tbsp lemon juice or cider vinegar	100ml (4fl oz / ½ cup)
200g (7oz / 1½ cups) Cheddar	1.5kg (3lb 8oz)
50g (2oz / ½ cup) smoked Cheddar	500g (1lb), or more plain Cheddar
2-3 tbsp parsley, finely chopped	70-100g (3oz / 1-1½ cups)
1 tsp dried herbs – thyme, mixed herbs, etc.	3 tbsp
1 tbsp Dijon or grainy mustard to taste	6-8 tbsp / ½ cup
1-2 tbsp capers, chopped (optional)	100g (3-4oz / ½-¾ cup) (optional)
125ml (5fl oz / ½ cup) sour cream or yoghurt	1l (2 pints / 4 cups)
approx. ½ tsp salt to taste	approx. 3-4 tsp
freshly ground black pepper to taste	1-2 tsp
1-2 tbsp olive oil to sauté	100ml (4-5fl oz / ½ cup), or as required
approx. 2 tbsp pumpkin, sesame or sunflower seeds to decorate (optional)	approx. 100g (4oz / 1 cup) (optional)

1. At least 3 hours before serving time, scrub the potatoes and spread them out on metal baking trays. Pre-heat the oven to 200°C (400°F / Gas Mark 6). Jab the potatoes in several places with a skewer. Bake for up to 1½ hours for the small quantity and 2 hours for the large quantity. Turn over after 40 minutes to ensure even cooking. They are ready when they are soft to squeeze and a knife will plunge through easily. It's important to test all the potatoes for softness, as they seem to possess an annoying habit of cooking at different rates! Leave any that aren't cooked through to bake for longer. When they are done, reduce the oven temperature to 180°C (350°F / Gas Mark 4).

2. Cover the eggs in cold water. Bring to the boil and simmer vigorously for about 10 minutes. Drain and cover with cold water (this is reputed to prevent a grey ring forming around the yolk).

3. As soon as the potatoes are cool enough to handle (or later, if more convenient), halve them lengthways. Scoop out most of the inside, leaving the skin sitting intact, like a boat, with only a thin layer of potato still supporting the shell. Place the potato pulp in a bowl, and line up your fleet of potato boats in lightly oiled baking dishes.

4. Crack and peel the hard-boiled eggs – leaving them in the cold water while you peel them helps the shells slip off more easily, as water will seep under the shell and loosen it. Chop them finely.

5. Sauté the onion or leek in olive oil with a pinch or two of salt, and the dried herbs. Add the courgette to the softening onion after 5 minutes. Stir in the lemon juice or cider vinegar and cook for a couple more minutes.

6. Grate the cheeses and mix together. Set one-third aside, ready to go on the top of the potato halves later.

7. Mash up the potato with a fork or masher. Mix in the onion mixture, chopped parsley, mustard and capers (if using). Remove some of the mixture for special diets at this stage, then mix in the sour cream / yoghurt, two-thirds of the grated cheese and the chopped eggs. Mix well. Seasoning to taste with salt, pepper and more mustard. If required, add some cooked lentils (see non-dairy diets option below) to the special diet portion, and season this.

8. Now use the filling to stuff the potato shells, pushing the mixture well to the edges and heaping it up. Sprinkle the remaining grated cheese on top and then sprinkle with pumpkin, sesame or sunflower seeds, if desired.

9. Place the stuffed potatoes in the oven and bake for about 30 minutes. When ready, the potatoes should be hot through, with the cheese melting temptingly and beginning to turn golden-brown.

For non-dairy diets: Leave out the cheese and sour cream or yoghurt. Vegans can also replace the eggs with 170g / 6oz / 1 cup (small quantity) / 1.3kg / 3lb (large quantity) of cooked red lentils (use just under half these weights if starting with dry lentils).

Monkey-nut stew

This wholesome peanut-enriched sweet-potato-based stew is a favourite dish in West Africa and is popular in South Africa too, which is where former participant and volunteer Sij Davies grew up. Sij first came to the College to study ecological design with Victor Papanek, back in the early 1990s. Luckily for us, she stayed on to share her great artistic and culinary skills, and this stew is one of several delicious meals that were cooked for all to share – and continues to be made at the College.

'Ground nuts', as peanuts are agriculturally known – or 'monkey nuts', as they are fondly nicknamed – are not really nuts at all. Rather, in the eyes of botanists, they are legumes (pulses) that have evolved a habit of thrusting their flower stems into the ground after pollination so that the fruit pods develop underground. The peanut thrives in tropical and subtropical climates and was first grown in pre-Inca times in Ancient Peru. The plant spread from 'New' to 'Old' World at the end of the fifteenth century thanks to the voyages of Christopher Columbus, and is now one of the world's major food crops, grown in many countries including the USA, Africa, India, China and Australia. With a protein content of 30 per cent, it has a vital role to play in nutrition as well as in economics.

For 6-8	For 45-50
1 medium aubergine (approx. 500g / 1lb), cubed	6 medium (approx. 2.5kg / 6lb)
225g (8oz / 1½ cups) onions, sliced	1.4kg (3lb)
1 tsp garlic, crushed	2 tbsp
⅛-¼ tsp cayenne pepper to taste	1-1½ tsp to taste
280g (10oz / 2 cups) cabbage, shredded	1.7kg (3lb 12oz)
500g (1lb 2oz) sweet potato, approx. 2cm / 1" cubes	3kg (7lb)
2-3 medium tomatoes, chopped	15 (1kg / 2lb)
700ml (24fl oz / 3 cups) tomato juice (or whizzed-up tinned tomatoes + water)	4.2l (7 pints / 3 US quarts) (use a 2.5kg / 5½lb tin of tomatoes + water)
225ml (8fl oz / 1 cup) apple juice	1.4l (2½ pints / 3 US pints)
1 tsp root ginger, grated	2 tbsp
1 tsp salt to taste	1 tbsp to taste
1 pinch black pepper to taste	1-2 tsp to taste
2 tbsp coriander leaf, chopped	70g (2½oz / 1 cup)
125ml (4fl oz / ½ cup) peanut butter	750ml (1¼ pints / 3 cups)
25g (1oz / ¼ cup) red-skinned peanuts, chopped	175g (6oz / 1½ cups)
A little peanut oil (or sunflower or olive oil) to sauté	approx. 100ml (4-5fl oz / ½ cup)

1. Slice the aubergine into generously sized chunks and toss with salt. Leave for half an hour to sweat.

2. While the aubergine is sweating, fry the sliced onions in the bottom of a large saucepan until they are beginning to soften. Add the garlic and cayenne.

3. After a few minutes, add the cabbage and sweet potatoes. Stir and cook for a further 10 minutes.

4. Rinse the sweated aubergine with cold water, drain and pat dry if necessary. With your eye now on two pans, sauté the aubergine in the oil until soft and well cooked. For the large quantity, blend the tinned tomatoes with a rod blender.

5. Add the cooked aubergine, tomatoes, tomato and apple juices, ginger, salt and black pepper to the sweet potato / cabbage stew. Stir well, cover and simmer gently until the sweet potato and cabbage are tender.

6. Mix the peanut butter with some of the cooking liquid to make a paste. Stir this into the stew and continue to simmer on a low heat for just a few more minutes, stirring regularly to prevent sticking. Check the seasoning and adjust to taste.

7. Just before serving, stir in half the freshly chopped coriander leaf. Use the rest to garnish the stew, along with the coarsely chopped red-skinned peanuts.

8. Serve with brown rice or, as an alternative, millet.

Quinoa goulash with blue cheese & leeks

Anna Lodge, Schumacher College's former Publicity Coordinator, is a passionate and dedicated woman with a career and a family, including two little boys. She has to juggle work with a home life run on wholesome values – and is just the kind of person Nigel Slater's book *Real Fast Food* is aimed at.

As Food Columnist for *The Observer*, cookery writer and TV chef, Nigel Slater is a busy man and someone well practised in the art of whipping up quick, healthy meals in 30 minutes or less. He believes, as I do, that "fast home cooking can mean fresh food, bright flavours and relaxed eating" and says his best-selling book is written for "anyone who enjoys good food eaten informally" – especially those who "lack the time to cook it". After all, cooking with a few fresh ingredients and your store-cupboard or garden favourites involves no more time than it "takes for a supermarket cook-chill supper to heat through".

While at Schumacher College, Anna used to cook this delicious quinoa goulash. Based on a recipe in *Real Fast Food*, the dish would sometimes include leeks and sometimes mushrooms – or both. The cheese selection too is adapted to locality: we tend to use a Devon blue, but you could use almost any cheese: Stilton, Gruyère, Taleggio, mozzarella or Cheddar. Quinoa is a great partner for blue cheeses, and the sweetness of leeks nicely offsets the bitter-blue edge.

For 6	For 45-50
3-4 tbsp olive oil	approx. 250ml (8-10fl oz / 1 cup)
6 sprigs fresh thyme or 1-2 tsp dried mixed herbs	12-20 sprigs fresh *plus* 2-3 tbsp dried
2 bay leaves (optional)	4-6 (optional)
6 small or 3 medium leeks (700g / 1lb 8oz), trimmed and shredded	6kg (13lb) trimmed
3 cloves garlic, sliced	2 heads
350ml (12fl oz / 1½ cups) dry white wine	1l (1¾ pints / 2 US pints)
	100ml (4fl oz / ½ cup) cider vinegar / more wine (for large quantity only)
300g (10oz / 1¾ rounded cups) pale quinoa	2.4kg (5lb)
900ml (1½ pints / 3 cups) hot vegetable stock	5l (9 pints / 5 US quarts)
200g (7oz) blue cheese, cubed or crumbled	1.6kg (3½lb)
1-3 pinches each of salt and pepper	1-3 tsp each
approx. 2 tbsp fresh parsley to garnish	4-6 tbsp (⅓ cup)

1. Begin by gently warming the oil with the thyme leaves, and a few bay leaves if you have them. Use a good-sized pan that will hold all the ingredients with room for expansion.

2. Add the shredded and rinsed leeks and the sliced garlic. Cook for 5-15 minutes, stirring from time to time, until the leeks begin to soften and turn a little translucent. Add the white wine.

3. If making the small quantity, add the quinoa to the pan with the white wine. Let the wine bubble away, allowing much of its liquid to evaporate while its flavour remains. (Nigel says "you need its flavour not its liquid"). Once the liquidity has reduced considerably, pour in the hot vegetable stock and stir well. Simmer and stir occasionally for 10-15 minutes, watching that it does not catch on the bottom. (Move on to Step 5).

4. If making the large quantity, cook the quinoa separately in the oven. This is the tried-and-trusted way at the College of cooking large amounts of quinoa. Combine the dry quinoa grain with 1-2 tbsp of dried mixed herbs in a large heatproof bowl. Add the hot stock, stir and cover with a close-fitting lid or foil. Place this carefully in a pre-heated oven at 180°C (350°F, Gas Mark 4). The quinoa will continue to expand without the risk of burning or the bother of stirring. After 30 minutes it should be cooked: add it to the leek/garlic mixture, along with the extra white wine or vinegar, and continue to cook until the liquid is absorbed or evaporated and the quinoa is well flavoured.

5. In the case of both quantities, the meal is ready when the liquid levels have been sufficiently reduced, the vegetables are tender and the quinoa is well expanded and no longer crunchy. At this point, stir in most of the crumbled/cubed cheese. Season with salt and pepper to taste, tip into a serving dish and serve straight away with a garnish of fresh parsley and the remaining crumbs of blue cheese.

For vegan diets: Leave out the cheese and substitute with roast cashews to taste if you like.

Whole mushroom & wild garlic (or spinach) quiche

Whole, succulent, deliciously dark-brown field mushrooms on the top of a tart are a wonderful sight to behold. Not only this, but the depth of flavour is magnificent – even more so when coupled with garlic. At Schumacher College, we're lucky to be surrounded by areas of open woodland that become carpeted with lush wild garlic (ransoms) in spring, which we use eagerly. At other times, finely sliced garlic cloves and garden spinach make for another winning marriage of flavours.

I also use this basic recipe to make a pure spinach quiche – and a pure sorrel quiche (see variations in ingredients list). The distinct lemony flavour of sorrel, combined with cheese, provides a taste sensation so uniquely pleasant that it needs to be tasted to be imagined – and has resulted in more sorrel beds being planted in the College vegetable patch!

For 8+ (1 large round quiche)	For 50 (6 large round quiches)
(1 x 28cm / 11" loose-based flan tins, 3-4cm / 1-1½" deep)	(6 x flan tins, same dimensions)

Pastry

175g (6oz / 1 heaped cup) plain white flour	1kg (2lb 4oz)
50g (2oz / rounded ⅓ cup) brown or rye flour	350g (12oz)
150g (5oz) butter, cold	900g (1lb 14oz)
¼ tsp fine salt	1½ tsp
1 tbsp sesame seeds	6 tbsp
approx. 4 tbsp cold water	350ml (12fl oz)

Filling

500g (1lb) medium open mushrooms	3kg (6lb 12oz)
225g (8oz) onions	1.3kg (3lb)
1 hand-bunch wild garlic, rough-chopped or 4 cloves garlic, sliced and 200g (7oz) spinach	6 bunches (up to 450g / 1lb) or 2 heads and 1.2kg (2½lb)
2-3 tbsp parsley, finely chopped (optional)	70g (2½oz / 1 cup) (optional)
5 eggs	30
125g (5oz) cream cheese	750g (1lb 10oz)
100g (4oz) Cheddar, grated	600g (1lb 6oz)
25g (1oz) smoked Cheddar, grated	150g (6oz)
175ml (6fl oz / ¾ cup) cream, sour cream or yoghurt	1l (1¾ pints / 2 US pints)

100ml (3½fl oz / ⅓ cup) milk	600ml (1 pint / 1¼ US pints)
1-2 tsp Dijon mustard	2-3 tbsp
1-2 pinches salt	approx. 2 tsp to taste
1 pinch black pepper	1 tsp to taste
A little olive oil to drizzle and sauté	approx. 100ml (4fl oz / ½ cups)

1. *Preparing the pastry:* Measure all the dry ingredients into a spacious bowl. Cut or grate in the cold butter. Rub the butter and flour between your fingers, lifting up to get air into the mix. Continue to 'rub in' until a breadcrumb-like consistency is obtained – avoid pushing the crumbs together at this stage. Trickle in the water and stir with a wooden spoon until absorbed – the dough should not be either very sticky or very fragmented. Now push together and divide into portions equal to the number of tarts you are making. Shape into balls and flatten these down into 2-3cm (1")-thick 'frisbees'. Pop on a saucer in a plastic bag or between sheets of baking parchment on a baking tray. Leave to rest in a cool place for 15-20 minutes. If leaving for longer, you may need to unchill your 'frisbees' at room temperature for 15 minutes or so to get them ready to roll. Roll the pastry out on a floured work surface with a floured rolling pin, lifting and re-positioning the pastry every now and then so it doesn't stick. When you've got it to about 3-4mm (⅛") thick throughout, roll up loosely on your rolling pin, then lightly unroll over your flan tin. Ease well into the corners and trim the pastry 0.5cm (¼") above the top of the tin before fluting the edge with your fingertips, or simply tidying it. Chill until needed.

2. Pre-heat the oven to 190°C (375°F / Gas Mark 5).

3. *Filling:* Peel, halve and slice the onions into narrow half-moons. Peel and finely slice the garlic cloves, if using. Sauté both in olive oil for a few minutes, until begining to go translucent.

4. Check over and brush the mushrooms, slicing off the tip of the stalk if it looks tough. Place two-thirds of the mushrooms on a baking tray, still whole. Drizzle minimally with olive oil then sprinkle with a little salt. Bake for 15-20 minutes until some juices begin to leak out and the mushrooms are just beginning to soften (they will cook more later). Remove from the heat and set aside.

5. Slice the remaining mushrooms and add to the almost cooked onions. Sauté for 5-10 minutes. If using wild garlic or spinach, wash and shred this, then add to the onions and cook briefly until wilted. Leave to cool. Season minimally with pepper and salt. Stir in the parsley, if using.

6. Combine the eggs, mustard and all dairy ingredients for the filling *except* the Cheddar cheeses. Whisk these together until a homogeneous 'custardy' consistency is obtained. Grate the Cheddar cheeses.

7. Sprinkle a little of the grated cheese in the base of the quiche. Follow this with the onion mixture and some more grated cheese, reserving a little cheese for the top. Next, fill the quiche cases up with about three-quarters of the 'custard' – covering the vegetables, and coming to about 1cm (½") from the top of the tin.

8. Now lay the whole cooked mushrooms decoratively on top of the mixture. Spoon the remaining 'custard' over the top of the mushrooms, making sure you don't drown them into invisibility. Finally, sprinkle the remaining grated cheese over the mushrooms. Place the quiche carefully in the hot oven for 45 minutes, until set and golden-brown on top. If your oven is blessed with good underneath heat, make sure your quiche spends at least half its 'oven time' close to the bottom, so the bases get well cooked. Allow the quiche to sit for 5 minutes or so before removing the edges of the flan tin and serving.

Variations: Substitute spinach, chard or sorrel for the mushrooms, using 500g (1lb 2oz) total per quiche. For vegan diets, use margarine in the pastry and substitute the three cheeses with tofu (same total weight). Blend in a food processor with half the onions, soya milk instead of the cream and milk, and nutritional yeast flakes (1 tsp small quantity / 2 tbsp large quantity). The seasoning and mustard may also be added at this stage.

Creamy risotto with nasturtium & squash

The joyful nasturtium plant hails from South America but is now common in cottage gardens throughout England and especially Devon, growing well on poor soil. With a pleasantly peppery taste, the flowers, leaves, stalks and seeds are all edible. Used fresh, nasturtium flowers make a brilliant adornment for any green salad. Used cooked, you can include much more of the plant, as the spiciness will be considerably reduced.

Creamy risottos are a development of what was originally a peasant dish made in the rice-growing areas of Italy. Though not always vegetarian, this typically included fungi gathered from the local forests. In the true spirit of this opportunistic strand of localized cooking, former Schumacher College course designer Toni Spencer, along with her friend Dolly, took up the baton of the latter-day peasants when they determined to transform a garden overrun by nasturtiums into good food. One of the results is this remarkably sensational risotto.

For those who do not have gardens, or want to make a vegetarian risotto outside the summer season, try using more roast squash – or make a mushroom risotto with porcini and field mushrooms (see variations on page 88).

For 6	For 45-50
30-50g (1-2oz) nasturtium flowers	250-400g (8oz-1lb)
80-100g (3-4oz) nasturtium leaves + upper stalks	600-800g (1lb 4oz-2lb)
15g (½oz / ½ cup) dried porcini mushrooms (if available)	120g (5oz / 4 cups)
2 small onions, peeled and chopped	1.8kg (4lb)
3 garlic cloves, peeled and finely chopped	2 heads
4 stalks celery, finely chopped	4 heads
100g (4oz / 1 cup) Parmesan-style cheese, grated	approx. 800g (1lb 12oz)
500g (1lb 2oz / 3 cups) Arborio or carnaroli rice	4kg (8½lb)
250ml (8fl oz / 1 cup) white wine	2l (3½ pints / 2 US quarts)
1.25l (2 pints / 2½ US pints) vegetable stock or water	10l (16 pints / 10 US quarts)
2-3 pinches each of salt and black pepper	1-2 tbsp salt, 2 tsp pepper, to taste
A squeeze of lemon juice (if needed at end)	Juice of 1-2 lemons
approx. 4-6 tbsp olive oil	approx. 400ml (¾ pint / 1½ cup)
approx. 4 tbsp flat-leaved parsley	100-150g (45 oz / 2-3 cups)
For squash risotto variation: 1-1.5kg (2-3lb) squash	8-10kg (17-22lb) whole weight
For mushroom risotto variation: 900g (2lb) field mushrooms, sliced	7kg (15lb)

1. Soak the dried porcini mushrooms (if available) in warm water for an hour, then simmer for 20-25 minutes and drain through a sieve to remove any grit. Some of the strained cooking water can be used in the risotto, though you should not use too much when making a nasturtium risotto, as the colour will be muddied.

2. Harvest the nasturtium flowers and leaves/stalks into two different containers, bearing in mind that you will only be using the top 10cm (6") of the stalk, which is the part where there is the highest concentration of vitamins and minerals.

3. Rinse the leaves in cold water, drain, then chop into roughly 1cm (½")-wide ribbons. Likewise, cut the stalks into 1cm lengths. Divide into two piles, one for longer cooking and the other to be added towards the end for brightness. Rinse the flowers (to flush out earwigs!) if you think necessary. Reserve a few whole flowers for garnishing at the end. The rest can be pinched in two at the stalk end and put with the second pile of chopped leaves, to be added at the end.

4. If you are including squash with the nasturtium (see variation overleaf), prepare it now, to have it roasting in the oven before you go on to the next step. For mushroom risotto (also see overleaf), it is convenient to get your mushrooms in the oven at this point – whisking them out after about 15 minutes, when they are ready. Set aside until needed.

5. Prepare your onion, garlic and celery, and grate the Parmesan-style cheese. You are now ready to begin cooking the risotto – and to give the cooking process your full attention. Start an hour before serving time, if you are making the large quantity; 35 minutes before if you are making the smaller amount. For this quantity, begin by heating 3 tbsp of olive oil in the bottom of a large thick-bottomed saucepan. For the larger quantity, use two large saucepans with about 200ml (8fl oz / 1 cup) olive oil in the bottom of each. Add the celery and onion and soften for 5-6 minutes. Add the garlic, cook briefly and then add the rice. Stir to coat each grain with the oil and allow it to become opaque – this may take 2-3 minutes.

6. Now add the white wine. Cook gently for 5 minutes so the rice absorbs the flavour of the wine, then begin adding the water or stock, ladle by ladle, only adding more when the previous amount has been absorbed. Add the porcini mushrooms (if using) and some of their (strained) soaking liquid. Also add half the shredded nasturtium leaves. Continue the process of cooking, stirring and adding liquid until the rice becomes al dente – about 15-30 minutes depending on scale. Now stir in half the Parmesan-style cheese, followed by the rest of the chopped leaves, and the stalks and flowers. Also add the chunks of roast (peeled) squash if making a squash or combined risotto. Cook for a couple of minutes only. Adjust the seasoning, using a squeeze of lemon if desired.

7. Serve the creamy risotto in a warmed baking dish, drizzling the top with olive oil and grated hard cheese. On top of this, add a scattering of bright nasturtium flowers. (Any remaining grated cheese can be served separately.)

Variations:

For vegan diets: Leave the cheese out and sprinkle some roasted cashews (roast for 10 minutes) on top for extra protein.

Squash risotto: Combine nasturtium with squash – or make an entirely squash risotto, as we often do. First, select a good orange variety of squash, such as butternut, 'Crown Prince' or 'Red Kuri' squash. Wash and cut the squash in half. Pre-heat your oven to 220°C (425°F / Gas Mark 7). Scoop out the seeds and then cut each half into 4-6 chunky half-moon-shaped pieces, each a couple of centimetres (an inch) thick. Place these on a baking tray. Toss with olive oil and season with salt and pepper. Cook until soft (and probably browning at the edges) – allow 20-30 minutes. Cool a little, then peel the skin off and (if making the purely squash risotto) mash two-thirds of it with a fork and add this to the risotto halfway through cooking. Cut the rest (or all for the combined version) into chunks to be added at the end.

Mushroom risotto: Toss the sliced mushrooms in olive oil, season and roast in the oven (for approximately 15 minutes). Use the porcini and its soaking water to flavour the rice at the beginning of cooking, as described in Step 6, and add the roast mushrooms to the risotto towards the end – as well as plenty of freshly chopped flat-leaved parsley.

Red kidney-bean burgers

After a mere five thousand years of cultivation, the first of the domesticated beans to arrive in England from South America in the sixteenth century were a dark red, kidney-shaped variety. This gave rise to the common English name 'kidney bean', while in France the Aztec name for this whole family of beans, *ayecotl*, meant they became known as one of the 'haricots'.

In this recipe, well-cooked red kidney beans are mashed and mixed with green lentils and other vegetables to make very tasty bean cakes, which can be fried briefly to give a crispy outside, and finished off in the oven. The accompanying red onion marmalade (see page 91) is spiced up deliciously with fresh ginger and rosemary, and 'pinked up' with cranberries.

For 6 (approx. 12 burgers)	For 45-50 (85-100 burgers)
125g (4½oz / ¾ cup) red kidney beans	1kg (2lb 4oz)
1 stick kombu seaweed (if available)	1-2 sticks
125g (4½oz / ¾ cup) green lentils	1kg (2lb 4oz)
approx. 1l (2 pints) water	approx. 6l (14 pints)
1-2 bay leaves	2-4
3-4 sun-dried tomatoes, rehydrated and minced	30 (200g / 7oz / 2 cups)
1 medium-large onion, finely chopped	8 (1.5kg / 3lb 5oz)
1 clove garlic, minced	1 good-sized head
1 medium carrot (85g / 3oz), grated	700g (1½lb)
1 small red pepper, finely chopped	8 small peppers or equivalent
1-2 tsp fresh thyme or rosemary, finely chopped (or half as much dried)	3-4 tbsp (or half as much dried)
3 tbsp wheat flour (or maize flour for gluten-free diets)	225g (8oz / 1½ cups)
2 tsp Dijon mustard	4-6 tbsp
2-3 pinches each salt and black pepper	1-2 tbsp salt and 1-2 tsp pepper
4-5 tbsp olive or sunflower oil to sauté and fry	approx. 500ml (1 pint / 2-3 cups)

1. The day before you want to make the bean cakes, soak the red kidney beans in twice their depth of water overnight. Include a stick of kombu seaweed, if available, to assist with detoxification. Also soak the sun-dried tomatoes – using water or a little spare red wine, if you have any to hand. (You can also use deliciously moist sun-ripened tomatoes such as you find at a delicatessen's counter, without any need to soak.)

2. Next day, drain the beans and refresh them with clean water, using half the amount listed above. Bring to the boil and boil vigorously for 10 minutes to remove any toxicity, before reducing to a simmer. Cook the green lentils at a simmer in the rest of the water with bay leaves. When the pulses are soft (1-1½ hours for the kidney beans; 30-40 minutes for the lentils), drain. It does not matter if the pulses begin to break up.

3. Fish the bay leaves out of the drained pulses and mash them together – by hand or in a food processor, though it's not necessary for the blend to be completely smooth. Season well with salt and pepper. Set the mixture aside, covered to prevent it drying out.

4. Use a large frying pan and some olive oil to sauté the onion, garlic, carrot and red pepper. Keep stirring the vegetables until they are beginning to soften and turn a light golden-brown. Stir in the thyme or rosemary and turn off the heat.

5. Drain and chop up the sun-dried tomatoes, until you have what resembles a coarse tomato purée. Thoroughly mix the vegetables and tomato together with the mashed beans, mustard and one-third of the flour (1 tbsp for the small quantity; 70g / 2½oz / ½ cup for the large).

6. Dampen your hands and shape spoonfuls of the mixture into 6cm (2½") round patties. Place on a sheet of baking parchment or a lightly oiled plate or baking tray. Cover them and leave them in the fridge to chill until needed – if possible for a whole hour. (In our two-hour cooking shifts at the College, half an hour must suffice, and we speed up the chilling/melding-together process by putting the bean cakes in the freezer if there's room. We also minimize the frying time by finishing them off in the oven – see next step.)

7. Coat/dip each pattie in flour to prevent sticking when frying. Get a shallow pool of oil hot (but not smoking) in the frying pan, then sizzle the burgers at a medium heat, allowing about 3 minutes for each side, or 1 minute on each side to lightly brown and then a further 15-30 minutes in the oven at 180°C (350°F / Gas Mark 4) – you can put them back on the oiled or baking-parchment-lined baking trays they were sitting on in the fridge.

8. Serve with a fresh green salad, and a chutney or relish – such as Rosemary, red onion & cranberry marmalade (see opposite). For Hilary Nicholson, who introduced bean cakes to the repertoire of evening meals at the College back in the '90s, home-made chips or (slightly more healthy) potato wedges – roast with their skins on – were always an essential part of the menu!

Red onion, rosemary & cranberry marmalade

This simple relish resembles an exceptionally thick-cut orange marmalade, and can be eaten hot or cold. It is lovely not just with bean cakes but also with nut roasts and other non-vegetarian dishes. With the addition of cranberries, it's delectable.

For 6-12	For 45-50
300g (12oz / 3 cups) red onions	1.5kg (3lb 12oz)
2-3 'little-finger-length' sprigs rosemary	10-15
1 tbsp fresh ginger root, grated	5 tbsp
1 tbsp organic orange zest, thinly peeled and chopped	5 tbsp
2 tbsp fresh orange juice	150ml (5fl oz / ½ cup)
225ml (8fl oz / 1 cup) white wine	1.25l (2 pints / 5 cups)
3 tbsp white wine or cider vinegar	225ml (8fl oz / 1 cup)
2 tbsp light muscovado sugar	150ml (5fl oz / ½ cup)
20g (½oz / 2 tbsp) dried cranberries	100g (3½oz / ½ cup)
½ tsp salt	2-3 tsp
¼ tsp black pepper	1-1½ tsp
2 tbsp olive oil to sauté	125ml (5fl oz / ½ cup)

1. Peel the onions and slice into narrow 5mm (¼") rings. Cut the largest rings in half. Sauté the onion rings and whole rosemary sprigs in olive oil, stirring frequently, until the onions are golden and beginning to caramelize. If making the large quantity, make sure you use a fairly wide pan, as you will want to maximize the evaporative surface area later on, when you reduce the liquid.

2. Grate the ginger root on the coarse side of your grater – the one you would use for carrots or Cheddar cheese. Peel strips of rind from the oranges using a potato peeler, avoiding picking up too much of the bitter white pith. Chop the rind into fine slivers, and squeeze the juice from the oranges.

3. Add the grated ginger, orange zest, sugar, cranberries and white wine / vinegar to the saucepan. Heat up until the mixture is simmering. Add salt and pepper, then reduce heat and cook slowly for an hour or more – until most of the liquid has evaporated and the mixture is reduced to a 'marmaladey' consistency. Stir in the fresh orange juice you have set aside, make a final taste check, and remove from the heat. The rosemary sprigs can be fished out or left in to add a little rustic charm (and keep your diners on the alert, since they will need to push them aside). Serve either warm or cold with the hot bean cakes.

Old Postern pasties

Individual pastry turnovers filled with moist vegetables and cheese are Schumacher College's version of the traditional Cornish pasty. These pasties have been made for generations and were a characteristic way of wrapping up a picnic lunch long before polystyrene boxes enclosed Indian takeaways or newspapers enfolded fish and chips. In fact, the reputation that our neighbouring county of Cornwall gained for making pasties was once so pervasive that, according to food writer Theodora FitzGibbon, it was said that "the Devil would never cross the river into that county for fear of the Cornish woman's habit of putting anything and everything into a pasty". The corners would often be marked with the recipients' initials, and sometimes pasties were made large enough for a whole family to eat, with a savoury mix at one end and a sweet filling at the other.

Feel free to substitute other vegetables for those given here, as the seasons offer them and as they take your fancy.

For 6-8 pasties	For 45-50
1 medium) onion (140g / 5oz / 1 cup), finely chopped	1.1kg (2½lb)
100g (4oz / 1 cup) leeks, fine chopped	900g (2lb)
1 stalk celery (½ cup), finely chopped	1 large head
180g (6oz / 1½ cups) carrots, finely diced or grated	1.25kg (2lb 12oz)
50g (2oz / ½ cup) swede, peeled and diced (if available)	400g (1lb)
140g (5oz / 1 cup) potatoes, finely diced	1kg (2lb 4oz)
70g (2½oz / ⅓ cup) cottage cheese	500g (1lb 4oz)
85g (3oz / ¾ cup) Cheddar, grated	650g (1½lb)
1 tsp dried mixed herbs	2-3 tbsp
2-3 tbsp fresh parsley, finely chopped	70g (2½oz / 1 cup)
1 tsp bouillon stock powder/cubes (as needed)	2-3 tbsp (as needed)
1 tsp mustard	3-4 tbsp
2-3 pinches each of salt and pepper to taste	1-2 tbsp salt and 1-2 tsp pepper
approx. 2 tbsp olive oil to sauté	approx. 100ml (4fl oz / ½ cup)

For vegan diets: Textured vegetable protein (TVP) can be used instead of cheese. Soak it in boiling water for 15 minutes and squeeze in a sieve to remove excess moisture. Alternatively, use chopped nuts or crumbled tofu. For the pastry, substitute butter with margarine or use bought (usually frozen) puff pastry. You'll need 450g (1lb) of pastry for the smaller quantity and 3.5kg (8lb) for the large quantity. Water or soya cream / vegan 'milks' can be used to stick the pastry together. Soya cream can also be used as a glaze and to hold on seeds.

Shortcrust pastry

For 6-8

250g (9oz / 2 scant cups) plain flour
(include a quarter to a third brown flour if you like)
140g (5oz / 1¼ sticks) butter
2 tsp sunflower oil
¼ tsp salt
A little milk or water to bind (50ml / 3 tbsp)
1 egg, beaten, for glazing (optional)
1-2 tbsp sesame seeds for sprinkling (optional)

For 45-50

2kg (4½lb)

1.1kg (2½lb)
4 tbsp
2 tsp
approx. 400ml (14fl oz / 1¾ cups)
1-2 (optional)
approx. 125g (4½oz / 1 cup)

1. Prepare the filling well in advance, so that the mixture can cool down before using. This will prevent it from softening the pastry, making it more difficult to handle. Begin by boiling the diced potatoes and, in another pan, sautéing the chopped onion with the dried herbs in a little olive oil. After 5 minutes add the leeks, celery, carrots and swede to the onion. Any pieces of carrot or swede over 0.5cm (¼") are best boiled with the potatoes. Drain the potatoes/carrots/swede when just tender, and remove the sautéed vegetables from the heat when tender.

2. Combine all the cooked vegetables with the fresh parsley, and season with the stock powder, mustard, salt and pepper. Allow the mixture to cool, and when almost cold, add the cheeses. If using rehydrated TVP, crumbled tofu or chopped nuts, add these instead. Adjust the seasoning to taste and allow the mixture to cool completely.

3. Prepare the pastry as usual (see page 85, but use the ingredients above). This can be done shortly before you want to make the pasties, allowing 20-30 minutes for the pastry to rest in a cool place for ease of handling. If you've made the pastry further in advance, you'll need to allow it to soften at room temperature for 20-30 minutes, so it's easy to roll out. Roll out the prepared pastry thinly – but not so thinly that you can see the worktop through it! A couple of millimeters (¹⁄₁₆") thick is about right. Pre-heat the oven to 200°C (400°F / Gas Mark 6).

4. Cut the pastry into roughly 14cm (5½")-square pieces. Put a dollop of filling mixture in the middle – an oval-shaped dollop, tapering down towards two diagonally opposed corners and higher in the middle, will work well. You'll need at least half a cup of mixture in each pasty, but be careful not to go too close to the edges. Paint two adjacent edges (forming a wide V-shape) very sparingly with milk, then bring them together with the two unpainted edges over the top of the filling. With two corners meeting to form a point at the top, press the edges together, sealing in the mixture. Flute together with your fingertips down the spine of the pasty. (An alternative style is to cut out circles of pastry around a saucer, paint half the edge, place the portion of filling slightly off-centre, then fold the larger half of pastry over and fork or flute around the semi-circular edge as it lies flat on the surface, rather than across the back). Once you've made a few pasties you will soon get a sense of how much mixture to use: overfilled, they will split apart in the oven; underfilled, they will not be so satisfying!

5. Line up the completed pasties on an oiled baking tray or, better still, one lined with parchment. Leave 1cm (½") between each pasty. Paint with beaten egg if you want them shiny – this will also stick down sesame seeds. Lastly, pierce each pasty on one or both sides with a skewer – fairly near the top, so juice is less likely to ooze out. This will allow the warm air to escape without the pastry being forced apart.

6. Bake in the hot oven for 30 minutes. Reduce the temperature to 180°C (350°F / Gas Mark 4) if they seem to be cooking too fast. When golden-brown, remove from the oven and allow to cool slightly before serving.

Gluten-free pastry

This pastry can be used instead of a traditional wheat-based pastry. It's not as elastic, so is more difficult to roll out, but it is easily pressed together, so requires a slightly different technique. It needs the support of the tin edge to hold its shape without cracking, and is therefore unsuitable for stand-alone pastries such as pasties – which are best converted into small pies formed in muffin tins. However, it can be successfully used and adjusted for the tart and pie recipes given on pages 66, 84, 148, 156 and 170, where the pastry is mainly underlying. We usually use a pre-packed white organic gluten-free blend as our white flour component. (This can be substituted with a mix in equal parts of potato flour, rice flour and tapioca flour. Soya flour can also be added.)

For 8+
(1 x large round 28cm / 11" tin, 2-3cm / 1" deep)

85g (3oz / ½ cup) gluten-free plain white flour
85g (3oz / ½ cup) maize flour
85g (3oz / rounded ½ cup) buckwheat flour
125g (4½oz) butter or margarine
2 tsp tahini (if using margarine)
¼ tsp salt
1 tsp xanthan gum* for binding (if available)
1 egg yolk for good binding (if not making vegan pastry)
approx. 4 tbsp cold water (less if using margarine)

For a sweet version
2 tbsp icing or caster sugar
+ ½ tsp cinnamon (as required)

For 50
(6 x large round tart tins)

500g (1lb 2oz)
500g (1lb 2oz)
500g (1lb 2oz)
750g (1lb 12oz)
4 tbsp (if using margarine)
2 tsp
2 tbsp
1 egg + 1 yolk (if not vegan)
350-500ml (12-18fl oz / 2 cups)

85g (3oz / ½ cup)
+ 3 tsp

1. Combine the dry ingredients in a bowl, then rub in the diced butter or margarine/tahini until the mixture resembles fine breadcrumbs.

2. Add the egg yolk (if using), followed by the cold water bit by bit. Blend together with a wooden spoon as you go. As soon as the mix comes together as a malleable, not-too-sticky dough, stop adding the liquid. (Less liquid will be required if you're using margarine, owing to its greater water content.)

3. Turn the pastry out on to a board dusted with gluten-free white flour. Dust your hands and knead it briefly until it forms a smooth lump. Leave to rest for 10 minutes in a cool place.

4. If you've added xanthan gum, roll out the dough and press it into your lightly oiled tart tin. If this proves too difficult, or if you haven't used xanthan gum, take sections of the dough and press together in the tin, 'patchwork' style. Flute and chill your pastry case as usual

*Xanthan gum is used to improve crumb structure and reduce crumbling. The Xanthomonas campestris bacterium is cultivated through the fermentation of (usually) sucrose or glucose. This by-product is then dried and powdered, ready to form a gum when liquid is added. Xanthan gum is also cultivated on a lactose substrate for commercial use.

Sprouting seeds & pulses: a quick guide

It is extremely simple and rewarding to sprout your own pulses and seeds. By doing this you will gain access to one of nature's greatest and most vitality-packed nutritional bonanzas. Sprouts are rich in enzymes, minerals, proteins and vitamins – with the vitamin C levels increasing by *600 per cent* during sprouting.

The most successful sprouts we make at Schumacher College are with green lentils, puy lentils, brown lentils, mung beans and fenugreek seeds. Chick peas, black-eyed beans and aduki beans can also be sprouted, but we find that these larger pulses are less popular.

Sprouting generally takes about 3-5 days – depending on the ambient temperature. Be careful about which water you use – at Schumacher College we use tap water because we know it's drinkable, but in other parts of the world it may be advisable to use bottled water for bringing your sprouts into life.

1. When calculating how many dry lentils, seeds or small pulses to sprout, bear in mind that the volume is going to increase by at least four times. So, for 1 cup of dry mung beans, for example, you'll end up with at least 4 cups sprouted – more if you let the shoots develop.

2. Begin by finding a suitable bowl, such as a pudding basin, and a plate that fits over the top like a lid. Alternatively, use a lidded plastic box (this is the method advocated by Schumacher College's House Manager, William Thomas, in *Gaia's Kitchen*). Put ½-1 cup of seeds or pulses in the basin and cover with two or three times their depth of pure, clean, fresh water. When you want to get your sprouts going quickly, use clean, lukewarm or body-temperature water – these are plants that have evolved in warmer climates than the UK, and they will respond to it. Leave to swell overnight, or for up to 24 hours. Keep out of direct sunlight.

3. Next day, drain through a sieve and rinse thoroughly with fresh water. Return the soaked seeds/pulses to the bowl and again cover with the plate or lid. There's no need to add more water – they will already be damp enough to begin their journey into sprouthood, and the lid will prevent them drying out. Keeping them in a warm spot such as an airing cupboard will hasten the process, if you're in a hurry.

4. The following day, again drain them through a sieve, splash with fresh water and return them to the bowl. Continue this rinsing process at least once, or preferably twice, a day. (Alfalfa seeds will need to be washed more frequently to prevent them rotting.) Stop using the sieve as soon as you see little tails bursting from the seeds – they can get caught in the mesh of the sieve and torn off. Instead, pull the plate (or lid) back a tiny crack and slowly drain out the old water, holding back the seeds within the bowl using the plate or lid. Splash with fresh water to rinse and drain this out too. Keep rinsing until the sprouts are 5mm (¼") long or as desired. When ready, consume or keep refrigerated to halt growth – you don't want them to start producing leaves: at that point, although still healthy, they will no longer be at their optimum nutritional value or taste.

Salads

Whirling seasons pasta salad

New potato, shallot & walnut salad

Carrot, strawberry & cranberry salad

Grape & almond coleslaw

Burgeoning butter-bean salad

Warm quinoa salad with marinated tofu, squash & fennel

Orange-marinated tofu

Wild rice, asparagus & tofu salad

Millet salad with leek, courgette & chestnut

Marinated mushroom salad

Celery, celeriac & apple salad

Apple cottage salad

Spinach & carrot weave

Roast vegetable couscous salad

Puy lentil & fennel salad

Kalifornian kale salad

Twirling seasons tricolour rice salad

Pink & purple salad

Portuguese marinated carrots

Warm parsnip & hazelnut salad

Whirling seasons pasta salad

In its modest spring attire this salad consists of pasta, flageolet beans and/or goat's cheese, sun-dried tomatoes, wild garlic, black olives and seasonings. In the abundance of late summer and early autumn it becomes more showy: the seasonal safe is unbolted and the salad reconstructs itself with colourful gems in the form of courgettes, green beans and roasted red peppers sparkling with olive oil. Fresh cherry tomatoes can also be substituted for the sun-dried ones. Thus a staple ingredient such as pasta (or indeed rice) responds joyously to the dance of the seasons and reflects their rich ebb and flow back to us.

For 6	For 45-50
Common ingredients (including dressing)	
150g (6oz / 2 cups) penne	1.4kg (3lb)
40g (1½oz / ¼ cup) black kalamata olives	300g (12oz / 2 cups)
75g (2-3oz / ½ cup) firm goat's cheese or feta (optional)	600g (1lb 4oz) (optional)
1 tbsp lemon juice or cider vinegar	125ml (4fl oz / ½ cup)
3 tbsp olive oil	350ml (12fl oz)
½ tsp grainy mustard	1 tbsp
1 pinch salt	1-2 tsp salt
Sprinkling of freshly ground black pepper	½-1 tsp
1 small clove garlic, crushed (when wild garlic not included)	6-8 cloves
Late autumn / spring options	
4-8 (15g / ½oz) tender punchy leaves of the season (e.g. young dandelion leaf, wild garlic, mizuna or rocket leaf/arugula, as available)	1 big bunch (150g / 5oz)
50g (2oz / ⅓ cup) dried flageolet beans	400g (14oz / 2 cups)
6 sun-dried tomatoes	200g (7oz / 2 cups)
Summer / early autumn options	
1 smallish courgette (in later summer/autumn)	8 medium
1 small or half a large red pepper (approx. 100g / 4oz)	approx. 1.5 kg (3lb)
8-10 fresh cherry tomatoes (approx. 100g / 4oz)	800g (1lb 12oz)
8-10 fine green beans (approx. 100g / 4oz) (French best; alternatively runner beans)	800g (1lb 12oz)
approx. 4 tbsp parsley, chopped (optional)	1-2 cups (optional)
approx. 4 tbsp basil, chopped or torn (optional)	1-2 cups (optional)

1. Soak the flageolet beans in three times their depth of water overnight.

2. Soak the sun-dried tomatoes for at least one hour in warm water, or overnight in cold water. When ready, slice into strips and put aside.

3. Next day, cook the flageolet beans in plenty of fresh water, allowing 45-75 minutes. When they are just pleasantly soft but still holding their shape, stir a pinch or two of salt into the water. Wait a minute or two and then drain. Drench in cold water to halt cooking if they are flaking. Spread out to cool.

4. Cook the pasta in plenty of salted water until al dente. Drain and remove from heat. Stir in a little of the olive oil to keep the pieces of pasta separate. The revived sun-dried tomatoes can also be added at this stage.

5. Wash the wild or cultivated leaves in cold water and dry as required (sometimes wild leaves have been cleaned to perfection by the early morning dew and need no further attention). Cut across the leaves' centre-folds into 1.5cm (½") strips – not too wide, as the wild garlic can be strong and the dandelion can be tough.

6. If a garlic clove is being included, crush and stir it into the lemon juice with the mustard, salt, pepper and about three-quarters of the olive oil.

7. Halve the black olives, removing stones if necessary. Mix together the pasta, lemon juice or cider vinegar, remaining olive oil, mustard, salt and pepper, then add the flageolet beans, sun-dried tomatoes (if not already added), olives and leaves. Taste and adjust. Goat's or feta cheese can also be added, instead of or as well as the flageolet beans. Heap into an attractive bowl to serve.

Summer / early autumn version:

Prepare the pasta as above (Step 4). Crush the garlic clove into the lemon juice with the seasoning and olive oil (Step 6). Then pre-heat the oven to 200°C (400°F / Gas Mark 6) and continue preparing the other ingredients as follows.

Courgettes: Slice either in 0.5cm (¼") disks or in 4cm (1½")-long batons (quartering, or sixthing, sections of the courgettes lengthways). Toss these in olive oil, then salt and roast in the oven until just tender.

Red pepper: These are very nice charred and peeled before slicing into 1cm (½")-wide strips, which could be as long as your little finger. However, it may be easier to cut them into strips and roast them with their skins on, in the same way as for the courgettes.

Green beans: Top and tail, then cut to about the same length as the pasta pieces. Cook in boiling salted water until just cooked and still bright in colour.

Cherry tomatoes: halve these (or quarter if much larger than usual!)

When all the ingredients are cooled, toss them carefully together. Taste and adjust the seasoning (less oil may be necessary in this version, as the courgettes have been roasted in oil). Parsley or basil can also be roughly chopped (or torn, in the case of basil, which bruises easily) and added to the summer salad. As with the late autumn / spring version, 'bring on the cabaret' and toss or layer in chunks of goat's or feta cheese as well – making the salad a balanced meal in itself.

New potato, shallot & walnut salad

My father and stepmother were great devotees of new potatoes, and it was at their dinner table that I first learned the trick of combining them with walnuts – and of not being quite so determined as my grandmother was to scrape off every last flake of potato skin. She always insisted it was easy, but I have learned to like the skin – and, so long as the potatoes are organic, it's good for you.

For 6	For 45-50
600g (1lb 4oz) new potatoes (preferably small ones)	5kg (11lb)
400g (14oz) shallots or red onions	3.2kg (7lb)
85g (3oz / ⅔ cup) walnuts or pecans	600g (1lb 4oz)
1 good bunch of fresh mint (if available), stalks and all	A couple of bigger bunches!
20g (1oz / ½-¾oz / ¼ cup) flat-leaved parsley, chopped	140g (5oz / 2 cups)
1-2 cloves garlic	8-15 to taste
4 tbsp lemon juice	120ml (8fl oz / 1 cup)
100ml (4-5fl oz / ½ cup) olive oil	600ml (1 pint / 2½ cups)
1 tsp grainy mustard	3 tbsp
½ tsp salt to taste	3-4 tsp
1-2 pinches freshly ground black pepper	1-2 tsp

1. Place the potatoes in a sink with plenty of very slightly warm water and rub-a-dub them between your hands as if you were scrubbing clothes. This process enables them to knock the mud off each other without too much individual attention. Rinse and repeat the process.

2. Pop the potatoes into a deep saucepan, cover with cold water and add a pinch of salt. Bring to the boil, then reduce to a simmer. Cook for 15 minutes and then add the mint to flavour them. Cook for another 10 minutes then check: if the largest potatoes feel just soft enough to eat when pierced with a knife, remove them from the heat and drain. When the potatoes have cooled, remove the mint.

3. Pre-heat the oven to 190°C (375°F / Gas Mark 5). Peel the shallots or red onions and cut them into quarters lengthways from root to shoot. Toss the pieces in about half the olive oil and season with salt and pepper. Spread out one layer thick on a metal baking tray and roast in the oven for 20-25 minutes until soft. Chop up the parsley.

4. Crush the garlic and stir it into the lemon juice. Add salt and pepper, then pour in the remaining olive oil. Whizz together with a rod blender (or shake up in a jam jar). Stir in the grainy mustard.

5. Set aside some of the nuts and parsley for garnishing. Combine all the remaining ingredients. Mix carefully and minimally with a wooden spoon, or your clean hands, until the potatoes are well coated with dressing. Taste and adjust the seasoning if necessary. Transfer to a serving dish and sprinkle with the reserved nuts and parsley.

Carrot, strawberry & cranberry salad

This lovely combination of grated carrot and berries was introduced to us by Susie Smith, who first arrived at Schumacher as a maternity cover for our Publicity Coordinator. Dried cranberries, in contrast to strawberries, can be bought at any time of year. Revive them and add to your cooking when you need to bring a touch of luxury to your menu. They travel light, last long and are full of vitamin C.

In the USA, cranberries were used, both fresh and dried, by the Native American people long before the settlers arrived. They contain a natural preservative, benzoic acid, which makes them very suitable for drying and keeping. Because of this they were transported on long journeys across the ocean long before refrigeration, and rank alongside spices as one of the most ecologically low–impact kinds of food to import. By contrast, strawberries are best eaten fresh and sourced locally.

For 6	For 45-50
450g (1lb / 3 cups) sweet young carrots	3.5kg (8lb)
60g (2½oz / ½ cup) dried cranberries	400g (14oz / 3 cups)
125g (5oz) fresh strawberries	1kg (2lb)
Juice of a half or 1 lemon	Juice of 4-6 lemons
2-3 tbsp olive oil	300ml (10fl oz / 1¼ cups)
2-3 pinches salt	2-3 tsp
1 pinch freshly ground black pepper	1-2 tsp

1. Cover the cranberries with very hot water and leave them to soak for just 10-15 minutes, before draining.

2. Scrub then top and tail the carrots. If they are new carrots, it shouldn't be necessary to peel them, but if there is any blemishing on the skin or if they are not organic you must peel them, as this will look better, taste better and be healthier. Then grate them.

3. Mix the grated carrots with the lemon juice and cranberries.

4. Remove the hulls from the strawberries and rinse them very briskly in cold water. Leave to drain in a colander or pat dry. Halve about 3 (or 10 for the larger quantity) and put aside for garnishing. Cut the rest from top to bottom to produce heart-shaped slices about 0.5cm (¼") thick. Some variation in size is fine – though giant strawberry pieces are best halved (lengthways).

5. Add the olive oil, salt and pepper to the grated carrot mixture. Check and adjust the seasoning and then lightly toss in the strawberries. Tip the salad into your serving dish and decorate with the reserved strawberry halves, cut side down. Serve immediately.

Grape & almond coleslaw

This fresh and fruity reincarnation of a bog-standard cabbage-mayo salad puts coleslaw back within the domain of things that are interesting and tantalizing to munch on. You could easily forget that it's a close relative of the ubiquitous salad found at every motorway café. Schumacher chef Wayne Schroeder first encountered this sophisticated 'slaw when holidaying in France, and since then he has morphed it into a favourite lunchtime salad, which appears in almost every season.

Admittedly the currency of this dish has more to do with the natural long life of local white cabbages than the very limited availability of local grapes. Our neighbours in southern Europe, however, boast long grape seasons. From these treasure troves come the grapes that go into this therapeutic salad – kindling our imagination with the vision of bunches of fruit dripping down juicily from the roofs of Mediterranean verandas, where people sit happily sipping wine in vine-dappled sunlight . . .

For 6	For 45-50
375g (14oz / 3-4 cups) white cabbage	3kg (6½lb)
250g (9oz / 1½ cups) seedless black grapes	2kg (4½lb)
25g (1oz / 2-3 tbsp) flaked almonds	200g (7oz / 1½ cups)
3 spring onions or a quarter of a red onion	3-4 bunches or 2 red onions
2-3 tbsp flat-leaved parsley, chopped	70-100g (3oz / 1-1½ cups)
75ml (3fl oz / 5 tbsp) mayonnaise	600ml (1 pint / 2¼ cups)
4 tbsp thick full-fat yoghurt or sour cream	500ml (16fl oz / 2 cups)
½ tsp Dijon mustard	3-4 tsp
1 pinch salt	approx. 2-3 tsp
1 pinch freshly ground black pepper	1-2 tsp

1. Pre-heat the oven to 200°C (400°F / Gas Mark 6).

2. Remove any tough or dried outer leaves from the cabbage, and rinse it in cold water. Cut it in half, through the trunk, and then into sixths or eighths, depending on how large it is. Cut out the core and shred the wedges of cabbage crosswise, as finely as you can.

3. Rinse the grapes and slice lengthways to get oval halves. Add them to the bowl of shredded cabbage.

4. Toast the flaked almonds on a metal baking tray in the hot oven for about 5 minutes until they are golden-brown at the edges. Allow to cool.

5. Chop the parsley finely and toss most of it in with the cabbage. Finely slice the onion and add this too.

6. Combine the mayonnaise, yoghurt or sour cream, mustard, salt and pepper. Add to the cabbage and mix well, being careful not to break up the grapes. Taste and adjust the seasoning if necessary.

7. Toss in half the flaked almonds and give the coleslaw a quick stir. Tip into a serving dish and garnish with the rest of the almonds and parsley.

Burgeoning butter-bean salad

This wholesome salad, with its bounty of butter beans, can be served at any time of year as it easily adapts to the winter months when dried herbs and tomatoes can be substituted for fresh. The marinating of the mushrooms in the tomatoey juices gives a lovely flavour to both the mushrooms and the beans.

Butter beans are a variety of the lima bean grown in the USA. Large and flat, these white beans have a good flavour and protein-rich generosity to them, which will appease any reluctant vegetarian. This nutritional value must be why their cultivation spread steadily outwards from Ancient Peru (where traces of lima beans were found in archaeological sites dating back to 7000 BC) to the rest of the American continent and beyond.

For 6	For 45-50
150g (6oz / 1 cup) dried butter beans or 500g / 1lb 2oz cooked	1.2kg (2½lb) dried
2 large fresh tomatoes or 4-6 sun-dried	1.5kg (3lb 4oz) fresh or 200g (7oz / 2 cups) sun-dried
1 small red onion (or half a large)	4-5 good-sized red onions
1 stalk celery	1 head
225g (8oz / 2-3 cups) mushrooms (button or open type)	1.8kg (4lb)
1 bay leaf	2-3 only
1-2 sprigs basil, freshly chopped	50g (2oz / 1 cup)
2-3 tbsp olive oil	300ml (10fl oz / 1 cup)
1-2 tbsp lemon juice	100ml (3fl oz / ⅓ cup)
1 tsp cider vinegar	2 tbsp
1 tsp grainy mustard	2-3 tbsp
2 cloves garlic, crushed	10-15 cloves
2-3 pinches each of salt and black pepper to taste	2-3 tsp salt, ½-1 tsp pepper
1-2 tbsp parsley and chives, chopped (optional extra!)	½-1 cup (optional)

1. Soak the beans overnight. Next day, cook them up in *fresh* water with a bay leaf, for an hour or so, until tender but still holding their shape. Add a spoonful of salt to the water for the last 5-15 minutes of cooking to help the beans keep their shape. Drain.

2. If the tomato season is over, use sun-dried tomatoes. Soak them in water for 1-2 hours, then slice into fairly narrow strips. If using fresh tomatoes, prepare them by skinning them (see tip opposite), then halve and slice.

3. Slice the onion in fine half-moons, the celery in fine diagonal slices across the stem, and the mushrooms in elegant 0.5cm (¼")-thick slices.

4. Sauté the onion and celery in some of the olive oil until soft. Add the mushrooms and cook for another 5 minutes, adding more olive oil if required. Remove from heat before adding the prepared fresh tomatoes (or sliced sun-dried tomatoes) and the chopped basil.

5. Now stir in the lemon juice, vinegar, mustard, garlic, salt and pepper.

6. Finally, add the cooked butter beans to the mixture. If possible, leave it to stand for 20 minutes to marinate. Stir in any additional fresh herbs and tip into a serving dish.

Tip: To skin tomatoes, dunk them in boiling water for a few minutes or until the skins split apart immediately on piercing with a knife. Drain, then use a fork to hold the tomatoes in place as you peel them. If using for a salad, make sure you peel immediately the skin reaches splitting point, to ensure a nice smooth, not fuzzy, surface texture. Some people like to cross the tomato with a knife before dunking.

Warm quinoa salad with marinated tofu, squash & fennel

As the summer begins to turn to autumn, a warm salad brings a sense of comfort and refreshment, like a soft eiderdown. The mellow tastes and textures of richly coloured squash, orange-marinated tofu and anise-flavoured fennel go beautifully together. Indeed, this salad is so brimful of protein and other goodness it could be a meal in itself. Normally, however, we serve it with bread, soup and maybe some additional greens (raw or cooked).

For 6	For 45-50
250g (9oz / 1 pack) tofu	2kg (4½lb / 8 packs)
350g (12oz / 2½ cups) orange-fleshed squash	2 large squash (2.8kg / 6lb)
135g (5oz / ¾ cup) quinoa	1.1kg (2½lb / 6 cups)
1 fennel bulb + 1 tbsp fennel leaf, chopped	8 bulbs (2kg / 4lb 6oz) + 3 tbsp
30g (1oz / 4 pieces) apricots	270g (10oz / 1½ cups)
30g (1oz / 4 tbsp) cashews	225g (8oz / 1½ cups)
½ tsp dried oregano	1 rounded tbsp
3 tbsp flat-leaved parsley, chopped	100g (4oz / 1½ cups)
250ml (8fl oz / 1 cup) boiling water	2.1l (3¾ pints / 4½ US pints)
approx. 2 tbsp olive oil	approx. 250ml (8-9fl oz / 1 cup)
1-3 pinches salt, 1-2 pinches freshly ground black pepper	2-3 tsp salt, 1 tsp pepper

Dressing

approx. 1 tbsp marinade (see page 108)	6-8 tbsp to taste
1-2 tsp lemon juice	Juice of 1 lemon

1. The day before, prepare the marinated tofu, cutting it into generous 2cm (¾") cubes (see Orange-marinated tofu recipe, page 108). In emergencies you can save time by doing this early on the same day, but at least four hours in advance.

2. On the day, pre-heat the oven to 170°C (325°F / Gas Mark 3). Place the quinoa in a heatproof bowl with the dried oregano and the boiling water. Stir briefly and cover with a close-fitting lid or foil. Place in the warm oven for about half an hour and leave to swell. When ready, the quinoa will have absorbed all the water, with the individual grains still separate. Remove from the oven and give it a good stir – if there are still specks of white in each grain, indicating a hard centre, allow it to go on cooking in its own heat with just the lid on. If, on the other hand, the quinoa is well cooked and might go sticky if left in its own heat any longer, spread it out using an additional container and place in a breezy spot such as on a windowsill. This allows steam to escape rapidly, halting the cooking process.

3. Turn up the oven to 200°C (400°F / Gas Mark 6). Next, prepare the squash. Peel, de-seed and cube into generous 2cm (¾") chunks, comparable in size to the tofu. Tip into a roasting tin, massage with olive oil and sprinkle with a little salt. Mix to ensure an even coating of oil, and spread out the squash so it's only one piece thick.

4. Now prepare the fennel. Chop off the stalks of the bulbs, retaining some of the greenest of the feathery leaves to chop finely and add to the salad at the end. If the outer petals of the fennel are very brown and dried, these will also have to be discarded, as will the root end. Slice the bulb in half from tip to root, then lay the cut side flat on the work surface and slice the fennel up lengthways into fairly narrow 0.5cm (¼") pieces. If any pieces seem too large, cut them through the core. Spread the fennel pieces out on a baking tray and, as with the squash, mix with a drizzling of olive oil and sprinkle with salt. Roast both the fennel and the squash in the hot oven for 20-30 minutes.

5. Chop the apricots and add to the cooling quinoa.

6. Spread the cashews out on a metal baking tray and roast in the oven alongside the fennel and squash for 8- 10 minutes. When ready, they should be lightly browned in places. Leave to cool before adding to the quinoa.

7. Fish the tofu out of the marinade with a slotted spoon (reserve the marinade for another occasion). Remove most of the garlic slices and add to the quinoa. Also remove the orange peel, which can be sliced finely and added to the quinoa (or composted). Spread the tofu out on a baking tray, one cube deep (with gaps between) and bake in the same oven for 15-20 minutes. The tofu will puff up slightly and become a little firmer. Turn it gently with a wooden spatula halfway through cooking.

8. Now that all the ingredients are ready, the salad can be put together in an attractive serving dish using one of the following two methods. The first is quicker but depends on a light touch. The second (layering) is more foolproof, especially when making the large quantity, since it avoids too much stirring of breakable ingredients.

Method A: First, reserve some of the roast squash, tofu and cashews for the top. Next, stir the lemon and marinade dressing into the quinoa, then mix in all the other ingredients. Taste and adjust seasoning if required, then heap into a bowl and toss the reserved squash, tofu and cashews on top.

Method B: Gently stir together all the ingredients *except* the squash and tofu. Add the lemon and marinade dressing, stir and taste. Spoon half or one-third of this mixture into the base of your serving dish, then add half or one-third of the tofu and squash. Follow this with another layer of the quinoa mixture, then another layer of the squash and tofu. (If using thirds, repeat with another layer of each.) Finish the final layer of squash and tofu with cashews sprinkled on top, ready to serve.

Orange-marinated tofu

With the price of nuts rising steadily, tofu contributes a valued source of vegan protein to our diet at Schumacher College. We use organic tofu made locally from organic Chinese soya beans, and look forward to the day when more beans are actually grown locally, as has been shown to be possible in the east of England. Tofu, also known as bean curd and used in many Asian cuisines, is made by coagulating soya milk and then pressing the resulting curds into soft white blocks.

This is a variation of the marinated tofu recipe that appears in *Gaia's Kitchen*. It is mellower, lighter in colour and doesn't rely on opening a bottle of wine. As with the other recipe, the marinating process gives a new dimension of exciting fruity flavour to what is otherwise a rather plain and tasteless form of protein.

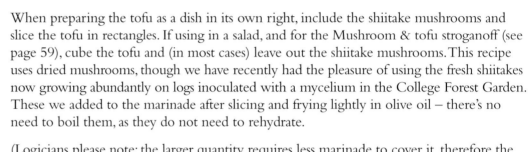

When preparing the tofu as a dish in its own right, include the shiitake mushrooms and slice the tofu in rectangles. If using in a salad, and for the Mushroom & tofu stroganoff (see page 59), cube the tofu and (in most cases) leave out the shiitake mushrooms. This recipe uses dried mushrooms, though we have recently had the pleasure of using the fresh shiitakes now growing abundantly on logs inoculated with a mycelium in the College Forest Garden. These we added to the marinade after slicing and frying lightly in olive oil – there's no need to boil them, as they do not need to rehydrate.

(Logicians please note: the larger quantity requires less marinade to cover it, therefore the liquid ingredients have been scaled up to a lesser degree than the tofu.)

For 6	For 45-50
500g (1lb / 2 packs) plain tofu	4kg (16 x 250g packs) / 8½lb (17 x 8oz packs)
6 (10g / ½oz / ½ cup) dried shiitake mushrooms	50-85g (1 small bag / 2-3oz / 2-3 cups)
3-4 strips orange zest	8-10 strips (from 3-4 oranges)
100ml (4fl oz / ½ cup) orange juice (from 1 orange)	600ml (1 pint / 2¼ cups) (6-8 oranges)
100ml (4fl oz / ½ cup) cider vinegar	600ml (1 pint / 2¼ cups)
100ml (4fl oz / ½ cup) tamari or soy sauce*	600ml (1 pint / 2¼ cups)
1-2 cloves garlic, crushed or sliced	12 cloves / 1 good-sized head
150ml (5fl oz / ⅔ cup) water	900ml (1½ pints)
100ml (4-5fl oz / ½ cup) olive oil and/or sunflower oil	600ml (1 pint / 2¼ cups)
1 pinch freshly ground black pepper	1 tsp
2 tsp fresh herbs (e.g. tarragon, chives or marjoram), coarsely chopped, or 1 tsp dried	4 tbsp fresh or 2 tbsp dried

*For gluten-free diets, make sure you use tamari, not ordinary soy sauce, which contains fermented wheat or barley. Tamari is a by-product of miso making and is gluten-free.

1. Begin by pressing the tofu – this is not absolutely essential, but will greatly help to increase its absorbency. Drain the tofu in a colander, to remove the surplus water, then place each lump well apart in a rectangular baking tray or dish. Cover with a sheet of baking parchment or greaseproof paper and then place another flat-bottomed baking tray or dish on top. Fill this with heavy objects (baked bean tins, etc.) and leave for several hours or overnight to press out excess moisture.

2. Remove the pressed tofu and drain off the liquid. Slice or cube the tofu according to your recipe: make rectangles that are about 0.75cm (just over ¼") wide from the shorter side of the tofu, or cubes that are roughly 2cm (¾") square.

3. If cutting the tofu in rectangles for serving as a dish in its own right, stack the slices in your baking dish so that they overlap like tiles on a roof. Cubes of tofu can just be plonked on top of each other in a more random fashion.

4. Now prepare the marinade. Begin by simmering the dried shiitake mushrooms in the water in a lidded saucepan for about 15 minutes. Using a peeler, slice 3-4cm (1-1½") strips of zest from the oranges and put aside. Squeeze the oranges and put the juice (minus pips!) in a deep pan with the tamari / soy sauce, cider vinegar and oil, crushed (or finely sliced) garlic and pepper. (If you have access to a fairly cheap olive oil, use this, otherwise combine olive oil with sunflower oil or use all sunflower oil, depending on your budget.) Add the simmered shiitakes with their water and bring to the boil. Add the orange zest and simmer for 5 minutes.

5. Pre-heat the oven to a mere 150°C (300°F / Gas Mark 2).

6. Add the freshly chopped or dried herbs to the hot marinade and pour it over the tofu. Cover with a lid or foil and put in the warm oven for 30 minutes or so. Remove from the oven and, when the mixture has cooled down a bit, gently reverse some of the cubes/rectangles with a wooden spatula or your fingers, so that the lighter top side is now immersed in the darker under-layer of the marinade, below the oil. Leave for several hours or overnight.

7. To serve the orange-marinated tofu, fish the tofu rectangles out of the juices and arrange on a platter with plenty of the shiitake mushrooms, orange zest, herbs and garlic – and just a little of the liquid. A scattering of fresh herbs can be added as an additional garnish if desired.

8. Surplus marinade liquid can be kept in the fridge for a few weeks and used once more to marinate more tofu. I add a little extra orange juice and tamari to revitalize the mixture, and again heat it up to boiling point before it is poured on top of the prepared tofu.

Wild rice, asparagus & tofu salad

At Schumacher College, as everywhere, we need to adapt to both seasonal and market availability of foods. Thus, this delicious salad offers options for varying the inclusion of the more expensive or seasonally limited ingredients. Wild rice is sometimes substituted with aduki beans, and asparagus (which has a fairly short growing season, in late spring and early summer) is very often replaced with broccoli or calabrese. Wild rice and asparagus represent the more expensive options: I leap at the opportunity to use them when they are available, and like to maximize their value by spreading them out in an interesting salad mixture, where they are still the stars of the show.

For 6	For 45-50
375g (13oz / 1½ packs) tofu	3kg (6½lb / 12 packs)
170g (6oz / 1 cup) wild rice or aduki beans	1.4kg (3lb / 8 cups)
1 fennel bulb	8 bulbs (2kg / 4lb 6oz)
1 small red onion	6 medium (1kg / 2lb)
1-2 heads broccoli or 2 bunches asparagus (approx. 500g / 1lb 2oz)	8-12 medium heads or 16 bunches (4kg / 9lb)
1 clove garlic, crushed	6-8 cloves
2-3 tbsp flat-leaved parsley, chopped	70g (2-3oz / 1 cup)
1-2 tbsp lemon juice	100ml (¼ pint / ½ cup)
3 tbsp olive oil (2 tbsp for roasting, 1 tbsp for dressing if required)	100ml (¼ pint)
1-2 pinches salt to taste	A few pinches to taste
1-2 tbsp marinade to taste (see page 108)	100-250ml (4-8fl oz / ½-1 cup)

1. Prepare the marinated tofu as described in the Orange-marinated tofu recipe on page 108. This is best done the day before and left overnight.

2. Boil the wild rice or aduki beans in plenty of water until just cooked. In both cases, you want to avoid the individual grains or beans breaking up. The rice will cook more quickly than the beans (about 25 minutes, compared with 45-60 minutes). Drain, spread out and leave to cool. Pre-heat the oven to 200°C (400°F / Gas Mark 6).

3. Cut off the tough stalk and root of the fennel. Slice the bulb in half from stem to core, then cut out the core with two sharp diagonal incisions meeting under the core in a 'V' shape. Continue by cutting the fennel into narrow longish strips, again working downwards from stem to root. Toss the fennel in olive oil, sprinkle with salt and roast in the oven.

4. Slice the onion in half and then into fairly narrow half-moon pieces. Toss these in with the roasting fennel (it will cook a bit more quickly, so can join the fennel halfway through its cooking process).

5. Drain and bake the marinated tofu cubes in the oven as described in the Warm quinoa, squash & fennel salad on page 106. They should plump up a bit and become more robust to handle when tossed into the salad.

6. If using asparagus, cut or break off the fibrous ends. The spears will snap easily where the tender part of the asparagus begins, so you can feel your way along until you reach the snapping point, and be confident the fibrous part has been left behind. (This in turn can be pared down with a potato peeler and also used.) If using broccoli or calabrese, cut into neat florets, or (if enormous) half-florets, again salvaging some of the tender inner trunk by cutting away the tough outside skin. Blanch the florets of broccoli or asparagus in boiling salted water. When al dente, and still bright in colour, drain and spread out to cool. Cut the asparagus into 5cm (2") lengths.

7. Chop up the parsley and squeeze the lemon juice. Crush the garlic.

8. If you want to serve the dish as a warm salad, start combining all the ingredients straight away, otherwise let them cool for a little longer. Begin by mixing together the rice or aduki beans with the extra lemon juice, garlic, parsley, fresh olive oil and a few spoonfuls of marinade to taste. Add the roast fennel and red onion. Carefully stir in, or layer in, the more fragile broccoli or asparagus and the roast tofu, reserving a few attractive pieces for the top. Keep your handling of the salad ingredients light, loose and minimal, and do not press it down!

Millet salad with leek, courgette & chestnut

It is tempting to think of millet as a grain fit only for chickens, but the fact is that there are many different kinds of millet, and it still forms an important part of people's traditional staple diet in many hot, dry regions. In the West, too, people are becoming more interested in millet, and it's especially popular with wheat-avoiders – so is now readily available in wholefood shops.

In this recipe the trick is to cook the millet in such a way that it does not turn into porridge: if you can do this, you will be turning thousands of years of stodgy millet-eating upside-down – and you will have a lovely nutritious, loose-grained, right-brained salad! Quite a contrast to the coarse millet bread and porridge the Romans and Ancient Greeks were making – as long ago as 2000 BC.

For 6	For 45-50
125g (5oz / 1 cup) raw millet	1kg (2lb 4oz)
50g (2oz / ½ cup) dried chestnuts (or approx. 75g / 3oz / ⅔ cup fresh/hydrated)	450g (1lb) dried / 675g (1½lb) fresh/hydrated
1 medium courgette (approx. 200g / 7oz)	1.6kg (3½lb)
Half a medium or 1 small red onion (approx. 50g / 2oz)	500g (1lb 2oz)
3-4 mushrooms (approx. 50g / 2oz) (optional)	450g (1lb) (optional)
1 smallish leek (approx. 125g / 5oz)	1.5kg (3lb 4oz)
1 pinch thyme, mixed herbs or marjoram (optional)	1-2 tsp (optional)
4 tbsp parsley, finely chopped	100-150g (4-5oz / 2 cups)
½-1 tsp Pommery or grainy mustard	2 tbsp
2 tbsp lemon juice	200ml (8fl oz / 1 cup)
200ml (8fl oz / 1 cup) boiling water	1.5l (3 pints / 3¾ US pints)
Plenty of olive oil for roasting etc. (approx. 3-4 tbsp)	200-400ml (½-¾ pint / 1-1½ cups)
60ml (2fl oz / ¼ cup) good vinaigrette (see page 133)	400ml (15fl oz / 2 cups)
2-3 pinches each of salt and black pepper	1-3 tsp salt, 1-2 tsp pepper

1. If using dried chestnuts, soak them in plenty of water overnight. The next day, cook them in the same water until tender but still holding together. Drain, cool and pick out any obtrusively woody bits. Pre-heat the oven to 190°C (375°F / Gas Mark 5).

2. Heat a little olive oil in the bottom of a large pan, then stir the millet into this. Keeping stirring, cook for no longer than 5 minutes, by which time the millet should be beginning to sizzle slightly. Add the boiling water and a pinch of salt. Return to the boil with a lid on and continue to cook for 5 minutes. Switch off the burner and leave the millet to swell, still keeping the lid on to maintain heat. Drain off surplus water after 15 minutes and spread out the grain to ensure rapid cooling – all this has been done in an attempt to prevent the millet merging into a porridge, as it is well practised at doing! If some grains are still slightly crunchy, it doesn't matter, as they will continue to soften. However, if the gritty effect is pronounced, you'll need to re-boil for a couple of minutes to remove this edge.

3. Wash and cut the courgette into 0.5cm (¼") rings, discarding the tip of both ends. If using large courgettes, halve or quarter the rings. Spread out on a baking tray and drizzle with olive oil. Mix to ensure an even coating. Sprinkle with salt, and a few dried herbs if you like. Cook in the hot oven for about 15-20 minutes, until pleasantly cooked but not too brown.

4. Peel the red onion and cut into either rings or wedges. Toss them in olive oil (they will start to fall apart) and sprinkle with salt. Roast these alongside the courgettes.

5. Depending on the size and shape of the mushrooms, they can be either roasted whole (smallish buttons) or cut into halves, quarters or thick slices. As with the courgette and onion, toss in olive oil and sprinkle with salt before roasting in the oven for about 10 minutes.

6. Now for the leek. To avoid overdoing the oil in this salad, I prefer to semi-steam these until just cooked but still bright in colour. Discard the root tip, together with any very old or tough-looking outer leaves. Slit downwards through the top leaves until you get to the white part. Rinse the leek and then chop into chunky, finger-thick, white rings (which should hold together), as well as greener half-moon pieces (which are likely to fall apart). Fill a pan with about 2cm (1") of water. Add the leeks and a sprinkling of salt, then bring to the boil and cook briskly with a lid on until just soft and pleasant to eat – they may be a bit on the squeaky side but hopefully won't be too soggy! Drain immediately.

7. Mix the mustard into the lemon juice and stir into the millet, along with the chopped parsley. When the vegetables are ready, lightly toss them into the salad, along with the chestnuts. Be careful to keep this bejewelled melange loose and lively, rather than squashed down. Season to taste with additional salt and freshly ground black pepper – and a little vinaigrette or more olive oil if you feel the salad needs it. Heap into an attractive serving dish and serve cool or still warm.

Marinated mushroom salad

This marinated salad offers a sort of hybridized mushroom-eating experience that is halfway between a fried and a raw mushroom mouthful. I love edible mushrooms in all forms, and enjoy the slippery oyster-like tenderness marinated mushrooms offer. This may be compared (lovingly) with the deep-brown fungal squelch of the cooked 'shroom next to your fried eggs – and the light pink nibbliness a slice of fresh mushroom brings to a green salad. Both are delightful in their way, and will leave you feeling like a carnivore on the one hand and a caterpillar on the other . . . Try this recipe from Tchenka to feel like a mushroom gourmet! At the College we prepare this salad after breakfast, and leave it to chill in the fridge until lunchtime.

For 6	For 45-50
500g (1lb 2oz) button mushrooms	4kg (9lb)
125ml (5fl oz / ½ cup) olive oil	1l (2 pints / 4 cups)
4 tbsp cider vinegar	480ml (16fl oz / 2 cups)
1 tbsp orange juice, freshly squeezed	120ml (4fl oz / ⅓ cup)
1 tsp clear honey*	3 tbsp
1-2 cloves garlic, crushed	8-14 (or 1 head)
1 tsp mustard seeds	2½ tbsp
1 tbsp juniper berries (if available)	50g (2oz / ½ cup)
½ tsp salt	4 tsp
1 pinch freshly ground black pepper	1-2 tsp
3-4 tbsp parsley, finely chopped	150g (5oz / 2 cups)

1. For the small quantity, brush or wipe the mushrooms to clean them. For the large quantity, save yourself some time by rinsing them very quickly in cold water, splashing and rubbing them together a bit so any loose soil comes off. Leave to drain in a colander.

2. Mix together all the other ingredients except the parsley. For the small quantity, you can place them in a jam jar and shake them. For the large quantity, put them in a jug and stir or hand-whisk together.

3. Going back to the clean, drip-dried mushrooms, cut off any very brown or tough-looking ends and then slice them all into 6mm (¼") slices – not too thin, or they will become floppy. When making the large quantity, it is a great bonus to have a food processor or a willing team of helpers available, as slicing so many mushrooms can be a tedious and time-consuming job for one person.

4. Pour the well-mixed marinade over the sliced mushrooms and stir them gently until every mushroom is coated. Clean hands are good for this. Then put the mushrooms in the fridge.

5. After 3-4 hours marinating in the fridge, the mushrooms will have shrunk to about half their original size. They are ready for a final stir and the addition of the chopped fresh parsley. Once you've done this, transfer the salad to an attractive serving dish.

*For vegan diets use agave.

Celery, celeriac & apple salad

Bursting with silicon and mineral salts, celery is very good for you and aids digestion. The cultivated celery and celeriac we use today are both descended from the wild umbellifer found in hedgerows, also known as 'smallage'. In this recipe, the two are combined with apple and walnuts for a delightfully crunchy Waldorf-style salad, with a delicious yoghurt–mayo dressing.

For 6	For 45-50
2 crisp medium dessert apples	16
approx. 1 tbsp lemon juice	Juice of 2-3 lemons
250g (9oz / 2 cups) celeriac	2kg (4½lb)
2-3 stalks celery	2-3 heads (1.5kg / 3lb 10oz)
50g (2oz / ½ cup) light brown walnuts or pecans	450g (1lb / 4 cups)
1-2 tsp parsley or lovage, chopped	3-4 tbsp

Yoghurt–mayo fusion dressing*

1 heaped tbsp mayonnaise	150ml (5fl oz / ⅔ cup)
1 tbsp thick whole yoghurt	100ml (4fl oz / ½ cup)
¼-½ tsp Dijon mustard	1 tbsp
1 tbsp fresh orange juice	125ml (4fl oz / ½ cup)
1 tsp honey	2 tbsp
Half or 1 clove garlic, pressed	2-3 tsp
1 pinch ground ginger	1 tsp
½ tsp curry powder (optional)	1 tbsp (optional)
1-2 pinches fine sea salt and 1 pinch freshly ground black pepper	1-3 tsp salt and 1 tsp pepper

If using this dressing to dress coleslaw, or other salads where lemon not already included, add 1 tsp lemon juice (2 tbsp for large quantity).

1. Rinse the apples in cold water, then slice into eighths. Cut out the core and then slice into 1-1.5cm (½-¾")-wide pieces. Toss the apple in the lemon juice to prevent discolouring.

2. Peel the celeriac with a small knife and grate. Mix with the apple. Cut the base and top leaves off the celery, then rinse in cold water. Slice the stalk at an angle to get attractive curved pieces, about 0.5-1cm (¼-½") wide. Add to the apple and celeriac.

3. Sort through the walnuts and remove any dark or woody pieces. Set aside a few of the best for garnishing, then rough-chop or halve the rest and add to the apple mixture. Rough-chop the parsley or lovage. Keep a little of this aside for garnishing, then chop the rest a little finer.

4. Combine the ingredients for the dressing in a bowl and mix well. Mix the dressing with the salad ingredients and finely chopped herbs. Taste and adjust the seasoning if needed. Heap into a serving bowl and decorate with walnuts.

*For dairy-free diets, substitute the yoghurt with more mayonnaise. For vegan diets, simply use the vinaigrette on page 133, omitting the honey.

Apple cottage salad

The relatively high protein and low fat content of cottage cheese make it a popular food supplement at Schumacher College. Skimmed milk is mixed with starter culture and vegetarian rennet, left to set, then cut into tiny squares with wires and gently heated until it separates. The whey is drained off from the curds, and a creamy dressing added. In this salad, cottage cheese melds deliciously with sweet crisp apples and poppy seeds – both staples of a classic cottage garden. Indeed, we can imagine that the ancestral 'cottager's cheese' was once made in such a home alongside other simple 'bag cheeses' and clotted cream.

For 6	For 45-50
500g (1lb 2oz / 2 cups) cottage cheese	4kg (9lb)
2 medium eating apples	16
Juice of half an organic lemon + 1 pinch zest	Juice of 4 lemons + 2-3 tsp zest
50-60g (2oz / ½ cup) hazel or cashew nuts	450g (1lb / 4 cups)
4 tbsp sunflower seeds	250g (9oz / 2 cups)
2 stalks celery	2 heads
4 tbsp raisins	250g (9oz / 2 scant cups)
2 tbsp poppy seeds	125g (5oz / 1 cup)
1 tbsp honey	120ml (4fl oz / ½ cup)
1 bunch watercress to garnish (optional)	3-4 bunches (optional)

1. Pre-heat the oven to 190°C (375°F / Gas Mark 5). If using hazelnuts, spread them on a baking tray, one layer thick. Dry-roast for 10-15 minutes until the skins begin to split. Cool briefly, then rub the skins off between your hands, or bundle the nuts into a tea towel and give someone a 'hot nut massage' (see page 185). Then go outside with a colander, tip the nuts into it and shake them around. Most of the skins will fly away, but don't expect to remove every speck! If using cashew nuts, just roast them for 10 minutes until they are light brown, then leave to cool.

2. Repeat the dry-roasting process with the sunflower seeds, allowing 8-10 minutes.

3. Grate a little of the outermost zest from the lemon and stir into the cottage cheese. Juice the lemon and reserve the juice to mix with the apples.

4. Wash and quarter the apples. Cut out the core with a knife to remove the pips, etc. The colourful skin of the apple is very much a feature of this salad, but if you are using windfalls or old bruised apples, you will be better off peeling them and removing any brown spots. Cut the apples into eighths and slice into small pieces. Mix with the prepared lemon juice to prevent discolouration. Wash and slice the celery into narrow pieces.

5. Combine all the ingredients except the watercress, reserving a few nuts for the top. Mix well and taste (the cottage cheese comes salted – but adjust with lemon and salt if you wish). Heap into a bowl, toss the remaining nuts on top, and garnish the edges with watercress.

Spinach & carrot weave

This is a lovely salad to make early in the season, when tender baby spinach first arrives on the menu. The bright slivers of vegetable give a loosely woven effect, like a bird's nest, and this allows you to adapt your use of the spinach for several months as the season moves on – removing more of the stalk as it gets tougher, and shredding the leaves into ever-narrower ribbons. Leave out the red peppers at the beginning of the year, as they have a shorter period of abundance than either the carrots or the spinach and are not really essential to this salad – nice though they are for the melding of juicy and crunchy elements.

For 6	For 45-50
225g (8oz / 1½ cups) carrots	2kg (4lb)
125g (4oz / 1 small bunch) fresh spinach leaves	1kg (2lb)
Half a medium red pepper (if in season)	4 medium or large
1 punnet (approx. 250ml / ½ pint / 1 cup) mustard & cress, alfalfa or fenugreek sprouts*	8 punnets (approx. 2l / 3½ pints / 8 cups)
3 tbsp sunflower seeds	200g (7oz / 1½ cups)
approx. 1 tbsp tamari	2-3 tbsp
4-5 tbsp vinaigrette (see page 133)	approx. 400ml / 14fl oz (see page 133)

1. Pre-heat the oven to 190°C (375°F / Gas Mark 5). Scrub the carrots and peel them, unless they are particularly fresh, clean and thin-skinned. Grate.

2. Wash, de-seed and slice the red pepper finely into narrow 3-4cm (1½")-long strips. Add these to the grated carrots.

3. Spread the sunflower seeds on a baking tray and roast in the hot oven for 8-10 minutes. Remove from the oven and sprinkle all over with tamari. Stir with a wooden spatula and return to the oven for a minute to 'steam-dry'. Remove again, scrape with the spatula to loosen the seeds and get some air on to them, and leave to cool. (If in a hurry, transfer to a ceramic dish to cool.)

4. Wash and dry the spinach. Remove the stalks and any yellowing leaves. Cut into fine strips, varying from 0.5cm to 1cm (¼-½") in width. This may be done by rolling up or stacking-up a few leaves and slicing them together. Though spinach is more robust than lettuce, try to avoid pinching or pressing it, to minimize bruising and maintain a fresher and brighter shade of bottle-green.

5. Cut the mustard and cress off its sod of earth, or remove from blotting paper if you have grown them yourself. Rinse this, or the alfalfa/fenugreek sprouts, and spin or pat dry with a clean cloth or kitchen paper.

6. Finally, 'weave' all the ingredients together with the vinaigrette by means of some light, airy tossing. Add only as much vinaigrette as you think tastes good. Serve straight away.

*See page 95 for sprouting instructions – you'll need to begin growing them 3-4 days before making this salad.

Roast vegetable couscous salad

For this salad, we have roasted the juicy Mediterranean vegetables of late summer and combined them with the fluffy yellow 'grains' of all seasons . . . Only they aren't grains! Couscous is made up of tiny granules that are formed by rubbing and sieving wholewheat flour and salted water together in such a way that minute balls of dough emerge around the bran and wheatgerm. These are then preserved by drying. Archaeological evidence suggests that this process originated in the tenth century in North Africa, and it is there that I first encountered it – steamed in the vapours of a hearty stew and served in a Moroccan children's home. Couscous rehydrates very quickly, and could indeed be described as the 'fast food' of the wholefood world.

For 6	For 45-50
Vegetables to roast	
250g (9oz) tomatoes (cherry ones are nice)	2kg (4lb 4oz)
Half a medium red pepper	4 medium
Half a medium yellow pepper	4 medium
Half a medium aubergine	4 medium
1 medium courgette	8 medium
1 small fennel bulb	8 small or 6 large
Half a large red onion	4 large
6 whole cloves or 1 clove garlic, crushed	40-50 whole cloves (4 heads) or 8 crushed
4-5 tbsp olive oil	approx. 500ml (15fl oz / 2 cups)
1-2 pinches each of salt and dried oregano	3-4 pinches
Soaking the grain	
140g (5oz / 1 cup) medium couscous	1.2kg (2½lb)
500ml (18fl oz / 2 cups) boiling water or veg stock	2.4l (4 pints / 5 US pints)
½ tsp vegetable stock powder (if required)	1 heaped tbsp (if required)
3-4 (15g / ½oz) sun-dried tomatoes	approx. 100g (4oz / 1 cup)
Later additions	
2 tbsp lemon/lime juice (and garlic, if using crushed)	225ml (8fl oz / 1 cup) (and garlic, if crushed)
1 pinch ground cumin	1 tsp
1 small pinch cayenne pepper	½-1 tsp
1-2 tbsp more olive oil (if needed)	125ml (4fl oz / ½ cup), if needed
4-5 fresh basil leaves, chopped or torn	100g (4oz / 1½-2 cups)
50g (2oz) firm goat's cheese / feta (optional)	700g (1½lb) (optional)

1. Cover the sun-dried tomatoes with some of the boiling water or vegetable stock and leave them to soak while you get on with the rest of the preparation.

2. Pre-heat the oven to 190°C (375°F / Gas Mark 5) and begin preparing the vegetables, washing them all and removing tough ends and stalks that will not cook down nicely.

3. Halve and de-seed the peppers, then cut into 2cm (¾") squares/diamonds. The fennel can be halved lengthways, then cut in narrow bands, reaching from stem to root. Cut the aubergine in half lengthways, then continue to cut each half lengthways into 6-8 more triangular-cross-section strips. Cut these up into 0.5cm (¼")-thick pieces. Toss all these vegetables in olive oil. Add a sprinkling of salt and oregano. Spread out one layer thick on metal baking trays and roast in the oven for 20-30 minutes. If you are making the large quantity, roast the aubergine separately, so you can finish it off in a frying pan if it doesn't cook easily.

4. Slice the courgette into 1cm (½")-thick rings and the red onion into 2cm (¾") square-ish pieces, similar in size to the pepper. Again, toss in olive oil and season with salt, before spreading out on a baking tray to roast for 20-30 minutes.

5. Peel the garlic cloves. If using the larger number of cloves whole, toss them in with the already-roasting red peppers. If you are crushing a smaller amount, add the crushed cloves to the lemon juice you'll be combining with the couscous later.

6. If you have cherry tomatoes, pierce them with a knife. Whole tomatoes can be cut in 4-6 segments, depending on size. Toss the tomatoes in olive oil, salt and oregano and spread out on a roasting tray as with the other vegetables. Roast separately for only about 15 minutes.

7. Strain and chop the sun-dried tomatoes, reserving the liquid for the couscous. Make the volume of liquid back up to the correct measure with water, i.e. 500ml (small quantity) or 2.4l (large quantity). Bring the liquid to the boil. Add a little vegetable stock powder, if required, to give a mild stock, then pour on top of the couscous. Stir and cover with a lid, and leave to stand for 5-15 minutes. Once all the liquid has been absorbed, add the lemon or lime juice, with the crushed garlic if you are not roasting the cloves whole. Also stir in the cumin, cayenne and chopped sun-dried tomatoes.

8. Test the roasting vegetables and remove them from the oven as they become pleasantly tender. Some of the edges may be slightly toasted and brown-looking. Remove a few of each cooked vegetable and put them aside on a saucer, for grain-free garnishing purposes. Chop or tear the fresh basil into fairly small pieces. Stir the basil and all the vegetables *except* the (more fragile) roast tomatoes into the couscous. Taste and add a little extra salt and olive oil as required.

9. To finish off the salad, just heap it into a bowl, tossing in the roast tomatoes layer by layer as you go. Adorn the top with the reserved roast veggies, and serve warm or cool.

Optional extra: Goat's cheese or feta go deliciously with this salad if you want to add more protein. Select a fairly firm (as opposed to oozing) goat's cheese and slice into 1.5cm (¾") cubes. Layer into the salad with the roast tomatoes. Feta cheese can be similarly combined or, alternatively, presented in slices tiled attractively around the top edge of the couscous and drizzled with olive oil and a sprinkling of basil or oregano.

Puy lentil & fennel salad

Lentils have been cultivated for thousands of years in Asia and Egypt. After the soya bean, they contain more protein (25 per cent) than any other legume or vegetable. For this reason, lentils have been enormously valued as a staple food in India, where they are eaten as dal. In European countries, Roman Catholics have also appreciated lentils when giving up meat for Lent – which, it is speculated, could well have derived its name from the little legume.

In contrast to common lentils, which merge into a lovely mush when cooked, the small, green, speckled *Verte du Puy* lentil from France retains its individual shape. Perhaps because of this feature, and also perhaps due to its relative costliness, it is the only one of its kind to achieve the status of a delicacy – indeed, rather a trendy one nowadays. This puy lentil salad is another delicious recipe brought to the College by Tchenka Sunderland. In its original form it contained only fennel, parsley and puy lentils – which tasted brilliant but looked rather dull. We brighten it seasonally with the addition of roasted red peppers and small cherry tomatoes, and sometimes surround the salad with a tiled circle of feta cheese. Enjoy adding to the recipe as the season progresses, starting with only fennel in July, adding tomatoes in August, and finally red peppers in September and October.

For 6	For 45-50
150g (6oz) puy lentils	1.2kg (2½lb)
1 bay leaf	2-3
2 fennel bulbs	16 medium (approx. 2.5kg / 5½lb)
1 red pepper	8 medium (approx. 1.6kg / 3½lb)
10 (approx. 200g / 7oz) cherry tomatoes	1.6kg (3½lb)
2 tbsp balsamic vinegar	225ml (8fl oz / ¾ cup)
2 tbsp cider vinegar	225ml (8fl oz / ¾ cup)
1 tbsp tamari or soya sauce	100ml (4fl oz / ½ cup)
4-6 tbsp olive oil	Up to 400ml (15fl oz / 2 cups)
Plenty of parsley, chopped (approx. ½ cup)	150-200g (5-8oz / 2-3 cups)
1-3 pinches each of salt and black pepper to taste	1-2 tsp of each to taste
250g (9oz) feta cheese (optional)	approx. 2kg (7lb) (optional)
2 pinches dried oregano, cayenne, paprika to taste (optional)	A little more to taste (optional)

1. Check over the lentils on a plate, to make sure there are no tiny stones masquerading as lentils. Place them in a saucepan with a bay leaf or two and cover with a couple of inches of water. Bring to the boil, reduce to a simmer and cook until tender – 25-40 minutes, depending on the amount. When cooked, drain immediately and mix with the balsamic vinegar, cider vinegar and tamari / soy sauce. Leave to cool.

2. Meanwhile, prepare the vegetables. Cut the fennel in half lengthways and remove the tough end bit and most of the stalk. Chop and retain some of the feathery fennel leaf to add later. Place the bulb on your chopping board, cut side down, and cut across into 0.5cm (¼") strips. Some of the pieces will be quite wide in patches because they are held together by areas of core – don't worry about this. It is a feature of the salad, and so long as the core is thin enough it will cook easily and should be delicious. Begin sautéing in some of the olive oil. Tchenka advises that covering with a lid can help speed up the cooking time, especially when making the large quantity.

3. Wash and de-seed the red pepper. Cut this too into 0.5cm (¼") strips, to match the size of the fennel strips. Add to the sautéing fennel and cook both until pleasantly tender. Add a pinch or two of salt. (If you wish, de-skin the peppers by charring them on a flame and scraping off the blackened skin with a table knife.)

4. Wash the cherry tomatoes. When the fennel and red pepper are just done, add the cherry tomatoes and sauté briefly until the skins begin to burst.

5. Gently mix together the cooked puy lentils and the sautéd vegetables, adding more of the olive oil, and salt and pepper to taste. Also add most of the parsley and the reserved chopped fennel leaf. Arrange in a bowl or platter, and scatter with the remaining parsley. If you are going to include feta cheese, slice it into fairly narrow rectangles and arrange them around the edge of the lentil salad, overlapping the slices like tiles on a roof. Drizzle the feta with olive oil and give it a sprinkling of dried oregano or cayenne/paprika if you like. This dish is delicious served with crusty bread and a leafy green salad.

Kalifornian kale salad

This scintillating kale salad was brought to us by Lindsay Toub, a gloriously tuneful participant-turned-volunteer. It includes a pioneering method of 'cold-cooking', whereby the cell walls of the kale are broken down through 'massaging' the leaves. Lindsay learned to make it at California's Esalen centre, which, like Schumacher College, specializes in alternative education. California is the home of the Raw Food movement and is also host to the plentiful avocados that go so well with this salad. Don't try skipping the kale massage, or you may find there is more wind about than in a Californian kale field! When making the large quantity, the massage could take 30 minutes, as only a small amount of kale can be dealt with at a time.

For 6	For 45-50
250g (9oz / 4 large handfuls) kale (The best kale is Dino, also called Lacinato or Cavolo Nero)	2kg (4½lb)
1 tbsp pumpkin seeds	50g (2oz / ½ cup)
1 tbsp sesame seeds	50g (2oz / ½ cup)
1 tbsp sunflower seeds	50g (2oz / ½ cup)
1 small red onion	4 medium or to taste
25g (1oz / 1 cup) alfalfa, fenugreek or lentil sprouts*	250g (9oz / 6-8 cups)
100g (4oz) goat's cheese (optional)	800g (1lb 12oz) (optional)
Summer option: 1 ripe avocado, not too small!	8-10
Winter option: 1 tennis-ball-sized beetroot or piece of squash plus a few splashes of olive oil, tamari and balsamic vinegar	8 (approx. 2kg / 4lb) plus a bit more to taste

Dressing	
2 tbsp tamari	250ml (9fl oz / 1 cup)
2 tbsp olive oil (or 1:1 olive oil and flax-seed oil)	250ml (9fl oz / 1 cup) (or 1:1 olive oil and flax-seed oil)
2 tbsp lemon juice	250ml (9fl oz / 1 cup)

1. Begin with the kale preparation. Strip the leaves off the stems and compost the stems. Now tear the leaves into small pieces – only about 1.5cm (½-¾") big. Collect these in a large bowl and then massage them firmly for a few minutes to break down the fibre – rub them against each other and between your fingers as if you were washing clothes. Do this for at least 3 minutes. Green leaves will look a little darker from bruising by the time you have finished.

2. Winter options: If using beetroot or squash, as opposed to avocado, pre-heat the oven to 190°C (375°F/ Gas Mark 5). Peel and slice the beets or squash in pieces about 1.5cm wide but only 0.5cm (¼") thick, so they cook easily. Toss them in olive oil, tamari and balsamic vinegar and roast in the hot oven for 20 minutes until tender. Alternatively, used boiled beets, and roast briefly in the above-mentioned mixture for added flavour.

See page 95 for sprouting instructions – you'll need to begin growing them 3-4 days before making this salad. See also note opposite, under 'Variations'.

3. Roast the pumpkin, sunflower and sesame seeds either in a frying pan or in the oven – allow 8-10 minutes in the oven at 200°C (400°F / Gas Mark 6) until golden-brown. The pumpkin seeds will be beginning to swell up and pop. Stir frequently if roasting on the hob – no oil necessary.

4. Combine the ingredients for the dressing in a bowl (use flax-seed oil as a substitute for half of the olive oil if you prefer). Peel and slice the red onions thinly and add to the dressing to marinate for at least 10 minutes.

5. Summer option: Peel the avocado and chop, or scoop out the flesh with a teaspoon. You want small but fairly chunky pieces.

6. Combine the kale with the dressing at the last minute before serving. Toss in the seeds and alfalfa or other sprouts (see below) and mix again – very lightly. The other more substantial additions (such as squash, beetroot and avocado) can be layered in with the kale mix as you transfer it to a serving bowl – this is to prevent them falling to the bottom of the dish and to keep the colours fresh. Otherwise just mix carefully and minimally, reserving a few roasted vegetable pieces or avocado chunks for the top.

Variations:

Fenugreek or lentil sprouts: Alfalfa goes particularly well with the avocado or squash – but avoid using them with beetroot, as they will stain and look miserable. In lieu of alfalfa, Lindsay has also been adding fenugreek sprouts or lentil sprouts, and thinks they go very well.

Goat's cheese: A firm goat's cheese also goes very nicely with the kale, alfalfa, squash and beetroot. Cut into 1cm (¼-½") pieces and toss in at the end.

Twirling seasons tricolour rice salad

When the juicy vine-offerings of summer are with us, this tricolour salad tangoes brightly on to the dance floor dressed in polka dots of yellow, black and red. During autumn, winter and spring, our salad waltzes demurely, as tomatoes, sweetcorn and olives are replaced by the mellower hues of squash and almonds. In its more muted attire, this salad is also nice served warm.

For 6

180g (6oz / 1 rounded cup) mixed rice
(e.g. 100g white or brown basmati plus
40g red rice, 40g wild rice)

1 good stalk celery, sliced thinly (and a few leaves if nice)

3 tbsp parsley, finely chopped

4-6 tbsp vinaigrette (see page 133)

Autumn/winter/spring options

5-6 (25g) sun-dried tomatoes

250g (9oz / 2 cups) butternut squash

40g (1½oz / ⅓ cup) whole almonds

2-3 tbsp red onion

Olive oil, salt and oregano for roasting squash

Summer options

170g (6oz / ¾ cup) sweetcorn kernels (fresh, frozen or tinned)

250g (9oz / 1 cup) firm red tomatoes

50g (2oz / ⅓ cup) pitted black olives, halved or quartered

2 spring onions, chopped into rings

For 45-50

1.5kg (3lb 5oz / 9 level cups)
(e.g. 800g + 400g + 300g
or 5 cups + 2 cups + 2 cups)

1 head

approx. 100g (4oz / 1½ cups)

approx. 500ml (1 pint /2¼ cups)

200g (7oz / 2 cups)

2-3 good-sized (approx. 3kg / 6½lb)

350g (12oz / 3 cups)

300g (12oz / 1½-2 cups)

100-150ml (approx. ¼ pint / ½ cup)

1.3kg (3lb)

2kg (2lb 4oz)

400g (14oz / 1½ cups)

300g (12oz / 2-3 bunches)

1. If you have bought pre-mixed rice, cook it according to the instructions on the packet. If you have obtained separate varieties of rice, make this an advantage and cook them separately. This will help maintain a slightly fresher distinction of colours. They also take slightly different lengths of time to cook, with the red rice taking longest. Use a ratio of one part rice to two parts water.

Autumn/winter/spring version:

2. Soak the sun-dried tomatoes in warm water for at least an hour. Once rehydrated, chop them into small pieces or strips. Pre-heat the oven to 200°C (400°F / Gas Mark 6).

3. While the rice is cooking and the tomatoes soaking, peel the squash and remove the seeds. Cut the orange flesh into 1.5cm (½") cubes. Toss these in olive oil with a sprinkling of salt and oregano. Spread out in a roasting tin, a single layer deep, and roast in the hot oven for 25-35 minutes. Check halfway through the cooking time and turn the tin if required, to ensure even roasting.

4. At the same time, spread the whole almonds out on a metal baking tray and roast for 10 minutes alongside the squash. When ready, the skins on some of the nuts will be splitting slightly. Leave to cool. Finely chop the red onion and set aside.

5. When the rice is ready the grains should still be separate. If necessary, drain off any surplus liquid and spread the rice out to prevent the grains trapping heat and continuing to cook – this is especially important when making the large quantity. You don't want the rice 'glued' together!

6. Make the vinaigrette (see page 133) and pour it over the warm rice. Add the chopped sun-dried tomatoes.

7. Once the squash is tender, remove it from the oven and allow to cool (when ready it will be slightly brown on some of the ridges but the prevailing colour will still be 'roast' orange).

8. Combine the rice with all other ingredients. Toss it together gently, so the tomatoes or squash don't become too smeary or broken. Taste, adjust the seasoning, then heap up in an attractive serving dish. This version of the salad is pictured above.

Summer version:

2. If using fresh sweetcorn, boil it and then cut the kernels from the cob. For frozen sweetcorn, cook in a little water. Drain tinned sweetcorn. Slice the tomatoes into 2cm (¾") chunks.

3. Follow Steps 5 and 6 of the autumn version (without the sun-dried tomatoes), then gently combine the rice with all the other ingredients, season and serve.

Pink & purple salad

Love it or hate it, the staining pink 'blood' of beetroot is a wonder to behold. In this raw beetroot salad, its transformative potential is put to shocking use as crisp white slices of apple turn a sparkling shade of pink. On special occasions, dried cranberries can also be added to the treasure trove, for an extra-pink twinkle – though for everyday it is more economical to stick with plain currants. All the berries will benefit from being softened in a little freshly squeezed citrus.

Beetroot has many virtues as a healing whole food – it is rich in silicone, and particularly good for the liver as well as for the heart and circulatory system. It can be stored for several months, so can be used from summer right through to late spring.

For 6	For 50
300g (11oz /2-3 medium) beetroot	2.5kg (5½lb)
30g (1oz / ¼ cup) currants or cranberries	250g (8oz / 2 cups)
1½ medium eating apples (150g / 6oz)	1.2kg (2lb 12oz)
2-3 stalks crisp celery	2 good heads
Juice of half an orange	Juice of 3 or 4
1-2 tsp lemon juice to taste	Juice of 1 lemon
2-3 tbsp olive oil	250ml (8fl oz / 1 cup)
1-3 pinches salt	2-3 tsp
1-2 pinches freshly ground black pepper	½-1 tsp

1. Squeeze the oranges and soak the currants and/or cranberries in the juice while you get on with the rest of the recipe.

2. Scrub, peel and grate the beetroot.

3. Wash the apples. Cut them into sixths or eighths (depending on size). Cut out the pips, then cut each segment into fine slices along the width of the piece. Bright streaks of apple skin is one of the features of this salad, so look out for crisp apples with some red in the skin, like Cox or Pink Lady. However, if the apples have been stored for several months you may find them so wizened that it's better to peel the leathery skin off.

4. Cut the end off the celery to separate and wash the stalks. Trim off the 'branches' but include some of the tender leaf from the heart if you like. Slice the celery stalks thinly across the stem.

5. Mix together the prepared beetroot, apple, celery, currants/cranberries, orange and lemon juice, olive oil, salt and freshly ground black pepper. Taste and adjust the seasoning as required. Toss gently until all the apple is stained pink. Serve heaped up in a bowl. If you like, garnish the salad with a circle of whole Lollo Rosso or, for contrast, a green lettuce or watercress around the edge.

Portuguese marinated carrots

This recipe is another of Wayne Schroeder's holiday souvenirs. Cooks are a bit like entomologists looking for rare beetles: they love to go exploring and come across new species of recipes! Like the Grape & almond coleslaw, this carrot salad brings a glamorous new look to a familiar vegetable. Bathed in their own flavoursome infusion, the carrots taste absolutely amazing.

For 6	For 45-50
700g (1½lb) carrots	5.5kg (12lb)
2 tbsp cider vinegar	250ml (½ pint / 1 cup)
2 tbsp lemon juice	250ml (½ pint / 1 cup)
2-3 cloves garlic	1 good-sized head
2 tbsp virgin olive oil	250ml (½ pint / 1 cup)
50g (2oz / ¼ cup) good-quality, pitted black olives (Kalamata, etc.)	450g (1lb / 2 cups)
1 pinch salt	2-3 tsp
1 pinch freshly ground black pepper	1-2 tsp
2 tbsp flat-leaved parsley, chopped	approx. 150g (5oz / 2 cups)

1. Scrub the carrots and peel if they are at all damaged by carrot fly or if they are not organic. Slice in narrow rings, to form attractive coin-like disks – which should indeed be about the thickness of a £1 piece (though I've seen the carrot prepared in other elegant shapes too).

2. Boil the carrots in salted water for about 10-15 minutes until just tender (al dente).

3. Meanwhile, crush the garlic and finely chop the parsley.

4. Mix together the cider vinegar, lemon juice and crushed garlic in a small jug.

5. Drain the carrots and tip them into a big bowl or back into the saucepan. Immediately pour the vinegar, lemon juice and garlic mixture over the hot carrots. Stir gently and enjoy the healing vapours as the steam rises. Five minutes later, add the olive oil. (Wayne adds all the liquids straight from the bottle, without measuring – glug, glug, glug . . . It is the sign of a confident chef, and something we all can do once we have got used to making a dish and developed a sense of how it should taste. But when making for the first time, try adding the measured amounts given above!)

6. Allow the carrots to cool before adding plenty of chopped parsley and black olives. Season with salt and pepper to taste.

Warm parsnip & hazelnut salad

A parsnip revival is surely much over-due. It is recipes like this one that will help to lift the image of this funny old root and bring it back into favour by giving it some new embellishments. Back in the medieval days, before the arrival of the potato from South America and sugar from the Caribbean, this semi-sweet, somewhat unusual-tasting vegetable was a staple source of starch in Europe. In addition, because of its sweetness it was used in cakes and puddings.

Parsnips can be conveniently left in the ground until needed, although they can grow so large and woody that the core needs to be removed. Indeed, parsnips are positively improved by a good frost, which causes the living root to convert some starch into sugar. Nowadays, the British are one of the few remaining cultures who reserve some genuine sense of gusto for the parsnip, happily serving it roasted on Sundays or mashing it up with potatoes. Christmas dinner would not be the same without the roast parsnips alongside the Brussels sprouts, carrots and potatoes.

In this recipe from Wayne, the parsnip skins are left on, since most of the flavour lies directly below them, and the parsnips are cut down to small chip size and roasted quickly. The magic touch is then the combining of roast parsnip with lemon and toasted hazelnuts – and serving the mixture still warm. This is an excellent salad for the autumn-to-winter period, when the first frosts have sweetened the parsnip to perfection and the tree-nut harvest has begun.

For 6	For 45-50
650g (1½lb) parsnips	5kg (12lb)
75g (3oz / ⅔ cup) hazelnuts	600g (1lb 4oz / 5 cups)
1-2 tbsp sunflower oil	approx. 150-200ml (5-7fl oz / ½-¾ cup)
2 tbsp juice + 1 tsp zest of an organic lemon	200ml (7-8fl oz / 1 cup)
2 tbsp olive oil	approx. 150-200ml (5-7fl oz / ½-¾ cup)
1-2 tbsp flat-leaved parsley, chopped	½-1 cup
approx. ½ tsp salt	approx. 2-4 tsp
approx. ¼ tsp freshly ground black pepper	approx. 2 tsp

1. Pre-heat the oven to 200°C (400°F / Gas Mark 6), then prepare the parsnips. If possible, choose smaller and younger specimens. Scrub in warm water and rinse. Cut out any blemishes and remove the tapering root end. Cut the parsnips across into 5-6cm (2-2¼")-wide 'logs', then cut these lengthways into smaller sticks or chips about 1cm (½") thick – the width of the log will now become the length of the chip. For the sprouting end, quarter it first, then cut out any earth, shoots and the tough part of the core (while it is quicker to slice the whole end straight off, some good vegetable can be salvaged this way).

2. Toss the prepared parsnip 'chips' in sunflower oil and sprinkle with salt. Keep the amount of oil added at this stage quite minimal, as more fresh olive oil will be added to taste later.

3. Roast the parsnips in the hot oven for about 30 minutes, turning halfway through. The parsnips are ready when they are beginning to brown lightly and taste good – soft, but not mushy.

4. While the parsnips are cooking, dry-roast the hazelnuts: spread them out on a metal baking tray and put them in the oven for 10-15 minutes. They are ready when the skins are beginning to flake apart, revealing kernels that are (mostly) beginning to turn a light caramel colour – not too brown. Remove from the oven and, when cooled enough to handle, rub off the skins between your hands – or use the technique described on page 185. Rough-chop the hazelnuts – with a big knife or few brief whizzes in a food processor.

5. When the parsnips are ready, mix them with the olive oil, lemon juice and zest, parsley, black pepper and more salt if necessary. Taste, then toss in the hazelnuts. If possible, serve while still warm.

Dips & spreads

Roast red pepper houmous

Lemon & honey vinaigrette

Aduki bean pâté

Spring pesto with almonds & spicy leaves

Garlic & herb cream cheese

Red pesto

Black olive & sun-dried tomato tapenade

Nettle & sunflower-seed spread

Mayonnaise & aioli

Avocado & coriander dip

Roast red pepper houmous

The unflagging popularity of houmous at lunchtime, and as a protein-rich snack to raid when after a bit of extra non-dairy protein, makes it worth putting this recent reincarnation down in print. It's a variation of the original houmous recipe in *Gaia's Kitchen* and is obtained by whizzing roasted red peppers in with the chick peas to give a delicious, coral-coloured spread. If you're cutting corners and using tinned chick peas, just multiply the weight of dry chick peas by three.

For 6-8	For 45-50
200g (7oz / 1¼ cups) chick peas	1kg (2lb 4oz)
3 medium red peppers	24 medium (4kg / 9lb)
2-3 cloves garlic, crushed	approx. 1 head (2-3 tbsp)
approx. 3 tbsp tahini	250ml (9fl oz / 1 cup)
4 tbsp olive oil + extra for drizzling	350ml (12fl oz / 1⅓ cups)
4 tbsp lemon juice	250ml (½ pint / 1 cup)
2 tbsp orange juice	150ml (5fl oz / ⅔ cup)
2-4 tbsp chick pea cooking water	150-300ml (5-10fl oz / ⅔-1¼ cups)
⅛ tsp cayenne or chilli pepper	½-1 tsp
½ tsp ground cumin	2-3 tsp
1 pinch paprika	1-2 pinches
3-4 pinches salt	2-4 tsp

1. Soak the chick peas overnight in twice their depth of water. Next day, transfer to a saucepan and bring to the boil. Simmer until very soft (1½-2½ hours). Use a pressure cooker, if available, to reduce the cooking time. Pre-heat the oven to 200°C (400°F / Gas Mark 6).

2. Drain the chick peas into a colander set over a saucepan or bowl. Reserve some of the cooking liquid and leave the pulses to cool.

3. Prepare the red peppers by cutting into finger-thick strips and removing the stalk and seeds. Massage with a generous drizzling of olive oil and a pinch or two of salt, then spread out on a baking sheet and roast until soft in the hot oven. When roasted, reserve several strips of pepper for decoration and then, using a food processor, blend the rest into the chick peas along with all the other ingredients *except* the tahini (which has a thickening effect), until fairly smooth. (For the large quantity, either blend in batches, or use a catering-size rod blender to blend the ingredients together in a big saucepan.) Once smooth, blend in the tahini as well. When making the large quantity, blend the tahini into a small portion of the houmous, then stir this portion into the rest until evenly distributed.

4. Taste and adjust the seasoning as required. Once you are completely happy with the taste of the houmous, and once it is completely cool, heap it into a bowl and drizzle with a little olive oil. Decorate the coral-coloured houmous with strips of red pepper and a sprinkling of paprika. Adorn with a few black olives, if you like.

Lemon & honey vinaigrette

A mild vinaigrette made with a good virgin olive oil and containing a little local honey will complement the subtle crunch of almost any green or bean salad without disguising it. Not only that, but the leaves will become easier to munch and the flavours will be enhanced, as oils and fats act as carriers for flavour molecules. Use half-and-half lemon juice and cider vinegar when lemons are in short supply.

To dress approx. 300g (10oz) salad

2 tbsp lemon juice
(or 1 tbsp lemon juice + 1 tbsp cider vinegar)
½-1 tsp smooth mustard (e.g. Dijon)
1-2 small cloves garlic, crushed (optional)
2-4 tsp honey (preferably runny)*
6 tbsp olive oil
¼-½ tsp salt
2 pinches freshly ground black pepper

To dress approx. 2kg (4½lb) salad

200ml (6fl oz / ⅔ cup)
(or 50:50 lemon juice / cider vinegar)
1-2 tbsp
8-16 (1 medium head)
6-8 tbsp
600ml (1 pint / 1¼ US pints)
2-4 tsp
1 tsp

1. Measure the lemon juice and vinegar, if using, into the bottom of a good-sized measuring jug that gives plenty of room for your total volume of dressing to splash around. Add the mustard, garlic (if using), honey, salt and pepper. Mix with a fork or hand-held rod blender.

2. Add the olive oil and blend again with a rod blender. The vinaigrette usually emulsifies as air is whipped in. This dressing can also be made in the time-honoured way, using a ceramic or glass bowl and a wire hand whisk. In this case, gradually add the olive oil while whisking to bring in air. The dressing should thicken to an opaque golden sauce.

3. Taste by dipping in a mild leaf. Adjust seasoning and oil/lemon/vinegar quantities if required.

4. Surplus vinaigrette can be stored in a jam jar or glass bottle. It does not need to be refrigerated (indeed, in a fridge the oil will congeal, so the dressing would need to sit at room temperature to thin out before use).

Variations: Consider blending some fresh herbs into the dressing! You could also experiment with other vinegars or try using some nut oils along the way.

*For vegan diets, use agave, maple syrup or sugar.

Aduki bean pâté

This bean pâté is not only very tasty but also very convenient to make at the last moment when you haven't had time for an overnight soaking of beans! Aduki beans are so small that they can be cooked from dry in an hour. In this recipe, finely chopped sun-dried tomatoes and chopped walnuts are stirred into the creamy bean purée to give extra taste and texture – but just leave them out when you hear the voice of simplicity calling!

For 6-8

200g (8oz / 1 cup) aduki beans

6 sun-dried tomatoes

1 bay leaf

2-3 cloves garlic, crushed

2 tbsp light tahini

2-3 tbsp lemon juice

3 tbsp olive oil

40g (1½oz / ¼ cup) walnuts

1-2 tsp thyme (or basil or parsley), finely chopped

1-3 pinches salt and freshly ground black pepper

For 45-50

1.3kg (3lb / 7 cups)

150g (5oz / 1½ cups)

3

1 head / 2-3 tbsp

200ml (8fl oz / ¾ cup)

200-300ml (8-12fl oz / ¾-1 cup)

300ml (12fl oz / 1¼ cups)

250g (9oz / 1½ cups)

3 tbsp

approx. 2-3 tsp salt and 1 tsp pepper

1. Place the aduki beans in a saucepan with plenty of water, a bay leaf or two and the sun-dried tomatoes. Bring to the boil, then simmer for about an hour until the beans are tender. When ready, drain the beans, reserving a cup of liquid in case it's needed later.

2. Fish the tomatoes out of the beans, chop them finely and set aside.

3. Put the beans in your food processor along with the crushed garlic, tahini, lemon juice and oil. Blend until smooth, adding a bit of the bean cooking water if necessary. Tip into a bowl. If making the large quantity, blend the beans in batches, distributing the liquids and tahini evenly between them – tahini has a thickening effect so don't be tempted to add it all in one go!

4. Chop most of the walnuts into small pieces, roughly matching the size of the chopped tomatoes. Set aside a few walnut halves for decoration.

5. Mix (most of) the chopped tomatoes, nuts and herbs into the pâté, setting aside a tiny bit of each for decoration. Season, mix well and check the seasoning, adding more lemon, salt and pepper if necessary. Likewise, adjust the consistency if required. Scoop the pâté into a bowl. Decorate with walnut halves – as well as with the remaining chopped nuts, sun-dried tomatoes and herbs.

Spring pesto with almonds & spicy leaves

This vibrant, spicy pesto simply oozes flavour, spelling a healthy assortment of flavonoids and antioxidants – especially when you are able to make it with freshly gathered leaves. You can use any combination of spicy, easily tearable salad leaves that grow in your garden (or indeed hedgerows, if you are confident about selecting the edible ones). Because the almonds are soaked overnight, the nutrients in them are made easier to digest than usual. Serve with warm crusty bread, or with pasta.

For 6+	For 45-50
100g (4oz / 1 cup) whole almonds	600g (1lb 6oz)
50g (2oz / ⅔ cup) Parmesan-style cheese	300g (10½oz / 3½ cups)
1 tsp (2-3 cloves) garlic (unless including wild garlic)	2-3 tbsp (approx. 8-10 cloves)
150g (5½oz) mixed spicy leaves, e.g. 80g (3oz) basil, mustard leaves, sorrel + 70g (2½oz) rocket, mizuna, wild garlic	800g (1lb 12oz), e.g. 400g (14oz) + 400g
Juice of just over half a lemon	Juice of 4 lemons
100ml (3-4fl oz / ⅓-½ cup) olive oil	approx. 600ml (1 pint / 2½ cups)
1 pinch salt and black pepper to taste	approx. 2 tsp salt, ¼ tsp pepper

1. Soak the whole almonds for several hours or overnight.

2. Blanch the soaked almonds by immersing in boiling water and then slipping off the skins.

3. Gather together your leaves. Rinse in cold water, then spin or pat dry. Remove any tough stalks or yellowing leaves, then rough-chop.

4. Grate the cheese. Peel and crush the garlic, if using.

5. Put the blanched almonds into your food processor with the oil, lemon juice and leaves. Using the knife attachment, whizz these up to a relatively fine pesto, adding more liquid if required. If you're making the small quantity, all the ingredients can be processed in one go; if making the large quantity, it'll take a few batches to blend all the leaves. Add the grated cheese towards the end of the blending.

6. Tip into a bowl for one last stir and adjust the consistency and seasoning as required. If possible, leave for 30 minutes to let the flavours develop before serving.

Variations:

Try using alternative cheeses, such as a hard goat or sheep cheese, or other local hard cheese – especially if you have not been able to get hold of a vegetarian Parmesan-style cheese. For a vegan version, simply leave out the cheese altogether.

For a milder pesto, include blander leaves such as mallow and tender young lime leaves in the blend. Try different leaf combinations as the season progresses.

Garlic & herb cream cheese

In spring and summer, when the cows go out to pasture, the full-fat cream cheese from the local Jersey herd is especially rich and creamy. We mix it with garlic and freshly chopped herbs from the garden, to make our own 'Boursin'-style soft cheese to spread on home-made bread and crackers. When the cheese is thick enough, it can be shaped into herb-coated rondelles and presented on a cheese board, to be cut with a knife. At other times, simply heap the delicious mixture into a ceramic bowl, to be served with a small spoon. The key thing is to allow a good hour for the flavours to develop after the garlic and herbs have been stirred into the cheese – and remember, cream cheese is very rich, so a little goes a long way!

For 6	For 45-50
250g (9oz / 1 cup) full-fat cream cheese	2kg (4lb)
2 cloves garlic, crushed	3 tbsp
1 tsp rosemary, chopped	2 tbsp
1 tsp thyme, chopped	2-3 tbsp
1 tsp marjoram or oregano, chopped	2-3 tbsp
2 tsp parsley, chopped	4-5 tbsp
1 pinch paprika or freshly ground black pepper to taste (optional)	½ tsp (optional)
1 tsp psyllium husk* (to thicken for rondelles)	3 tbsp (for rondelles)

Coating (if forming into rondelles)

40g (1½oz / ½ cup) parsley, finely chopped	300g (10oz / 4 cups)
1 tsp dried mixed herbs	3 tbsp

1. Peel and crush the garlic, then stir it into the cream cheese so it can begin to infuse.

2. Also add the small amount of psyllium husk to thicken the cream cheese, if you want to form small patties (rondelles) that can be shaped easily – otherwise leave this ingredient out (don't be tempted to add more than the stated amount or the texture will be impaired, becoming slightly slimy – so measure carefully).

3. Rinse and spin and/or pat dry the herbs. Remove any tough stalks, then chop finely with a large sharp knife or mezzaluna. Chop one kind of herb at a time, as the varying leaf shapes and strengths will each require slightly different kinds of knife work. If you are not going to make rondelles, reserve a few sprigs of herbs for garnishing.

4. Add the chopped herbs that go in the cheese and stir well. Set aside the parsley for the coating if you are going to make rondelles. Taste and add more herbs or pepper, if you want. Salt is not normally necessary, as it is already present in the cream cheese.

*Psyllium husk is a natural source of soluble dietary fibre, well appreciated in India, and increasingly in the West, for its nutritive and binding properties. It is available from wholefood stores.

5. To form rondelles, combine the dried herbs with the finely chopped parsley, then sprinkle a few spoonfuls of this mixture on to a plate or board ready for action. If making the large quantity, remove about one-eighth of the mixture and plop it down on to the herbs. Sprinkle some more herbs over the top and sides, then slap the edges into a round with a couple of flat wooden spatulas or your clean hands. Sprinkle on more of the prepared herbs as you go. When all – or almost all – the cream cheese is covered, place the rondel carefully on a plate or tray covered with baking parchment. Make the rest of your patties in the same way and leave them in the fridge for an hour (if possible) before serving.

6. If going for the simpler option, scoop the cream cheese spread into an attractive ceramic bowl and refrigerate for an hour to let the flavours develop. Before serving, garnish with a few sprigs of fresh herbs, and maybe a sprinkling of paprika.

Tara's tip: As an alternative to using psyllium husk, the cream cheese can be stiffened by substituting one-third of the cream cheese with a grated hard cheese such as Cheddar. Blend this in using your food processor and allow to rest for 1 hour in the fridge.

Red pesto

Rippling with the intense flavours of sun-dried tomatoes and roast capsicums, this red pesto makes a great alternative to traditional basil pesto. Stir it through your favourite pasta or use as a sauce to cheer up brown rice. If you catch the fleeting moment when red peppers are at their cheapest and closest, they can be roasted and bottled in olive oil, or roasted and frozen for converting into pesto later.

For 8-10	For 40-50
50g (2oz / ½ cup) sun-dried tomatoes	300g (10oz / 3 cups)
100ml (4fl oz / ½ cup) apple juice, orange juice or water	600ml (1 pint / 2½ cups)
2 large red peppers	12 large (2.7kg / 6lb)
150ml (5fl oz / ½ cup) olive oil	750ml (1¼ pints / 1½ US pints)
3-5 cloves garlic	18-25 (approx. 2 heads)
110g (4oz / 1 cup) cashews or sunflower seeds	700g (1½lb / 6 cups)
50g (2oz / ½ cup) Parmesan-style cheese, grated (optional)	300g (10oz / 3 cups) (optional)
2-3 tsp lemon juice to taste	Juice of 1-2 lemons
½ tsp dried basil	approx. 1 tbsp
¼ tsp cayenne pepper	1 tsp
approx. ½ tsp salt	2-3 tsp

1. Cover the sun-dried tomatoes in the juice or water and leave to soak for a couple of hours.

2. Pre-heat the oven to 200°C (400°F / Gas Mark 6). Halve the red peppers and remove the seeds. Cut into finger-thick lengths. Spread out on a baking tray and drizzle generously with some of the olive oil. Mix well, then sprinkle with salt and dried basil. The layer of peppers should be only one piece thick, to ensure even and speedy roasting.

3. Separate the garlic cloves and toss these whole over the peppers so they cook in their skins. Roast in the hot oven until both peppers and garlic are soft. (The tips of the peppers may be slightly charred or brown in places).

4. Spread the cashews or sunflower seeds out on another baking tray and roast at the same temperature for 10 minutes until lightly browned.

5. Drain the sun-dried tomatoes, reserving the liquid to add later if needed. Squeeze the pulp out of the roasted garlic cloves.

6. Put the sun-dried tomatoes, garlic pulp and the roasted red peppers and nuts into your food processor and blend together until fairly smooth. Gradually add a little lemon juice and the rest of the olive oil. For the large quantity, you'll need to do this in several batches, with the liquids spread out evenly between them.

7. Mix, or blend in, the grated cheese – omit if making a vegan version, or because you think it tastes great without any (as we have discovered!). Taste and adjust the seasoning with a little more salt, cayenne pepper, lemon juice, tomato-soaking liquid, etc. The pesto should be thick enough to spread on bread without dribbling off; likewise, it will cling to pasta.

Black olive & sun-dried tomato tapenade

This intensely tasty mahogany-coloured paste is delicious spread on fresh warm polenta bread, toast or bruschetta – and can also be eaten with slices of grilled polenta. Containing some potentially fairly costly ingredients, it could be regarded as the vegetarian equivalent of caviar. Luckily, a little goes a long way, and this tapenade is quick to whizz up to make appetizers for impromptu gatherings. When shopping for your olives, choose the ones preserved in olive oil if possible; otherwise, good-quality pitted Kalamata olives preserved in brine will do – and are what we use at the College. Semi-moist sun-dried tomatoes such as you find in a delicatessen can be used instead of dried ones, but you'll need almost double the weight.

For 6-8

50g (2oz / ½ cup) sun-dried tomatoes

115g (4oz / 1 cup) black olives, de-stoned

White wine or apple/orange/grape juice (etc.) for soaking

4 medium cloves garlic, crushed

4 tbsp olive oil

Juice of a half or 1 lemon, or 1 lime

A half or 1 fresh red chilli, with seeds removed, chopped

2-3 tbsp fresh coriander or basil, chopped

For 45-50

400g (14oz / 4 cups)

900g (2lb)

1l (2 pints / 4 cups)

1½-2 tbsp

350ml (12fl oz / 1½ cups)

Juice of 3-4 lemons or 5-6 limes

2-3

70g (2½ oz / 1 cup)

1. Soak the sun-dried tomatoes for a couple of hours, or overnight, in some leftover white wine or apple/orange/grape juice (plain ol' water can also be used, if you don't have any of these to hand or prefer a milder tapenade).

2. When the tomatoes are soft, drain them and set aside a few pieces for garnishing purposes, along with a few whole olives. Put the rest in your food processor along with the remaining drained black olives, crushed garlic, chopped chilli, olive oil and lemon or lime juice. Whizz this mixture to a smooth spreadable paste and adjust the consistency by adding more of the soaking liquid or more lemon/lime as required (the tapenade should have a consistency similar to that of houmous).

3. Chop the coriander leaf or basil finely, and stir this into the tapenade. Taste again, then tip into a serving bowl or, if keeping for some time, a container for the fridge. If possible, cover and leave for an hour or so at room temperature before serving, to let the flavours develop.

Variation: Leave out the chilli to keep things cool!

Nettle & sunflower-seed spread

This pâté ripples with the goodness of spring energy, capturing the vital nutrients of nettles and wild garlic as they first emerge from the hedgerows, reaching for the sun. Later in the year, the spread can be made with leafy, non-flowering nettle tips and other intense 'forest garden' leaves that can also be used in salads, for example nasturtium, sorrel, marsh mallow, boiled dandelion, cleavers (goosegrass), young beech and garlic mustard.

For 6-8	For 45-50
100-150g (5oz) young nettle leaves or leafy tips	600-900g (1lb 4oz-2lb)
10-15 leaves wild garlic (or 1 clove garlic, crushed, if no wild garlic available)	50-100g (2-4oz) (or 6-10 cloves)
Half an onion	3 large onions
50g (2oz / ¼ cup) sunflower seeds	300g (11oz / 1½ cups)
1-2 tsp tamari	2-4 tsp
100g (4oz) tofu or 2 hard-boiled eggs	600g (1½lb) or 12 eggs
2-3 tsp lemon juice	50-80ml (4-6 tbsp)
3 tbsp olive oil	300ml (½ pint / 1 cup)
Salt and freshly ground black pepper to taste	1-2 tsp salt and ¼-½ tsp pepper

1. Having harvested the nettles, remove the stalks (protecting your hands with rubber gloves). Check the weight, and then rinse the leaves in cold water and leave to drain in a colander. Also rinse and drain the wild garlic, or any other edible wild leaves you may be using.

2. Pre-heat the oven to 200°C (400°F / Gas Mark 6). Peel and chop the onion, and begin sautéing this in some of the oil in the bottom of a large, deep-sided frying pan or a saucepan. Also add the crushed garlic cloves, if using. Once the onion begins to turn translucent, stir in the nettles and other greens. For the large quantity, you may need to add them little by little, letting them wilt down in batches. Continue cooking until the nettles are soft and look a bit like cooked spinach. This will only take about 5 minutes – you don't want to overcook them, or the nutrient content will be diminished and the colour less appealing.

3. While the nettles are cooking, spread the sunflower seeds out on a baking tray and roast them in the hot oven for 8-10 minutes. Pull them out when they are beginning to turn light brown, and sprinkle with tamari. Stir with a wooden spatula, and then return to the oven for a few minutes to 'steam-dry'. Once the surplus moisture from the tamari has evaporated, remove the seeds from the oven, stir and leave to cool.

4. Crumble the tofu (or rough-chop the hard-boiled egg) and mix with the cooked onion and nettles. Transfer some of this mixture into your food processor and blend until smooth. Add half the roasted sunflower seeds to the pâté at this stage, either whole or blended in. Save the rest for garnishing. Add lemon juice, salt, pepper and more oil as you blend, checking the taste as you go. If you are making the large quantity, you may have to blend the ingredients in batches and do the final mixing in a bowl.

5. Scoop the finished pâté into a bowl and toss the remaining tamari-roasted sunflower seeds over the top. This vibrant nettle spread goes deliciously with bread and crackers, and is not too rich to be eaten on its own or with brown rice.

Tip: The tamari-roasted sunflower seeds described in Step 3 make a delicious snack at any time and keep well in an airtight jar.

Mayonnaise & aioli

When you have organic eggs in abundance, fresh lemons, and good-quality virgin olive oil in your cupboard, then the moment may have come to try making your own luscious mayonnaise. However, there is one more ingredient that is crucial to your success – calm, uninterrupted *time*. Sometimes, the sauce simply, infuriatingly, refuses to thicken – but I've found that success comes more often when I've been able to focus on what I'm doing and not had to rush it. So, choose your moment carefully! Aioli, the famous, throat-tingling garlic mayonnaise of Provence, makes a delicious and bracing addition to many vegetarian lunches, suppers and snacks. Once made, mayonnaise (both versions) can be kept for a week or so in the fridge.

To make approx. 300ml (½ pint)	To make 1 litre (1½ pints)
2 egg yolks, at room temperature	6 yolks
250ml (½ pint / 1 cup) good olive oil	750ml (1½ pints / 3 cups)
Juice of half a lemon	Juice of 1½-2
1 tsp Dijon mustard	1 tbsp
½-1 tsp fine sea salt	2-3 tsp
1 pinch pepper (cayenne or freshly ground black)	½ tsp
For aioli: 6-8 cloves garlic	18-20 (2 good-sized heads)

1. For the aioli, mash the peeled raw cloves with the salt using your pestle and mortar until a thick pulp is formed. Alternatively, crush the raw cloves and mix with the salt on your chopping board using the sharp tip of your knife.

2. Squeeze the lemon and strain the juice through a sieve. Measure out your olive oil so it is ready to use.

3. Separate the (room temperature) eggs and put the yolks together in a ceramic or glass bowl. Add the mustard, pepper and salt (or salt and garlic) to the yolk with just a few drops of the lemon juice. Mix with a wooden spoon for a minute or two until the yolk begins to thicken slightly.

4. Still using a wooden spoon, or a flat sauce whisk, begin stirring the olive oil into the egg yolk, drop by drop. Mix as you go, using one hand for pouring and one hand for stirring. As the mixture becomes very thick, add a few drops of lemon juice to loosen it.

5. As the volume of the mayonnaise grows you can increase the amount of olive oil you add from a drop to a steady trickle and then to a thin stream, *but* keep watching what you are doing. If you start to add the oil faster than the sauce can absorb it, it will curdle. Should this happen, go back to the beginning with a fresh egg yolk, and gradually add the curdled mayonnaise to the new mix, stirring all the while. When all the oil has been absorbed, taste the mayonnaise and adjust the flavour with a little more salt, mustard, lemon juice or oil, as needed.

Blender method: For the large quantity, an alternative to hand-mixing is to put the yolks, seasoning and lemon juice in a blender. Begin whizzing at slow speed, then pour the olive oil gently through the hole in the top of the goblet: keep the stream slow and steady, so air gets in too.

Variations: Finely chopped fresh herbs are delicious stirred into mayonnaise. Vinegar can also be used as a substitute for lemon juice.

Avocado & coriander dip

Blending sour cream, garlic and coriander with ripe avocado is a delicious way to make something special go a little further. This simple dip is a smooth, mild green alternative to your classic rugged, tomato-rich guacamole. Other fresh herbs, such as parsley, basil and tender young mint can also be used to ring the changes and will complement the avocado. Serve with salads and crudités.

For 6	For 45-50
2 large or 3 medium soft, ripe avocados (450g / 1lb)	16-24 (3.5kg / 8lb)
1 tsp lemon juice, freshly squeezed	approx. 2 tbsp to taste
200ml (8fl oz / ¾ cup) sour cream or crème fraîche	1.5l (2¾ pints / 3½ US pints)
1-2 cloves garlic, crushed	2-4 tsp
25g (1oz / ½ cup) coriander or basil, chopped	200g (7oz / 3-4 cups)
¼ tsp salt to taste	2-3 tsp
1 pinch freshly ground black pepper	½-1 tsp

1. Wash the fresh herbs in cold water, then spin and/or pat dry. Strip the leaves from the stalks. Set aside a few sprigs for garnishing and chop the rest quite finely.

2. Halve the avocados and remove any browned flesh. If making the large quantity, try putting the avocado stones in the bowl with the flesh as you process the rest, to prevent it discolouring (this is a traditional Brazilian cooking technique. Remember to remove the stones when all the avocados have been gutted!) Add the sour cream / crème fraîche, fresh herbs, crushed garlic, lemon juice, salt and pepper. After a quick preliminary mix, transfer some (or all, if it will fit) of the mixture into your food processor and whizz until smooth using the knife attachment – several batches of blending will be required if making the large quantity. When all the mixture is blended and returned to the mixing bowl, taste and add more salt and pepper if necessary.

3. Just before serving, transfer the avocado dip into an attractive serving bowl. Garnish with the remaining sprigs of fresh coriander or basil.

Desserts

Rhubarb & strawberry crumble

Pear & chocolate tart

American apple pie

Topsy-turvy puddings (Apple & sultana; Chocolate & pear)

Rainbow's roulade

Honey-kissed lemon tart

Zesty almond-polenta cake (with reversible berry option!)

Chocolate pavlova (with pears or berries)

Rhubarb & strawberry trifle

Twinkling berry cheesecake

Avocado-chocolate truffle torte

Spicy pumpkin pie

Strawberries & cream flan

Rhubarb & strawberry crumble

My memories of Fritjof Capra's regular courses at Schumacher College are punctuated by memories of his wife Elizabeth Hawk perching in the Schumacher kitchen, lapping up the atmosphere and contributing interesting nuggets of conversation to the general hubbub. While Fritjof was busy teaching, Elizabeth would often be found doing her own unofficial bit of awareness-raising and networking. Like her husband she is a polymath, but not of the scientific kind. Elizabeth is an extremely

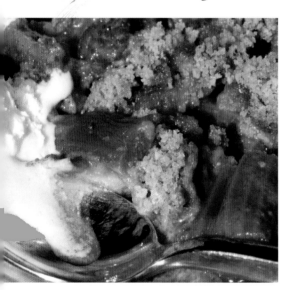

practical and well-informed person: a passionate gardener and campaigner who has done all sorts of things in her life – from making costumes for elephants to writing and illustrating a book about super-hero mermaids, from learning to fly a bird of prey to bringing up their daughter Juliette . . . She is also someone who loves to cook, and to describe so temptingly the mouth-watering dishes she has eaten that it makes you want to cook them!

Here is a gorgeous version of rhubarb crumble, which I started to bake after Elizabeth mentioned how wonderfully deep pink rhubarb becomes when you include strawberries with it . . . The good thing about using strawberries in cooked desserts is that you don't have to worry about air miles, because you needn't use fresh fruit. If, during the strawberry season in the summer, you have put some aside in the freezer or as a whole preserve, you can use them to add a hint of luxury to a cooked or puréed dessert. We need to allow fruit to alter what it contributes to the menu when it is used out of season, rather than try to replicate its fresh state with jet-set fresh fruit. Fruit flown in from afar will never taste as good as the same fruit does when in season on your own doorstep.

Rhubarb can be pulled from spring to early summer. By the end of the season, strawberries are also becoming abundant, so the harvesting time for the two overlaps. Rhubarb can also be cut and frozen raw to extend its availability. When not using strawberries with the rhubarb, the ginger element of this dessert can be enhanced, by doubling the ground ginger in the crumble and adding slices of crystallized ginger to the rhubarb (about 50g / 2oz for the small quantity; 100g / 4oz for the large).

For gluten-free diets: Substitute the flours with gluten-free flours, such as buckwheat flour or GF oat flour for the brown; and soya flour, tapioca flour, maize flour or pre-packed white GF flour for the white.

For vegan diets: Just use margarine in place of the butter.

For 6	**For 45-50**
(1 x 28cm / 11" round or oval baking dish)	(3 x 30cm- / 12"-long oval baking dishes)

Fruity part

700g (1½lb) rhubarb stalk, chopped	4kg (9lb)
1 large punnet (350g / 12oz) strawberries	1.5kg (3lb)
85g (3oz / ½ cup) golden granulated sugar	450g (1lb / 2½ cups)
A little water (approx. 100ml / 4fl oz / ½ cup)	A little more (about 450ml / 15fl oz / 2 cups)

Crumble top

140g (5oz / 1 cup) white flour	550g (1½lb / 5 cups)
70g (2½oz / ½ cup) brown, barley or spelt flour	350g (12oz / 2½ cups)
50g (2oz / ½ cup) ground almonds	280g (10oz / 2½ cups)
2-4 tbsp flaked almonds (optional)	100-200g (4-8oz / 1-2 cups) (optional)
125g (4½oz / ¾ cup) light muscovado sugar	450g (1lb / 2½ cups)
125g (4½oz / 1 stick + 1 tbsp) butter	625g (1lb 6oz / 5½ sticks)
½ tsp cinnamon	2 tsp
½ tsp ground ginger	2 tsp
½ tsp salt	2 tsp

1. Combine the ingredients for the crumble in a bowl. (For the GF option, use gluten-free flours; for the vegan option, use margarine instead of butter.) Break up the butter and rub in with your fingertips – or, if the butter is cold, grate it in and rub a little to break it up further. Once you've obtained a breadcrumby texture, toss in the flaked almonds, if using. Set aside for later.

2. Cut off the rhubarb leaves and discard them – they contain large amounts of the toxin oxalic acid and must not be eaten, though they will be fine for the worms in your compost heap. The white tip where the rhubarb stalk has been pulled up is, by contrast, particularly sweet, so don't cut it off (just trim off any brown). Rinse the rhubarb stalks in cold water and chop into 2cm (1") pieces, filling one medium-small or three larger baking dishes as you go.

3. Pre-heat the oven to 180°C (350°F / Gas Mark 4). Rinse and de-hull the strawberries, if using fresh ones. Keep any small or medium ones whole, but halve any enormous ones. Mix these in with the rhubarb. Frozen or preserved ones can go straight in – no need to defrost, as they will hold their shape better if added frozen (Elizabeth emphasizes that there is a particular joy in finding them still whole when you eat this pud). Sprinkle the golden granulated sugar over the top and then pour a little water over – a mere 0.5cm (¼") of liquid is enough, because the rhubarb will produce a lot more juice as it cooks. If using bottled strawberries, use their liquid in place of the water and some of the sugar.

4. Sprinkle the crumble mixture over the rhubarb and strawberries. Go right up to the edge of the baking dish, and heap the crumble up until it is about 2cm (1") deep in the middle, where it will be thickest. No need to press down – leave the crumble characteristically loose, so it will be nice and crumbly.

5. Cook in the middle of the oven for 30-40 minutes (small quantity) or 45-60 minutes (large quantity). When ready, the top should be lightly browning, with pink juice beginning to ooze up in places around the edge of the crumble. Stick a skewer down through the crumble in the middle to check that the rhubarb is nice and soft. Serve warm with cream, ice cream or custard.

Pear & chocolate tart

I bake this tart once or twice a year, during the autumn and winter months – when the summer fruit is over and the English apples and pears have become our staple dessert fruit for the duration. The combination of pear and chocolate is always a winner, and works especially well when woven together in the form of a creamy baked chocolate-custard with melt-in-the-mouth chocolate pastry. The original recipe was from Delia Smith, queen of contemporary British cookery writers, and it was brought to me by Hilary Nicholson, our former administrator – and another great dessert chef. This tart is a three-stage process (pastry, pears, filling) and so takes a bit of time, especially when made in large quantities. This, together with the cost of organic chocolate, is the only reason I don't make Pear & chocolate tart more often, but when I do make it, it is always well worth the effort – and I always promise to make the lovely concoction again soon!

For 6 (1 medium (23cm / 9") tart)	**For 50** (5 large (28cm / 11") tarts)
Chocolate pastry	
140g (5oz / 1 cup) plain flour	750g (1lb 11oz)
40g (1½oz / 3 tbsp) ground almonds	250g (9oz / 2½ cups)
20g (2 tbsp) cocoa powder	120g (4oz / 1 cup)
25g (1oz / 2-3 tbsp) caster sugar	150g (6oz / 1 cup)
100g (3½oz) butter	550g (1lb 4oz)
1 egg yolk	1 egg + 1 yolk and a little cold water
1 pinch salt	1 tsp
1 tsp polenta or semolina (for sprinkling)	2 tbsp
Filling	
4-5 good-sized ripe pears, peeled and cored	24-30 (4kg / 9lb)
110g (4oz) dark chocolate (minimum 70% cocoa)	700g (1½lb)
60g (2oz / 4 tbsp) sugar	180g (12oz / 2 cups)
1-2 tbsp flaked almonds	6-9 tbsp (80g / 3oz)
200ml (7fl oz / ¾ cup) whipping cream	1.2l (2 pints / 2½ US pints)
Juice from half an orange	Juice from 2 oranges
2 eggs	12

1. *Chocolate pastry:* In a large bowl, mix together the flour, ground almonds, sieved cocoa powder, sugar and salt. Cut up the butter and rub it into the dry ingredients in the bowl until the mixture resembles breadcrumbs. Add the egg and a little water to bind into a firm but malleable dough.

2. Divide the pastry into five for the larger quantity. Form into balls then press these down into 'frisbees'. Place these on a plate or baking tray and cover with a plastic bag or greaseproof paper, so the surface doesn't dry out. Leave in a cool place to rest for 20 minutes – this will make it easier to roll out the pastry.

3. *Pears:* Next, peel the pears, remove the stalks and cut into quarters, lengthways. Remove the core minimally. Squeeze a little orange juice over the pieces to help prevent browning. Cover with a lid or cloth and set aside.

4. Retrieve the pastry from your fridge or pantry. Lightly oil the tart tins (I usually use the ones with removable bases). Roll out the pastry thinly on a floured surface and line the tins with it, making sure that it is pressed snugly into the corners. Flute the edges if you like – the pastry should normally rise up slightly above the edge of the tin, giving a total depth of about 3cm (1¼"). The pastry cases can also be prepared in advance and left in the fridge until you are ready with the pears. Some people even make their pastry cases days or weeks in advance and freeze them.

5. Sprinkle the base of the pastry with flour or polenta. This will help absorb surplus fruit juices, preventing the pastry from getting soggy. Arrange the pears in a circle on top of the dusted pastry base, with the fatter side outermost and the tips facing in – like a daisy. Return to the fridge or a cool place until you have prepared the rest of the filling. Pre-heat the oven to 190°C (375°F / Gas Mark 5).

6. *Filling:* For the chocolate 'custard', break or chop the dark chocolate roughly into smallish pieces and heat gently in a bowl set over a saucepan filled with about 5cm (2-3") of simmering water. Use a bowl that will be large enough to hold the rest of the filling ingredients (not the pears) as well.

7. Heat the cream gently until just simmering. Pour it little by little on to the melting chocolate and mix with a wooden spoon until the mixture is smooth. Remove from the heat.

8. Stir the sugar into the chocolate and cream mixture. Crack the eggs into a bowl and beat, then add these too to the now-cooler chocolate mixture and mix well. (Avoid adding the eggs when the mixture is still very hot, as this will scramble the eggs! Warm is OK.)

9. *All together now!* Fetch your pastry cases. Carefully ladle the chocolate-custard over the pears, making sure an equal amount goes into each tart. Sprinkle the top of the custard with the flaked almonds. Move the tart carefully to the middle or bottom of the oven (a position where you know the base will get a good baking but not burn). After 10 minutes, reduce the temperature to 180°C (350°F / Gas Mark 4) and continue to cook for another 30 minutes. The tart is ready when the custard is set and the pears noticeably softer when pierced with a knife. Delicious served warm or cold with cream or vanilla ice cream.

American apple pie

When it comes to pudding, a classic double-crust apple pie is as popular in America as apple crumble is in England. It seems that the medieval tradition of enclosing a filling between two layers of crust, pork-pie or 'coffyn' style, continued in America, while in England, from the seventeenth century, the habit of only bothering with an upper crust began to predominate. The occasional addition of sultanas, blackberries, blackcurrants, quince and rhubarb helps to bring variety to apple, whether in pie or crumble form, and is typical of Schumacher cooking. This recipe will work with whichever kind of apple is available (see Step 4 of method), but if you have the choice, go for a mix of tart cooking apples (Bramleys) and tasty dessert apples.

Because apple crumble is so easy and delicious, I had never developed a serious pie-making habit. However, during recent years of apple bounty, I began to quiz some keen American cooks among our postgraduate students on *the art of apple pie*. The key pieces of information garnered from Kathleen and Jessie were: a) cut your apple pieces very thinly, b) stack them very high, c) don't pre-cook them. Serve with ice cream or custard – or both! (Note: in this recipe, the metric makes slightly more than the imperial – so don't mix your measures.)

For 8-10 (1 x 23cm / 9" deep round pie)	**For 45-50** (5 x 23cm / 9" deep round pies)
Pastry	
300g (10oz / 2 cups) plain white flour	1.5kg (3lb 4oz)
170g (6oz / 1½ sticks) butter	850g (1lb 14oz)
½ tsp salt	2½ tsp
2-4 tbsp caster sugar (+ 1 tbsp for sprinkling on the top – optional)	150g (5oz / ¾ cup) (+ 5 tbsp – optional)
1 (level) tsp cinnamon or mixed spice	1½ tbsp
1 tbsp sunflower oil + extra for oiling the dish	75ml (2½fl oz / 5 tbsp) + extra
3-4 tbsp milk or water	250-300ml (approx. 9fl oz / 1 cup)
Filling	
1.25kg (2½lb / 6-7 cups) apples (e.g. dessert/cooker mix)	6.25kg (12½lb)
125g (4oz / ⅔ cup) brown sugar	525g (1lb 4oz / 3 cups)
¼ tsp cinnamon	1½ tsp
1 tiny pinch nutmeg, grated	½-1 tsp
1-3 tbsp blackberries or sultanas (optional)	150-450g (5oz-1lb / 2-3 cups) (optional)
1 tbsp cornflour (optional)	5 tbsp (optional)
A little lemon juice to taste (optional – for bland apples)	½-2 to taste (optional)

1. Ideally, select ovenproof ceramic or enamel pie dishes that are fairly deep (3-4cm / 1½"), with a rim and slanted sides. (Shallower pies can also be made, using less apple, for example a 'plate-pie' made in an enamel serving plate.) Grease with butter or oil.

2. Prepare the shortcrust pastry in the normal way (see page 85), adding the spices and sugar to the flour before rubbing in the butter and binding with the oil and milk. Form into flattened patties ('frisbees'), two for each pie. Cover and leave to chill in the fridge for 20 minutes or so.

3. Peel the apples and cut each into six to eight segments. Cut out the core and slice into thin pieces. Check the weight and bulk up a bit if there has been a lot of wastage and the amount per pie has dropped significantly below 1kg (2lb).

4. Collect the apple in a bowl and mix with the brown sugar, spices and berries or sultanas (if using). If the apples are very bland, add a squeeze of lemon juice and a pinch of salt. If they are very tart, add a bit more sugar – or if they are sweet, add less. Watery apples can have a tablespoonful of cornflour mixed in with them to absorb some of the juices during cooking. Pre-heat the oven to 200°C (400°F / Gas Mark 6).

5. Remove the chilled pastry from the fridge. Roll out on a lightly floured surface and use to line your buttered/oiled pie dishes, making sure the pastry fits snugly into the corners and is not stretched over them. Cut generously around the rim. Sprinkle the bases with flour or polenta to absorb excess juices and prevent the base getting too soggy.

6. Fill the pie cases neatly with layers of sliced apple, heaping these up into a rounded mountain that rises some 4cm (1½") above the edge of the pie dish at the highest point. Press down gently. Dot with butter if you like.

7. Roll out a circle of pastry for the top. Paint the exposed pastry rim in the dish with milk or water and cover with the circle of pastry you've just rolled out. Press down gently around the rim and trim a few millimeters (⅛") wide of the edge. Flute the edge with your fingers, if you like, or press with a fork. Prick the top in a few places with a skewer or cocktail stick to let out steam when cooking. If there is surplus pastry, you may like to decorate the top with pastry shapes (love hearts, stars, etc.) – using milk painted on the underside of the shapes as your 'glue'. (Alternatively, the pie can be covered with a latticed layer of pastry strips.)

8. Bake in the hot oven for 10 minutes, then reduce the temperature to 180°C (350°F / Gas Mark 4) and continue to bake for 45-60 minutes, until golden-brown on top and tender in the middle. Test the apples for readiness by plunging a skewer down through the middle of the pie. To finish, sift the top with a little cinnamon and caster sugar if you like (our chef Ruth Rae, a great apple pie aficionado, likes to paint her pies with milk and sprinkle with golden granulated sugar before they go in the oven).

Tip: The cooking position in your oven is critical to get the base well done – so choose a position where there is good heat on the base for at least the first 20-30 minutes. Normally this will be near the bottom of the oven.

Topsy-turvy puddings (Apple & sultana; Chocolate & pear)

These two puddings are basically upside-down variations of two fruity cakes that appear in the cake section. Rather than being prepared as sandwich cakes, or iced, they are instead served hot from the oven, showing off a temptingly syrupy top layer of fruit on what was once their base. These 'puds-*tatin*' are delicious served with ice cream or custard, and are very simple to make and easy to re-heat at the last moment. (For a gluten-free topsy-turvy option, see the Zesty almond-polenta cake on page 158.)

For 8-10 (1 x 23cm / 9" round cake tin or 4cm- / 1½"-deep pyrex dish)	**For 45-50** (5 x 23cm / 9" tins/dishes)
For both puddings	
100g (3½oz / 1 stick) butter + a little extra	500g (1lb 2oz / 4½ sticks) + a little more
100g (3½oz / rounded ½ cup) brown sugar	500g (1lb 2oz / 3 cups)
2 eggs	10
125g (4½oz / scant ½ cup) plain flour	625g (1lb 6oz)
2 tsp baking powder	3 tbsp + 1 tsp
1 pinch salt	½ tsp
2-3 tbsp milk	approx. 150ml (5fl oz / ½ cup)
125ml (4fl oz / ½ cup) golden syrup	600ml (1 pint / 2½ cups)
Apple & sultana pudding additions	
2-3 medium cooking apples (400g / 14oz)	10 medium (2kg / 4lb 4oz)
50g (2oz / ⅓ cup) sultanas	250g (9oz / 1-2 cups)
½ tsp cinnamon	2½ tsp
2 tsp mixed spice	2½ tsp
1 pinch salt	½ tsp
Zest of half an organic lemon or orange (optional)	Zest of 2½ (optional)
Chocolate & pear pudding additions	
4 medium pears (500g / 1lb 2oz)	20 medium (2.5kg / 5lb 10oz)
25g (1oz / 3 tbsp) cocoa powder	150g (5oz / 1 cup)
Zest of half an orange (optional)	Zest of 2 (optional)

1. Combine the butter and sugar in a bowl and leave in a warm spot to soften.

2. Measure together the dry ingredients, including spices / cocoa powder, as required. Set aside for later.

3. Butter your pyrex dishes or cake tins. Avoid selecting tins that have detachable bases, as the juices will ooze out during cooking (however, if this is all you have, just cut a ring of parchment 1-2cm (½") larger than the base and stick the edges to the walls of the tin using butter, so the gap is covered). Drizzle the golden syrup over the base of each tin and leave it to spread out over the whole area while you prepare the fruit.

4. Select even-sized apples or pears and peel them. Core the apples through the middle and cut into fairly narrow (5mm / ¼") rings. Cut the pears lengthways into six or eight pieces and minimally remove the core.

5. For a little added enrichment (which is nice though not strictly necessary!) add a hasty grating of butter over the golden syrup – just one or two scrapes from the coarse side of the grater will be enough to bring out the flavours.

6. *Apple & sultana pudding:* Follow the butter / golden syrup with a tiny dusting of cinnamon, then arrange the apples in a ring of overlapping circles around the edge, with one or two circles of apple in the middle. Each 'wheel' of apple should just about cover the hole in the middle of the apple before it (you can also make the arrangement using boat-shaped segments rather than wheels). Toss some of the sultanas over the apples, to fill in the gaps.

7. *Chocolate and pear pudding:* Arrange the segments of pear over the golden syrup so that the narrow ends point inwards. If you have pear pieces to spare, put a couple in the middle, ying & yang fashion, or as you please.

8. Chop any remaining fruit and set aside to add to the cake mixture later. (If there isn't any remaining, that's fine!)

9. Pre-heat the oven to 180°C (350°F / Gas Mark 4).

10. Return to the softened butter and sugar mix. Add the orange or lemon zest, if using. Stir in the eggs, one by one (or two by two!). Fold in the dry mixture, half at a time (for the apple version this will also include the leftover sultanas). Add a dash of milk after the first addition of flour. Once you have a soft, dropping mixture, stir in any remaining chunks of fruit. Divide the cake-pudding mixture equally between all your prepared containers – remembering to leave at least 1cm (½") of edge exposed for the cake-pud to rise into. Place centrally in the warm oven and bake for 30 minutes or so, until well risen – a knife or skewer inserted in the middle will come out clean and moist, with no mixture sticking to it.

11. Serve immediately or put aside to warm up later. Just before serving, go around the edge of the tin or dish with a knife to loosen, then place a large serving plate over the cake-pud and, grasping both securely together with a tea towel, flip them over. Remove the tin to reveal what will (hopefully) be a lovely glistening arrangement of fruit. Serve with ice cream, cream or custard.

Rainbow's roulade

This chocolate roulade is part of the culinary repertoire of Lou Rainbow, Head of Fundraising and Events at Schumacher. It looks spectacularly impressive and difficult to make – but when you have the 'know-how' it becomes easy and fun. It is great for special occasions such as the gourmet fundraising banquets inspired by Lou, because you can make the cake part the day before and then roll it up shortly before serving. And, in case you're wondering, Rainbow is a family name that betrays Lou's gypsy origins: her ancestors were known as the Rainbow People because they dressed in colourful cloth they had dyed themselves.

For 8-10	**For 45-50**
(1 x baking tray – dimensions below)	(4 x baking trays – see below)
Roulade	
150g (6oz) very good dark chocolate (70% cocoa)	600g (1lb 5oz)
50g (2oz / ½ cup) cocoa powder	200g (7oz / 2 cups)
150g (5oz / ¾ cup) golden caster sugar	600g (1lb 5oz)
6 large eggs	24
1 pinch salt	½ tsp
½ tsp vanilla essence	2 tsp
Cocoa and icing sugar for dusting	A little more as required
Filling	
300ml (10fl oz / 1¼ cups) double cream	1.2l (2 pints)
25g (1oz / 3-4 tbsp) icing sugar	100g (4oz / ⅔ cup)
5 tbsp raspberry/strawberry jam or spread	1 jar (340g / 12oz / 1½ cups)
300g (10oz / 2 cups) raspberries (optional)	1.2kg (2lb 10oz) (optional)

1. Lightly oil your shallow baking trays (28 x 36cm / 11 x 15" – and at least 2cm / 1" deep), and line the base with baking parchment.

2. Rough-chop the dark chocolate and melt it gently in a bowl set in a saucepan containing some simmering water. Cover with a lid.

3. Separate the eggs. Combine the yolks with the caster sugar and vanilla extract in one bowl and whisk at high speed until the mixture has doubled in volume and is pale in colour – this can take 5-10 minutes. Pre-heat the oven to 180°C (350°F / Gas Mark 4).

4. In a clean, grease-free bowl, whip up the egg whites until they form soft peaks. Add a little salt as you go.

5. Quickly stir the hot melted chocolate into the beaten egg yolk mixture. Give the egg white a few rejuvenating extra whisks, then fold one-third of it into the chocolate mixture using a large metal spoon. Next, fold in the cocoa powder, and then the rest of the whipped egg white – fold gently, don't beat. You want to keep the mixture as bubbly as possible.

6. Pour the mixture into the prepared tins: it should be no more than 1cm high (and just less than ½"!) – any thicker and it is more difficult to

roll and more prone to cracking. Bake in the oven for about 20 minutes until the mixture is just set but not at all dried out. A skewer inserted in the middle should come out clean. Leave the roulade to cool in the tin. Cover with cling film or a damp tea towel if leaving overnight.

7. When you are ready to roll, go around the edges of the roulade with a knife to check it is not sticking. Dust it through a sieve with cocoa powder and then cover with a piece of parchment slightly bigger than the roulade itself. Place a large tray or chopping board over this and then, gripping all firmly together, flip the baking tray over so the roulade falls out on to the parchment on the board or tray. Peel off the lining paper.

8. Prepare the filling: carefully whip the cream until it begins to form smooth, soft, dune-like peaks, then stir in the sieved icing sugar minimally.

9. Spread the chocolate roulade first with a very thin layer of raspberry or strawberry jam and then with a generous layer of whipped cream. If you are including raspberries, scatter these over the cream and press down.

10. Now comes the skilful part! Holding the underlying parchment paper, roll the roulade up widthways, so the width becomes the length. It may help to ease the first and tightest part of the twist by cutting a little nick 1cm (½") in on either side of the roulade, so the first edge folds over more readily. Lou was observed to guide the rolling quite firmly by pushing the paper over the growing log at an angle and by smoothing the roulade through the paper. If the cream starts oozing out, you know you are pushing too firmly and need to take a bit of pressure off. Don't worry if some small cracks appear, as these add an attractively bark-like effect that enhances rather than detracts from the appearance.

11. Leave the roulade in the fridge, wrapped in the parchment, until just before you need to serve it. Complete with a final dusting of cocoa powder just before serving – and a fresh fall of snowy icing sugar on top of this if you like.

Honey-kissed lemon tart

Nothing matches the mouth-watering tang of a seriously lemony tart: *so* lemony it would be unbearable – if it weren't also so sweet. Many cooks have made delicious lemon tarts with more or less cream and egg yolks to enrich the flavour and set them. Our twist is to add a little bee elixir: honey, with thanks to those tiny tiger-striped workers who have struggled so hard to survive in recent years. Indeed, for over a year, the College's dwindling supply of Dartmoor honey was kept locked up like gold, reserved only for 'medicinal purposes'.

A tiny pinch of precious saffron – the dried stigma of the crocus flower – can also be added to this lemon tart to intensify the colour, as well as to connect us further with the critical role bees play in the web of life. Because the crocus is a crop that manifests itself as fields of wall-to-wall flowers, yielding 4.5kg (10lb) of saffron per half hectare (1 acre), it reminds us of the importance of bees for pollinating so many other flowering plants on which we humans depend. Fruit and nut trees, for example, must welcome bees to their blossoms before producing what we harvest as food.

For 10-12
(1 x 28cm / 11" loose-based tart tin)

Pastry

200g (7oz / 1½ cups) plain flour
25g (1oz / 3 tbsp) icing sugar
115g (4oz / 1 stick) butter
1 tsp cinnamon
¼ tsp salt
1 egg yolk
1½-2 tbsp cold water

Filling

160g (6oz / 1 cup) golden granulated sugar
7 eggs
Zest of 7 organic lemons
300ml (12fl oz / 1½ cups) lemon juice
2 pinches (1½ tsp) saffron threads (optional)
75ml (2½fl oz / 5 tbsp) honey
250ml (9fl oz / 1 cup + 2 tbsp) double cream
1 tbsp polenta or semolina

For 40-48
(4 x 28cm / 11" tins)

800g (1lb 12oz)
115g (4oz / ¾ cup)
450g (1lb)
4 tsp
1 tsp
1 whole egg + 1 yolk
approx. 6-8 tbsp

675g (1½lb / 4 cups)
28
Zest of 28
1.2l (2 pints / 2½ US pints)
2g (2 tbsp) (optional)
300ml (½ pint / 1¼ cups)
1l (1¾ pints / 2¼ US pints)
approx. 4 tbsp

1. Begin by preparing the pastry and pastry cases in the usual way (see page 85 – but in this case using some egg yolk (or egg plus yolk for the large quantity), not only to help with binding but also to give a richer, more flexible pastry). Leave them in the fridge to chill until you are ready with the filling.

2. Grate the outermost yellow zest from the lemons, removing *as little as possible* of the white pith below, as this part of the lemon will contribute a taste that is more bitter than sour. The soulful sourness of citrus is what you are after – not its bitter edge! One scraping of lemon zest from each place is normally enough. Set aside.

3. If using saffron to intensify the yellow colour of the tart, mix the saffron threads with 2-4 tbsp of boiling water and leave this standing for at least 30 minutes while the natural colour rushes into the water, turning it a fantastic crocus-yellow.

4. Meanwhile, squeeze the juice from all the lemons and check that it comes to the required amount, adding or deducting as required. Fish out any pips that have slipped in – sieving if necessary. Pre-heat the oven to 190°C (375°F / Gas Mark 5).

5. Break the eggs into a large bowl, reserving one egg white to paint the pastry bases with later. Mix the eggs together with the sugar, zest and honey (which should first be very gently melted if it is stiff). Next mix in the cream. Finally, stir in the lemon juice and saffron-water – don't attempt an all-in-one method for putting together this mixture: if the cream goes in after, or with, the lemon juice, the fats can separate out rather than blend in smoothly.

6. Get the tart cases out of the fridge. Paint the bases with egg white and sprinkle with a fine layer of polenta or semolina, then carefully pour in the lemon mixture. Move very steadily to the oven (some people prefer to top up their tarts on a pulled-out oven shelf, and then gently push in the shelf, to avoid carrying very full tarts that could slop over – do this if you judge yourself to be a little shaky-of-hand!). Place the tart where you know the base will get a good blast of heat from underneath, which will vary from oven to oven, but is likely to be the bottom half of the oven. After 10 minutes, reduce the heat to 170°C (325°F / Gas Mark 3) for another 25-35 minutes. Strategically move around or rotate the tarts to ensure even browning – especially important when making the large quantity.

7. Remove from the oven when the lemon-custard is just set to a quiver – the middle will set last, so this is the part to check. The pastry will be lightly browned, and the lemon-custard may also be showing the first glimpses of turning a very light golden-brown around the edge.

8. Eat warm or cold with cream, crème fraîche or ice cream.

Zesty almond-polenta cake (with reversible berry option!)

Polenta-almond cakes have a gorgeous yellow richness to them that happily marries together the grittiness of polenta, the tang of citrus and the lightness of almond. My grandfather used to put sugar on his ice cream simply for the grit — it made what might otherwise seem like nursery food feel like something more solid! Similarly, there is something satisfyingly substantial about a zesty polenta cake, like a kind of Victoria sandwich with added bite. Polenta cakes are also great for people on wheat-free diets, since polenta is derived from maize, not wheat. This version can be baked successfully as a plain cake, or turned *officially* into a dessert by being baked upside-down with baked-in berries on what becomes the top . . . It may be served warm or cold, and as either a dessert or a cake.

For 8-10 (1 x 25cm / 10" round cake)	**For 24-32** (3 x 25cm / 10" or 2 x 28cm / 11" cakes)
Basic cake	
100g (4oz / ⅔ cup) fine polenta	300g (12oz / 2 cups)
225g (8oz / 1¼ cups) golden caster sugar	675g (1½lb)
200g (7oz / 1¾ sticks) butter (softened)	600g (1lb 5oz)
Zest of 2 organic lemons	Zest of 6
3-4 tbsp lemon juice	125ml (5fl oz / ½ cup)
Zest of 2 organic oranges	Zest of 6 medium
2 tbsp orange juice	6 tbsp (90ml / ⅓ cup)
100ml (3fl oz / ⅓ cup) sour cream or full-fat yoghurt	300ml (10fl oz / 1¼ cups)
3 eggs	9
½ tsp vanilla essence	1½ tsp
300g (10oz / 3 cups) ground almonds	900g (2lb)
1 heaped tsp baking powder (select gluten-free if required)	1 heaped tbsp
1 pinch salt	¼ tsp
2-3 tbsp pine nuts (optional)	50g (2oz / ⅓ cup) (optional)
2 tbsp flaked almonds (for plain version only)	6 tbsp
Topping for upside-down berry option	
350g (12oz / 2½ cups) fresh or frozen berries, e.g. raspberries, blackcurrants or forest fruits	1.2kg (2lb 10oz)
25g (1oz / 4 tbsp) golden caster or muscovado sugar	75g (3oz / ½ cup)

1. Place the butter and sugar in a bowl and leave in a warm place so the butter softens (this can be done several hours in advance of cooking).

2. Prepare your cake tins (spring-form ones are ideal, if you have them). Butter the tins and line them with a ring of baking parchment cut 1cm (½") larger than the tin – this is especially important if you are using a detachable-based tin and making the upside-down version, as you don't want the juices to ooze out. Smooth the edges of the baking parchment up against the wall of the tins – the butter will help stick it in place. Add a further strip of parchment around the inside edge. Now butter the top of the parchment on the base too.

3. For the upside-down berry version, now sprinkle sugar over the parchment-covered base of the tin and spread it out a bit. It will stick to the butter. Next, cover the base with fresh or frozen berries: the surface should be completely covered, with each fruit touching its neighbour. Follow this with another layer of berries tossed over the first, to fill in the gaps. The second layer will help to minimize any oozing-out from the cake mixture, which can diminish the fruity effect.

4. Cream together the softened butter and sugar until light and fluffy. Add the finely grated lemon and orange rind to this, and also stir in the sour cream or yoghurt.

5. Separate the eggs and stir the yolks into the creamed butter and sugar. Also add the vanilla essence and the lemon and orange juice.

6. Measure together the polenta and ground almonds. Add the baking powder and salt to these. (Also, for the plain version of the cake, add pine nuts – these go very well in the brew but are expensive and often difficult to get hold of, so must be regarded as optional). Pre-heat the oven to 180°C (350°F / Gas Mark 4).

7. Before adding dry ingredients to wet, beat up the egg whites until soft snowy peaks are formed. Now swiftly stir the dry ingredients into the creamed mixture, and then fold in the beaten egg whites, half at a time, incorporating gently with minimal stirring. Once the egg whites are fairly evenly distributed, stop mixing.

8. Pour the cake mixture into the prepared tins (over the fruit if making the upside-down version; otherwise straight on to the parchment). Spread gently to the edges of the tin. If making the plain version, toss flaked almonds and/or more pine nuts on top before baking.

9. Bake in the oven for about 35-45 minutes, until a knife or skewer inserted comes out moist but clean.

10. If you are going to serve the upside-down berry cake as a warm dessert, allow to cool and 'set' for at least 10 minutes before inverting on to a plate and carefully remove the baking parchment. If serving cold, allow to cool almost completely in the tin and then, when still just slightly warm, invert and carefully peel back the baking parchment to reveal the fruit layer.

Serving tips:

If you want to make the cake in advance and serve it later as a warm dessert, it is best to keep it in the tin, and re-heat in the tin – which is why lining with parchment around the edges is important, as it guards against discolouration of the cake by the tin, especially if it is an old tin.

The plain cake can be finished with a simple dusting of icing sugar on the top just before serving. It is also delicious served as a dessert with a fresh fruit salad and ice cream.

Chocolate pavlova (with pears or berries)

Helen Chaloner, Schumacher College's first Catering Manager, reminded me of this lush dessert when she returned to take a course many years later. Because in its original form it was not in any way, sense or form a healthy pud, it had been dropped from the menu.

Now reintroduced and applauded, this version includes a healthy layer of fresh berries or pears between the chocolate and cream. The meringue is still, of course, terribly sweet, but for lovers of crispy, melt-on-your-tongue meringue, there is really nothing to beat it. Indeed, it would be a shame if, with so much emphasis on healthy eating, the sweet-toothed got banished, to the verandas of life with their creamy confections . . . along with the smokers!

For 6 (1 big dinner-plate-sized pavlova)	**For 45-50** (4 x 30cm / 12" round or 5 x dinner-plate-sized)
Meringue	
4 egg whites	20
225g (8oz / 1¼ cups) caster sugar	1.125kg (2½lb)
¼ tsp ground cinnamon	1½ tsp
1 pinch finest salt	½ tsp
½ tsp sunflower oil (for trays)	2-3 tsp
1 tbsp cornflour (for trays)	approx. 50g (2oz / ½ cup)
Filling	
180g (6oz) dark chocolate	900g (2lb)
3-4 tbsp brandy (and/or orange juice)	300ml (10fl oz / 1¼ cups)
4 tbsp cream (any sort, e.g. whipping)	300ml (10fl oz / 1¼ cups)
4 egg yolks	14-20
300g (10oz) fresh raspberries, or drained preserved black cherries, or peeled pear chunks, fresh or poached	1.5-2kg (3-4lb)
300ml (10fl oz / 1¼ cups) whipping cream	1.5l (2½ pints / 3 US pints)
1 tsp caster sugar (optional)	2 rounded tbsp (optional)
For decoration	
1 pinch ground cinnamon	1 tsp
A few shavings of chocolate	25g (1oz)

1. Line metal baking trays with wall-to-wall baking parchment. To estimate the number of tins you will need, imagine placing dinner plates over the surface – each dinner plate represents a pavlova, and you should have a 4cm (1½") gap between each. (Large flan tins can be used, as long as the edges are also lined.) Spread a thin layer of sunflower oil over the paper (you can use kitchen paper to smear it around, to avoid excess). Sieve this all over with a thin layer of cornflour, then hold the tray up at an angle and tap the cornflour across so it sticks evenly in a single fine coating. Tip out any surplus.

2. Measure the caster sugar and keep it at the ready. Also have a large-nozzled, meringue piping bag at the ready – I use a large jug to keep it open, such that the nozzle points down inside the jug and the opening is pulled back over the edge of the jug for easy filling. Alternatively, using a metal spoon to sculpt the meringue nests gives an attractive dune-like effect. Pre-heat the oven to 180°C (350°F / Gas Mark 4).

3. Separate the eggs and whisk the egg whites in a large bowl. As air bubbles begin to appear, add the salt and continue until smooth, stiff white peaks are formed. Immediately (before the bubbles begin to collapse) whisk in the sugar, half at a time. Also add the ground cinnamon.

4. Fill the icing bag until it is about two-thirds full, and use it to pipe 1-6 circular meringue nests. Begin by piping the base, with a spiral of connecting meringue about 1cm (½") thick, then build up a shallow 4cm (1½") wall at the edge to contain the chocolate and fruit. Alternatively, sculpt a nest with more rounded walls using a metal spoon.

5. Bake in the oven for 5-10 minutes to set the shell and prevent spreading, then reduce the tempera-ture to 140°C (275°F / Gas Mark 1) for a further 1½ to 2 hours. If you have two ovens, have them both ready at different temperatures and simply transfer the meringue from hotter to cooler. When ready, the meringue nests will be stiff with slightly cappuccino-like peaks. The middle should still be slightly gooey – test with a knife or lift gently to inspect the base. Remove from the oven and leave to cool. (When completely cold, the pavlova bases can be stored in an airtight bag or tin to use another day.)

6. If you are filling the pavlovas with pears, they should be poached in advance, then left to drain and cool. If ripe, they can be used fresh. To poach the pears, peel, cut, core and chop them, then cover with water and a little sugar and simmer gently with a lid on until tender – a little white wine and orange juice may also be included in the poaching liquid. If using tinned or bottled black cherries, leave these to drain in a sieve. If using raspberries, rinse briskly and leave to drain and dry off.

7. Break up the chocolate and melt it gently with the cream, brandy and/or orange juice in a bowl set in a saucepan of simmering water. Once the chocolate has melted, turn off the burner and swiftly beat in the egg yolks, which will cook a little with the heat of the chocolate. Leave to cool at room temperature – in the fridge it will become too stiff to handle.

8. One hour before serving, fill the inside of the meringue nests with a 0.5cm (¼") layer of the chocolate cream. Spread the drained fruit on top this. (Pat dry soft fruit with baking paper if necessary.)

9. To finish, whip up the cream until soft peaks are formed. Stir in the sugar, if using, and spoon the cream over the fruit, concealing it and the chocolate layer. Decorate with a sprinkling of cinnamon and a few swirls of chocolate made by scraping at the side of a bar of chocolate with a potato peeler. Serve in big triangular slices.

Rhubarb & strawberry trifle

The great English trifle first appeared in a recipe book as long ago as 1596 – but it was only by the mid-eighteenth century that this dessert had begun to take the shape of the sweetly layered confection we know today. With its creamy top glistening with glacé cherries, angelica and candies, trifle has become a legend at children's birthday parties. Indeed, it was definitely not 'a thing of little importance' to the two children who scoffed a whole spongy trifle down secretly and felt dreadfully sick in the tale *My Naughty Little Sister* by Dorothy Edwards:

> "*Bad Harry said, 'Now we've made the trifle look so untidy, no one else will want any,*
> *so we may as well eat it all up,' so they dug away into the spongy inside of the trifle and*
> *found lots of nice fruit bits inside. It was a very big trifle, but those greedy children ate and ate.*"

Trifle purists might turn their noses up at the inclusion of jelly in this recipe, but I am keeping it in just for fun! I have noticed that many adults as well as children seem to enjoy the occasional appearance of this humorous substance wobbling in their pudding bowls – quite a rarity at Schumacher College. Note that you'll need to reduce the liquid by half if you wish to make a trifle without jelly, since only as much surplus liquid as can be absorbed by the sponge will then be required.

Rhubarb and strawberries (or raspberries) make a lovely combination for June and July – but substitute other berries and soft fruit (fresh and/or lightly stewed) to taste, depending on what's available. Tinned fruit can also be used. For a children's party, it may be a safer bet to leave out the more unusual phenomenon (rhubarb!) and double the soft fruit, including more strawberries, raspberries, or other fruit such as peaches or cherries.

For 15+
(1 x 4-litre / 7-pint / 9-US-pint glass bowls)

2-egg sponge (see Strawberries & cream flan recipe, page 172*)
1kg (2lb) rhubarb
100g (4oz / ⅔ cup) sugar
300ml (8-9fl oz / 1 cup) water
200ml (7fl oz / ⅔ cup) sherry
100g (4oz / ⅓ cup) raspberry jam or spread
500g (1lb) strawberries or raspberries
1.2l (2 pints / 2½ US pints) jelly
Apple juice / other fruit juice, as required
85g (3oz / rounded ½ cup) custard powder
1.2l (2 pints / 2½ US pints) milk

For 50+
(4 x 4-litre bowls or equivalent)

4-egg sponge (see page 172*)
3kg (6½lb)
300g (10oz / 2 cups)
600ml (1 pint / 2½ cups)
600ml (1 pint / ¾ US pint)
340g (12oz / 1½ cups)
1.5kg (3lb 5oz)
3.6l (6 pints / 7½ US pints)
As required
250g (9oz / rounded 1½ cups)
3.6l (6 pints / 7½ US pints)

But use a simplified version of that recipe – see Step 1 of method.

3 tbsp sugar	100g (4oz / ⅔ cup)
1 drop vanilla essence	½ tsp
1l (1¾ pints / 2 US pints) whipping cream	3l (5 pints / 6 US pints)
approx. 3 tbsp flaked almonds (optional)	50-100g (2-4oz / 1 cup) (optional)

1. Begin by making the sponge cake as described on pages 172-3. If you are making the small quantity, make a two-egg sponge and only use two-thirds of it in the trifle. For the large quantity, double this, so you're using four eggs. Simplify the recipe by leaving out the ground almonds and orange – substitute to the same amount with more flour. The sponge can be made up to a week in advance if you like – it doesn't have to be really fresh, but should be stored in a tin or plastic bag. The sponge can be made in rectangular or round baking tins (e.g. 1-3 x 24cm / 9½" round cake tins are convenient), and the mix should be about 1.5cm (¾") deep before baking.

2. On the day of your party (or the day before), wash the rhubarb and cut into 2cm (1") chunks, discarding the leaves and any brown parts at the base. Pre-heat the oven to 170°C (325°F / Gas Mark 3). Place the rhubarb in a baking dish and sprinkle with the sugar and water. Cover and bake in the oven for 20-30 minutes until it is just tender and still holding its shape.

3. While the rhubarb is cooking, get ready one to four glass serving bowls each with a 4-litre (7-pint) capacity (this volume can be made up with smaller or larger bowls, depending on what you have, but you do need dishes that are at least 18cm (7") deep to allow you to build up the layers). Spread jam over the cakes and cut into triangles. Arrange these at the bottom of the bowls and drench with the sherry. (A sweet white wine can also be used.)

4. Rinse the soft fruit in cold water and drain. Remove the hulls from the strawberries, and set aside a few perfect ones to use as decoration later on. Slice the rest. If using raspberries, keep them whole. Then use a slotted spoon to lift the rhubarb on to the cake, breaking it as little as possible. Add the hulled and sliced strawberries (or the raspberries) to the rhubarb, distributing them in an even layer.

5. Measure the remaining rhubarb liquid and make it up to the volume required using apple juice and water (or other fruit juices if you've used a different selection of cooked or tinned fruit). Make the jelly according to the instructions on the packet using this fruity liquid (normally the powder or cubes are dissolved in part of a boiling portion of the liquid, and then the rest of the liquid is added to help cool the mixture down). While it is still runny and quite hot, pour the jelly mix over the fruit and cake and leave in a cool place to set.

6. Once the jelly is set and cold, make the custard. For the large quantity, make sure you heat the milk to boiling point before adding the smaller amount of cold milk with the custard powder dissolved in it (refer to the instructions on the packet). This will help prevent the milk burning as the custard thickens – because it will thereby reach thickening point more quickly. Once the custard has boiled it won't thicken any more. Stir in the sugar and vanilla essence. The amount of custard powder listed here should give a fairly thick custard that will jellify as it cools down on the trifle – this is more than the amount recommended on many packets, which usually result in a more refined and runny custard. Allow to cool for 15 minutes with a lid on. If you are in a hurry, spread the custard out in a baking dish and stir it to let out the steam and prevent a skin forming on the surface.

7. Spoon the still-warm custard carefully over the jelly – don't pour it all in one place. When you have built up the custard layer, return the trifle to the fridge to chill.

8. When the custard is cold and set, finish off the trifle with a layer of whipped cream, making sure you don't over-whip the cream. It should be just thick enough to hold an impression, as it will continue to stiffen and set in the fridge. If it starts to look grainy, stop whisking immediately – it's on its way to becoming butter! Sweeten the cream with a little icing sugar if you want to. Spread or pipe the whipped cream over the custard, and return the trifle to the fridge until ready to serve.

9. Finally, decorate with the reserved strawberries. To this can be added lightly toasted flaked almonds (see tip), grated chocolate perhaps and maybe some edible flowers. For children, a decoration of glacé cherries, jelly babies and dolly mixtures may (or may not . . .) seem more appropriate!

Tip: Toasting nuts (& seeds) – the oven method. Heat your oven to 200°C (400°F / Gas Mark 6). Spread the nuts/seeds) out in one generous layer on a metal baking tray. Pop into the oven, and *put your timer on!* 10 minutes is usually sufficient – but for flaked almonds, because they are so thin, 7 minutes is better. When ready, the nuts should look lightly caramel-brown in places and satiny, because the oils have come to the surface.

Twinkling berry cheesecake

Here is a classic baked cheesecake made with full-fat cream cheese and a hint of lemon zest. It can be topped with whipped cream and whichever soft bright berries the summer offers. Out of the summer season, Tchenka has pioneered a delicious topping of apple purée and chopped roast hazelnuts (see 'Topping variations' overleaf). Other frozen or preserved fruits, such as blackcurrants or 'fruits of the forest', can also be used, their juices stiffened with a little arrowroot or cornflour (see page 167). For cheesecake purists, such as Schumacher College's House Manager William Thomas, however, there never seems any need to crown this rich species of dessert with any jewels, however fruity. It can be cooked and presented plain all the year round, resplendent in its magnolia glory.

For 6-12
(1 x 23cm / 9" loose-based, deep round tin)

For 45-40
(either 4 x 23cm tins or 2 x 28cm / 11" and 1 x 20cm / 8" tins)

Base

350g (12oz) wholemeal digestive biscuits (or graham crackers in the USA)	1.4kg (3lb)
125g (4½oz / 1 stick + 1 tbsp) butter	500g (1lb 2oz)
¼ tsp sunflower oil (for tin)	approx. 1½-2 tsp

Filling

170g (6oz / 1 cup) golden granulated sugar	700g (1½lb)
700g (1½lb / 2⅔ cup) full-fat cream cheese	2.8kg (6lb)
4 eggs	16
Juice and zest of 1 small organic lemon	Juice and zest of 4
1 tsp vanilla essence	4 tsp

Toppings

250g (8oz / 1½ cups) fresh seasonal berries, e.g. 150g (4oz) strawberries + 50g (2oz) redcurrants + 50g (2oz) raspberries/blackberries	approx. 1kg (2lb / 6 cups), e.g. 500g (1lb) + 250g (8oz) + 250g (8oz)
275ml (10fl oz / 1¼ cups) double or whipping cream	1l (2 pints / 2½ US pints)

1. Deep, loose-based cake tins (preferably with spring-locks on the side) are essential for a successful cheesecake. Smear very lightly with sunflower oil.

2. Crush the **digest**ive biscuits. This can be done by roughly breaking them, then whizzing them up in a food processor using the knife attachment. Alternatively, break the biscuits and place in a clean plastic or fabric bag and roll them with a rolling pin, until as finely crushed as possible.

3. Gently melt the butter without letting it burn. Remove from the heat and stir in the crushed biscuits, mixing thoroughly.

4. *Biscuit base:* Begin by placing several spoonfuls of the crumb mixture in each tin. This should be enough to cover the base, though you can, of course, adjust the amount as you go along. Use the back of a flattish metal spoon to smooth out and press down the crumbs, to give a layer about 4mm (just under ¼") thick. Next, spoon some more of the crumbs around the edge of the base and press this up against the side to create a circular wall 3-4cm (1½-2") high – again use the back of the spoon. This is a bit fiddly to do, but you soon get the knack of it and your fingers come in very handy! A straight-sided, flat-bottomed drinking glass or tumbler can also be useful for pressing the walls and floor of biscuit bases into shape. The bases can be prepared in advance and refrigerated.

5. Pre-heat the oven to 160°C (325°F / Gas Mark 3).

6. *Filling:* Scoop the cream cheese into a large mixing bowl and mix in the eggs, two by two. Add the sugar, vanilla essence, lemon juice and zest. Beat until smooth – an electric hand mixer or rotary whisk can be useful for getting rid of any lumps.

7. Pour the filling into the biscuit base and bake the cheesecake for about 60 minutes for the smaller size. The larger cheesecakes will take longer – up to 1½ hours. When ready, it should be beginning to turn light golden-brown at the edges and be set (not really wobbly) – even in the middle. Ideally there should be no puffing up like a soufflé, as this will impair the texture. Turn the heat off and leave the cheesecake to cool gradually in the oven for a further 30-60 minutes. Then chill in the fridge for at least 2 hours, or preferably overnight.

8. *Finishing touches:* For the summer topping, whip the cream until it is thick enough to hold an impression, but still lovely and smooth. If the cream starts to look at all grainy, stop whisking immediately – this roughening of the surface is a first sign that the cream is beginning to separate and you could soon be making butter! Spread the whipped cream generously over the tops of the cheesecake – right up to, but not over, the biscuit edge. The soft fruit should be picked over to remove leaves and stalks, but if you can avoid washing it, do so, as this can make it watery. If it needs washing, rinse briskly in cold water and leave to drain in a colander, then spread out on absorbent kitchen paper or a clean tea towel. If the strawberries are really enormous, you may want to cut them in half. Arrange the berries wall-to-wall on top of the cream, heaping them up if you have lots.

9. *Turning the cheesecake out:* Very gently, release the spring-lock on the tin, and if it appears that the biscuit crust is sticking at all, close it again and go around the edge with a small sharp knife to loosen the base. This can be done before or after decorating the cheesecake.

Topping variations: To top with apple purée, Tchenka-style, you'll need 400g / 14oz (small quantity) or 2kg / 4lb (large quantity) of cooking or tart dessert apples, which can be sweetened to taste. Peel, core and chop these and cook in a little water with a blob of butter and a pinch of cinnamon. When the apples are soft, and the water has mostly boiled away, purée with a masher or in a food processor. Leave to cool and spread over the cheesecake – omitting the cream. Decorate with 50g / 2oz / ½ cup (small quantity) or 300g / 10oz / 2 cups (large quantity) of

roasted, rough-chopped and whole hazels – from which you have rubbed away most of the skins (see Rich chocolate & hazelnut gateau method, page 185). Puréed rhubarb is also delicious used in this way.

Using frozen or tinned/bottled fruit: Again, leave the cream out. Drain tinned, bottled or defrosted frozen fruit gently in a sieve or colander and reserve any juice. To minimize handling that will mush up the fruit, place it on the cheesecake once it has drained well, carefully forming a generous fruit layer. Make a glaze by stirring 1 tsp / 4 tsp of arrowroot or cornflour into a little cold water or juice. Add this blend to 150ml / 5fl oz / ⅔ cup (small quantity) or 600ml / 1 pint / 1¼ US pints (large quantity) of reserved fruit juice per cheesecake. If necessary, make up volume with apple juice or water. Bring to the boil in a saucepan, stirring constantly until thickened and quite clear in colour. Pour over the fruit on the cheesecake. Leave to cool. Black cherries, blackcurrants and frozen raspberries or forest fruits are nice used this way – as are rehydrated, lightly stewed, dried apricots.

Avocado-chocolate truffle torte

At Schumacher College, avocados are a much-cherished treat and best eaten in the spring and summertime, when they are being harvested in southern Europe. It's only recently that we've started to blend them with chocolate to create this highly desirable truffle torte for the birthdays of our special-diet customers, inspired by nutritionist Dale Pinnock.

If using avocado in a dessert seems too weird for words, you need only have a conversation with a Brazilian to discover that this lovely pale green fruit is often blended with sugar and eaten as a sweet, rather than a savoury, dish. The principal contribution of the mild avocado to desserts is not taste but rather a smooth, buttery consistency and a healthy amount of unsaturated fat. For extra setting power we've also included cocoa butter and creamed coconut in the truffle blend of this dessert. However, as cocoa butter is an expensive ingredient, and not always easy to get hold of, more creamed coconut can also be used when required – and silken tofu may be very successfully substituted for avocado.

Avocados originated in South America and have been cultivated for over 7,000 years. In fact, their name comes from the Aztec word for testicle: 'ahuacatyl'. This was later corrupted into 'alligator pear' by the Spanish, and thence to 'avocado pear'. They are the highest in protein and oil content of all fruit, and contain many other beneficial ingredients. Avocados are harvested from the tree when fully grown and firm. They ripen in one to two weeks in a warm place, so get your avocados 4-5 days in advance. When ripe enough, keep them in the fridge so they don't become over-ripe or brown.

For 8 Small torte (20cm / 8" detachable-based flan tin)	**For 24** Large torte (1 x 28cm / 11" flan tin) or 3 x small tortes
Nut case	
150g (6oz) mixed nuts, quite finely chopped e.g. 50g (2oz) walnuts	500g (18oz), e.g. 150g (6oz)
+ 50g (2oz) cashews or more walnuts	+ 150g (6oz)
+ 25g (1oz) almonds or hazels	+ 100g (3oz)
+ 25g (1oz) ground almonds	+ 100g (3oz)
30g (1oz) creamed coconut	85g (3oz)
25g (1oz) cocoa butter (or more creamed coconut)	85g (3oz) (or more creamed coconut)
1-2 tsp honey or (for vegan option) agave syrup or fine sugar	1-2 tbsp to taste
1 small pinch fine sea salt	¼ tsp – 1 good pinch

Filling

2 medium ripe avocados (400g / 14oz whole weight) (or 300g / 10oz silken tofu)	6 (approx. 1.2kg / 2½lb whole weight) (or 900g / 2lb)
150g (5oz) organic dark chocolate (70% cocoa)	450g (1lb)
40g (1½oz) creamed coconut	125g (4½oz)
25g (1oz) cocoa butter (or more creamed coconut)	85g (3oz) (or more creamed coconut)
2-3 tbsp orange juice (or brandy or soya milk)	Juice of 1 orange (approx. 100ml / 4fl oz / ½ cup)
½ tsp organic orange zest, finely grated	Zest of 1 orange
1-2 tbsp honey or (for vegan option) maple syrup to taste	3-5 tbsp to taste

1. First, ensure that your avocados are perfectly soft and ripe. If you need to hasten the ripening, put them in a warm place or in a brown bag with some bananas. Oil your flan tin very lightly.

2. *Nut base:* Place the harder nuts (almonds, hazels) in your food processor first. Give them a good whizz and then add the softer nuts (walnuts, cashews) and blitz some more. The desired consistency is that of medium-sized breadcrumbs or fine shingle – you want there to be some texture, but also coherence.

3. Rough-chop the cocoa butter and creamed coconut and melt them gently in a bowl set in a saucepan quarter-filled with boiling water. When melted, remove from heat and stir in the finely chopped nuts, ground almonds, salt and sweetener (honey, agave or sugar). Mix well, then press into your oiled flan tin. Use a fairly flat spoon or a flat-bottomed glass to help you sculpt the nut mixture across the base and up the edges, in-filling as required. The nut walls should be about 3.5cm (1½") deep. Place in the fridge to set.

4. *Filling:* Break up the chocolate and place it in a heat proof bowl suspended over gently simmering water. Also add the second portion (the amount for the filling) of chopped cocoa butter and/or creamed coconut. As the mixture begins to melt, stir gently.

5. Halve the avocados and remove the stones. Scoop out the flesh into a bowl, removing any browning or bad parts. Place in a bowl and mash with your potato masher. (If using silken tofu to substitute for avocado, or make up their volume, simply remove from its carton, draining if required.)

6. Add the now completely melted chocolate mixture to the avocado (and/or silken tofu), along with the orange juice, zest and honey or maple syrup. Mix or mash them up, then transfer to your food processor and whizz until smooth – or use a rod blender in the bowl. When there are no green specks remaining, taste and add more sweeteners if required.

7. Now that the avocados have been completely overwhelmed by chocolate, with no green specks left showing, the mixture is ready to pour into the nut case. Spread gently to the edges as required, then return it to the fridge to set. Two or three hours later, gently ease off the edges of the tin and serve the torte. If you like, decorate with a few swirls of dark or white chocolate made with your potato peeler – or with toasted flaked almonds, or perhaps an edible flower, a ring of raspberries – or a few chocolate bay leaves (see page 200).

Spicy pumpkin pie

Almost every year at Schumacher College there will be Canadian or American students staying in November who want to celebrate Thanksgiving. When Mary Catherine Harmon (now known as Cathy Clipson) set out to make a pumpkin pie in the mid-'90s, I managed to track down a huge pumpkin for her in an unlikely place: it was under the bed of a telesales assistant who worked for one of our most mainstream catering suppliers! What Cathy really wanted was tinned pumpkin, so we steamed our pumpkin and blended it up to make it look like tinned. Later I realized that a good orange-fleshed squash, such as Crown Prince, will result in a much tastier pie. The squash we think of as a 'pumpkin' is often splendid to behold, and wonderful to make jack-o'-lanterns out of, but its pale flesh is somewhat bland, fibrous and full of water. It needs to be mixed with denser varieties of squash and spiced to improve the flavour. If you are not attempting to use up jack-o'-lantern pumpkin, then try to get hold of sugar pumpkins, which are intended for cooking and, again, can be mixed with other squash.

Thanksgiving commemorates the first meal the Pilgrim Fathers had with the Native American people back in the 1700s — a fleeting moment of hope, when they shared each other's food, before rivalry set in and turned the relationship sour. For those who celebrate the festival at Schumacher College, it remains a time of genuine thankfulness and sharing, rather than gift-giving — and this includes a great appreciation of the learning that has come from the first people of North America themselves, some of whom now teach at Schumacher College.

For 10+ (1 x 28cm / 11" loose-bottomed tart tin)	**For 45-50** (4 x 28cm / 11" tins)
750g chunked squash (1lb 10oz / 3 cups mashed)	3kg (6½lb)
175g (6oz / 1 cup) golden granulated sugar	700g (1½lb / 4 cups)
4 eggs	16
500ml (18fl oz / 2¼ cups) cream (single, double or whipping)	2l (3½ pints / 4¾ US pints)
1 tsp ground cardamom	1 rounded tbsp
1 tsp ground cinnamon	1 rounded tbsp
¾ tsp ground ginger	3 tsp
1 tiny pinch ground cloves	¼ tsp
½ tsp salt	2 tsp
approx. 1 tbsp pumpkin seeds and/or ½ an apple (optional – to decorate)	4 tbsp and/or 2 apples

Pastry

See recipe for pastry with cinnamon on page 156 (Honey-kissed lemon tart).
Leave out the cinnamon and add:

2 tsp ground cardamom and ½ tsp mixed spice	3 tbsp and 2 tsp

1. Prepare your pastry and line your tart tins in the normal way (see page 85), and leave to chill in the fridge.

2. Select a good flavoursome squash such as butternut or Crown Prince. Peel, de-seed and cut into chunks that weigh in at the specified amount. Steam these in a bamboo or metal steamer suspended above a saucepan of boiling water on the hob, the steam enclosed with a lid. When soft, remove from heat.

3. Blend the squash in your food processor, or mash well with a fork (the former will give a smoother finish, which is preferable though not essential). Add some of the eggs if the squash on its own is too stiff to process easily in a blender.

4. Pre-heat the oven to 180°C (350°F / Gas Mark 4).

5. Mix the pulped squash, sugar, egg, salt and spices together in a bowl. Stir in the cream and mix until evenly blended.

6. Pour the pumpkin pie mixture into the pastry cases. Sprinkle the tops with pumpkin seeds around the edge (and a few slices of apple, painted thinly with oil, if you like) and gently move to the oven. Try to ensure that for the first 15 minutes you have selected a position where the base will receive strong underneath heat and therefore cook well. Bake for 40-50 minutes until the filling is set and the pastry is golden-brown.

7. Serve warm with ice cream or whipped cream.

Strawberries & cream flan

This dessert is an absolute summer favourite, loved by children and adults alike. The winning formula is really simple: strawberries + sponge + cream! You can buy sponge flans ready-made in supermarkets, but it's much nicer to make them fresh and put the best ingredients into the mix. Ideally you will need a special rimmed flan tin to shape a cake with a 'crater' in the middle, which is perfect for holding strawberries and cream. If you don't have this, just make normal-shaped sponge cakes in sandwich tins instead, and layer these together with jam, chopped strawberries and whipped cream – with whole strawberries set in a layer of cream on the top. True, fatless sponge cake is wonderfully light and bubbly – and can also be used in other desserts, such as the Rhubarb & strawberry trifle on page 162.

For 8-10 (1 x 23cm / 9" round flan)	**For 50-60** (6 x 23 cm / 9" round flans)
Sponge cake	
110g (4oz / ⅔ cup) caster sugar	675g (1½lb / 4 cups)
110g (4oz / 1 scant cup) plain flour	675g (1½lb / 5 level cups)
25g (1oz / ¼ cup) ground almonds (or more flour)	150g (6oz / 1½ cups)
2 tsp baking powder	4 tbsp
½ tsp mixed spice	3 tsp
2 eggs	12
½ tsp organic orange zest	3 tsp
2 tbsp orange juice	100ml (5fl oz / ½ cup)
2-3 tbsp milk or water	150ml (8fl oz / 1 scant cup)
1 pinch salt	½-1 tsp
Filling	
2 tsp icing sugar	4 tbsp
600g (1lb 6oz / 4-5 cups) strawberries	3.5kg (8lb)
3-4 tbsp strawberry jam	1 jar (340g / 12oz / 1½ cups)
350ml (12fl oz / 1½ cups) whipping cream	2l (3½ pints / 4½ US pints)

1. Grease the tins liberally, preferably with butter, then – if you have rimmed flan tins – line the bases as follows. Use a compass or plate to match the size of the raised central area of the tin, so you can draw a matching circle on parchment. Cut this out and use it to line the flat centre of the tin. Using other plates (or a compass), draw two further rings around the first to obtain a narrow ring of parchment that will sit neatly at the bottom of the dipped area. Cut this out and use to line the base of the tin. (You'll have an in-between ring of parchment, which you can discard – this simply represents the sloped gap between the two flatter surfaces that need lining.)

2. Pre-heat the oven to 180°C (350°F / Gas Mark 4).

3. To make the sponge cake, begin by separating the eggs. Add the sugar to the yolks and beat until pale and creamy. Then stir in the orange zest and juice, followed by the milk or water.

4. Measure together the dry ingredients – flour, ground almonds, baking powder, salt and mixed spice. Set aside while you whisk up the egg white into stiff foamy peaks.

5. As soon as the whites are ready, blend the flour mix into the sugar/yolk mixture.

6. Gently fold in half the whipped egg white – if the mixture is stiff, the first addition of whites will help to loosen it. Fold in the rest of the whites, being very careful to preserve as many bubbles as possible – so *no beating*, only gentle folding, please! As soon as the egg white looks fairly evenly distributed, pour the cake mixture into the tins, leaving a good 1-2cm (½-¾") of the tin edge exposed for the cake to rise into.

7. Place the sponge cakes on the middle shelf of the oven and cook for approximately 30 minutes until golden-brown and well risen. A knife or skewer inserted in the middle should come out clean and the cake will be beginning to shrink away from the edge of the tin. Leave in the tin for a few minutes to cool, then go around the edge with a knife and invert on to a wire cooling rack.

8. Give the strawberries a brisk rinse in cold water, and leave them to drain in a colander or on a tea towel. (If rinsed in your own garden by the morning dew, omit this step – the lustrous patina of a strawberry is much better protected if left unwashed!). Remove the hulls of the fruit and select the best strawberries to go on the top – about half or two-thirds. Slice the rest into medium/small pieces.

9. Once the cake is thoroughly cool, you can assemble the filling. Whip the cream into soft smooth peaks that will just hold the impression of the whisk. If there is any sign of the cream becoming grainy, stop whisking – you don't want it to turn into butter! The sifted icing sugar can be added to the cream halfway through whisking, or folded in at the end.

10. If you have used a rimmed flan tin, spread a fairly thin layer of strawberry jam (3-4 tbsp for each cake) across the inside base of the sponge flan – in the mouth of the crater, so to speak. Cover this with a few spoonfuls of whipped cream (about one-quarter of the cream). On top of this scatter a thick layer of chopped strawberries. Conceal these with the rest of the whipped cream, which should bulge up out of the 'crater'. Arrange the remaining strawberries on top of the cream, point up, hull-side down. The strawberries should be close together and pressed in just enough to secure them. Leave the strawberry flan in the fridge until you are ready for it. Serve sliced into triangles that deliciously reveal the hidden layers of strawberries and cream . . .

Variations:

Include other summer soft fruits in the mix: blueberries, raspberries, redcurrants, etc.

For the layered strawberry sponge cake (if not using a rimmed flan tin), you'll need to double the amount of jam used and make 2 x 21cm (8") cakes for every one rimmed cake. Sandwich each cake lavishly together by spreading jam on the upturned base of the cake, followed by a layer of chopped strawberries, just under half the cream, then the second cake (again with the flatter, base surface downwards). Spread the rest of the cream generously on top, and plant with hulled or halved strawberries.

Cakes

La Gomera banana & chocolate marble cake
Lovely lemon gateau
Carob brownie slice
Transition plum & almond cake
Rich chocolate & hazelnut gateau
Pear & chocolate cake
Cardamom cake
Chocolate-courgette cake
Dundee fruit cake
Chocolate & almond sachertorte
Dartington apple cake
Polish walnut-coffee cake
Chocolate bay leaves
Coconut cake
Fruity bread pudding-cake
Date, walnut & carrot cake
Moist-as-moss ginger cake
Crystallized flowers

La Gomera banana & chocolate marble cake

I am including this recipe with thanks to Carrie from the unique hippie village of El Guru, La Gomera. Here, on her mosaic-encrusted veranda, she was known for providing an exclusive two-course, fixed Sunday lunch menu of pizza and banana cake to the many walkers who clambered the rugged slopes above Via Grande Rey. Since gleaning the recipe from her in a whisper, over ten years ago, it has become one of my favourite cakes to bake – one that always reminds me of the place and its originator, though I have seen neither of them since! Like Carrie, I often serve this cake warm from the oven – with the fragments of dark chocolate oozing temptingly from the folds of the yellow-and-brown, banana-hugging sponge.

The Canary Islands, off the coast of north-west Africa, have a remarkably temperate climate that allows for a long growing season. Where the land is flat and fertile enough to support agriculture, this allows for abundant crops. In coastal plantations such as Via Grande Rey, huge, eight-tier bunches of bananas hang from the trees. Sometimes, with plastic overcoats on for protection, the bananas can be seen growing as early as January.

1 medium round cake (serves 12) (1 x 22cm / 9" tin)	**2 large round cakes (serves 32)** (2 x 28cm / 11" tins)
Main mix	
250g (9oz / 2¼ sticks) butter, softened	750g (1lb 10oz)
250g (9oz / 1½ cups) golden granulated sugar	750g (1lb 10oz)
300g (10oz / 2 cups) plain or self-raising white flour	900g (1lb 14oz)
5 eggs	15
4 tsp baking powder (if using plain flour)	4 level tbsp
¼ tsp salt	¾ tsp
Additions	
3-4 medium peeled ripe bananas (300g / 11oz)	9-11 (900g / 2lb)
100g (4oz) dark chocolate	300g (12oz)
40g (1½oz / 4 tbsp) cocoa powder	120g (4oz / ¾ cup)
40g (1½oz / 4 tbsp) more flour	120g (4oz / ¾ cup)
approx. 120ml (4fl oz / ½ cup) milk	300ml (12fl oz / 1½ cups)
¼ tsp vanilla essence (optional)	1 tsp (optional)
approx. ½ tsp sunflower oil	approx. 1 tsp

1. Pre-heat the oven to 180°C (350°F / Gas Mark 4) and grease and line the tins with baking parchment.

2. Combine the sugar and softened butter in a mixing bowl and cream together.

3. Peel the bananas and check that the weight is roughly what you need – bananas can vary considerably in size. Begin your banana preparation by cutting just half a banana (small quantity) or one-and-a-half (large quantity) into narrow round slices, spread these out on a plate, and smear them very lightly with sunflower oil to prevent them drying out in the oven. Set aside to decorate the top of the cake with later. Chop the rest of the banana up more roughly – into chunks og about 1.5cm (½") thick – if too large they will sink inside the cake. Set aside.

4. Roughly chop the dark chocolate, making sure to include some good-sized shards of about 1cm (½") or so. Put a couple of tablespoonsful of the chopped chocolate on to a saucer and reserve for the top. You can also use chocolate chips, but chopping up a bar, as Carrie did, gives for a more interesting texture, and ensures there will always be a few potholes of oozing chocolate in the cake to look forward to.

5. Add the eggs to the butter and sugar mix, one or two at a time. Next fold in the flour, baking powder and salt.

6. Divide the main cake mixture in two, judging by eye – having two equal-sized mixing bowls will help you to do this. A measuring jug can also be used if you're unsure. To one half, stir in half the milk and the sifted cocoa powder. To the other, stir in the rest of the milk and the additional flour (plus vanilla essence, if you like). The cake mixtures should be soft and dropping, but not too runny.

7. Begin by spreading *half* the brown cake mixture across all the tins you are using. Toss over this half of the chopped chocolate. Over this spread a layer of yellow cake mixture, again using up only half of the total amount. Toss over about two-thirds of the rough-chopped bananas. Follow this with another layer of chocolate mixture, then more chopped chocolate *and* the rest of the rough-chopped bananas. Spread the final layer of (yellow) cake mixture on top of this and place the rings of banana carefully on top of it – oiled side up.

8. Bake on the middle shelf of the oven. After about 30 minutes, turn the temperature down to 170°C (325°F / Gas Mark 3) and cook for another 20-25 minutes. Cover with greased baking parchment / non-plastic butter wrappers once the cake has set on top, to help prevent the surface burning during this relatively long cooking time. When ready, the cake will feel softly firm to the touch, and a skewer inserted in the middle will come out clean (see tip below). Remove from the oven. If you have used tins with detachable bases (or are planning to serve the cake cold), immediately scatter the cake with the reserved pieces of chocolate. The heat of the cake will melt the chocolate, and a little light pressing down of the larger chunks will help them bond to the cake – don't spread them out; they will hold their shape as they cool and re-solidify. Cool the cake in the tin, removing it to a wire rack after 20 minutes to hasten the cooling process.

9. If you plan to serve the cake warm and *haven't* used a tin with a detachable base, wait for 5 minutes before turning out the cake, whisking off the lining paper and reversing it carefully back on to a plate, then toss over the chocolate shards as described above – or omit them, to avoid mess.

10. For a real treat, accompany with ice cream!

Tip: How to tell when a cake is ready. If you touch the cake gently in the middle, it will no longer feel wobbly because the egg has set. Instead, it will feel gently firm yet spongy – and if you insert a skewer or small knife in the middle, it will come out clean and moist, with no gooey cake mixture sticking to it. A further sign is that a tiny gap will have appeared between the cake and the edge of the tin.

Lovely lemon gateau

It is thought the vitamin-C-rich fruit of the *Citrus medica* tree originated in north India and only reached the Mediterranean when the Romans discovered a direct route from the Red Sea to India in the first century AD. Back in the Middle Ages the fruits were rare and expensive in England, known only as a luxury used by the rich to garnish fish. Meanwhile, in the kitchens of Italy, lemons were becoming more and more abundant, and cooks began to use them in sweet dishes too.

It is unlikely that the English cooking experience will ever be devoid of lemons again. Even if the import of Californian lemons loses its seasonal foot-in-the-door, as air transportation becomes restricted with the decline of cheap petroleum, we will in all probability continue to ship in lemons from southern Europe, with little need of refrigeration. Perhaps we will also return to growing lemons in orangeries, as the wealthy Victorians did! We will have to become more frugal, and more seasonally aware, in our use of lemons in vinaigrettes, etc., and go back more often to vinegar for our touches of sourness. The profligate, cavalier, use of lemon will, once more, be reserved for special occasions. This luscious lemon gateau is a cake for such an occasion (and, for those with lemons on their doorstep, it can also be cooked more often, and more simply, as a batch cake – see 'Variations' at end of the recipe).

1 small round cake (serves 8) (2 x 18cm / 7" round sandwich tins)	**2 larger round cakes (serves 40)** (4 x 28cm / 11" round tins)
110g (4oz / 1 stick) butter, softened	700g (1½lb)
110g (4oz / ⅔ cup) light soft brown / caster sugar mix	700g (1½lb)
2 eggs	12
150g (5oz / 1 cup) plain or self-raising white flour	900g (1lb 14oz)
2 tsp baking powder (if using plain flour)	4 tbsp baking powder
Zest of 1 organic lemon and 2 tsp lemon juice	Zest of 6 and juice of 1
1 pinch ground cinnamon	1 tsp
1 pinch salt	½ tsp
A little milk	approx. 200ml (6fl oz / ¾ cup)
200ml (7fl oz / ¾ cup) whipping or double cream (for filling)	600ml (1 pint / 1¼ US pints)
3-4 tbsp flaked almonds (for topping)	approx. 50g (2oz / ½ cup)

Lemon drenching syrup

Juice of 1 lemon (from lemon used in cake mix)	Juice of 5 (250ml / 8-9fl oz / 1 cup)
1 rounded tbsp light muscovado sugar	85g (3oz / ½ cup)
1 tbsp honey	100g (4oz / ½ cup)

Lemon curd filling

Zest of 1 organic lemon	Zest of 2
50ml (2fl oz / 4 tbsp) lemon juice	100ml (4fl oz / ½ cup)
100g (4oz / ⅔ cup) caster sugar	225g (8oz / 1¼ cups)
50g (2oz / ½ stick) butter	100g (4oz / 1 stick)
1 egg + 1 yolk	3 eggs

Lemon butter icing (optional)

100g (4oz / 1 stick) butter, softened	300g (10½oz / 2½ sticks)
300g (10½oz / 2⅓ cups) golden icing sugar	900g (2lb / 7 cups)
1-2 tbsp lemon juice and zest of 1 organic lemon	3-4 tbsp juice and zest of 3

1. Pre-heat the oven to 180°C (350°F / Gas Mark 4). Grease and line the cake tins with baking parchment.

2. Cream together the softened butter and sugar.

3. Zest, then juice, the lemons for the cake mix. Mix the zest and a small amount of lemon juice into the creamed mixture, reserving the rest for later.

4. Mix in the eggs, one or two at a time.

5. Combine the flour, baking powder, salt and cinnamon. Sift half into the wet mixture and mix, then add the rest. Add a splash or two of milk to give a soft, smooth, dropping consistency.

6. Spread the cake mixture into the prepared tins – it should be about 2cm (¾") deep. Bake, mid-oven, for about 25-30 minutes. When ready the cake should be well risen and golden-brown at the edges. A skewer poked into the middle will come out clean but moist.

7. While the cake is cooking, prepare the lemon drenching syrup. Measure then strain the lemon juice into a saucepan and combine with the sugar. Bring to the boil and simmer fairly vigorously for 2 minutes, then add the honey and turn off the heat (you can substitute the honey with more brown sugar if you like, cooking it all together).

8. Once the cakes come out of the oven, poke them all over with a skewer or cocktail stick: each jab should go right down to the base of the tin and they should be about 2cm (¾") apart. Then spoon the hot drenching syrup over the cake as evenly as you can. Leave the cakes to cool in the tins.

9. *Lemon curd:* This can be prepared in advance and kept in the fridge – the smaller quantity will make more than you need, giving you some extra to go on bread or toast (very nice!). Make a 'double boiler' by finding a ceramic or pyrex bowl that fits snugly into a saucepan filled with about 5cm (2") water. Combine the beaten egg, strained lemon juice, zest, chopped or grated butter and sugar in the bowl, then bring to a

simmer and stir continuously until the butter is melted and the mixture thickens. It will not be really thick until cooled, but should at least coat the back of your spoon (like runny honey). Pour the lemon curd into clean, warmed jam jars and screw lids on. Allow to cool before using – and keep refrigerated between use.

10. *Lemon butter icing:* Combine the sifted icing sugar and chopped butter in a bowl. Pop into a low oven for 5 minutes and then blend together with the zest and a little lemon juice – to taste. When ready the icing should be soft and creamy, a little warmer than room temperature, so it sets on the cake.

11. Prepare the flaked almonds by dry-roasting them in a fairly hot oven (200°C / 400°F / Gas Mark 6) or under a grill until flecked with light brown – keep an eagle eye on them, as you do not want them to burn. Stir with a wooden spoon to ensure even browning (see tip on page 164).

12. Just before you are ready to assemble the cake, whip up the cream until it forms smooth peaks that will hold their shape and not flatten out. Be careful not to over-whip – once you get a granular effect, you are on the verge of creating butter! Remember that whipped cream will set more once it is put in place – which is why the whipping is left to the end.

13. *Assembling the gateau.* Turn out the cakes and remove the paper. Rest the bottom cake, top down, on a plate or chopping board. Spread a layer of lemon curd 0.5cm (¼") thick, then spoon on a layer of whipped cream. There's no need to go right up to the edge, as the top cake will push the filling down and out a little more. Gently place the top cake, base-downwards, on top of the cream, lining it up with the bottom cake. Next, spread the butter icing over the top and sides using a spatula or table knife. Fork a few squiggles into the icing if you like and then sprinkle with the flaked almonds. In the spring we often decorate this cake with fresh or crystallized primroses as well (see page 205).

Variations: Leave out the butter icing and simply toss the (untoasted) flaked almonds on top of one of the cakes before baking, limiting your decorations to this. You may also wish to sandwich the cakes together with the butter icing, instead of the lemon curd and cream. For even greater simplicity, leave out the cream, lemon curd and icing and just bake this as a plain batch cake delectably infused with the tang of lemon syrup.

Tip: To obtain zest (the outermost rind of a citrus fruit), grate sparingly – just one scrape of your grater will remove the colourful zest; the white pith below is bitter, so avoid this. Always use organic fruit: this ensures that the zest is free from the chemicals that may collect in and on the skin of conventionally grown fruit.

Carob brownie slice

When mixed, these ingredients form a viscous, near-black, substance that looks a bit like crude oil! When baked, however, this carob brownie slice is fudgy, delicious and more-ish. You can also use cocoa powder in the mix – or indeed convert the recipe into a fabulously rich, dense, chocolate brownie formula by substituting the carob with dark chocolate. This recipe works perfectly well with ordinary wheat flour – so no need to go out and buy any special flour if everyone you are cooking for is OK with wheat. I usually bake this slice in bread tins, then cut into slices rather than squares.

Small (makes 12-16 small slices)
(1 x 1kg / 2lb loaf tin)

85g (3oz / ¾ stick) butter

140g (5oz / 1 scant cup) muscovado sugar

40g (1½oz / ⅓ cup) rice flour

2 eggs

45g (1½oz / ⅓ cup) ground almonds (or more rice flour)

25g (1oz / 4 tbsp) carob (or cocoa) powder

1 pinch salt

¼ tsp vanilla essence

Large (serves 50-70)
(6 x 1kg / 2lb loaf tins)

500g (1lb 2oz / 4½ sticks) butter

840g (1lb 14oz)

250g (9oz / 2 cups)

12

250g (9oz / 2½ cups)

150g (6oz / 1½ cups)

1 tsp

1½ tsp

1. Grease and line the bread tins with baking parchment. Pre-heat the oven to 180°C (350°F / Gas Mark 4).

2. Melt the butter gently in a saucepan. Break up any lumps in the sugar and stir it into the melted butter. (If you are making the luxury chocolate brownie variation (see below), melt the chocolate, broken, *with* the butter in a double boiler – a bowl suspended over gently simmering water – rather than on a naked flame, before adding the other ingredients.)

3. Stir in the eggs, one or two at a time. Add the vanilla essence.

4. Combine the rice flour, ground almonds (if using) and salt, and stir into the mix. Next, add the sifted carob (or cocoa) powder and stir again, until you have a dark, gloopy mixture.

5. Pour the brownie mix into your prepared bread tins and place centrally in the oven. Bake for about 25 minutes – if using larger tins it may take longer. When ready a knife or skewer inserted in the middle will come out clean but moist, with maybe one or two small grains sticking to it. The cake will also feel springy to touch, with maybe a slight tinge of darker brown at the edges.

6. Leave to cool, then slice across, 'bread-style', into narrow 1cm (⅜")-thick slices of dense, fudgy cake.

Variation: For rich, real chocolate brownies, add 70% dark chocolate: 200g (7oz) for the small quantity; 1.2kg (2lb 12oz) for the large. Omit the carob/cocoa and reduce the sugar to 100g (4oz) for the small quantity; 600g (1½lb) for the large.

Transition plum & almond cake

In 2007, Transition Town Totnes (TTT) – mother of the Transition movement – celebrated its first anniversary. Tamsin Pinkerton, author of the Transition book *Local Food*, asked me to make a cake for the birthday party. Clearly a cake for a movement that aims at promoting local resilience to external change – through seed-swaps, farmers' markets, food hubs and by planting nut trees, etc., etc., would have to have a locally inspired cake ... Well, the plums were dripping off the plum tree in the Old Postern garden, and Riverford Dairy's delicious double cream was calling fatteningly from the fridge. The chickens were laying in the long grass at School Farm. And nuts – the recipe had to include nuts, even if the newly planted Totnes nut trees were still too young to produce any ...

1 medium round sandwich cake (serves 10) (2 x 23cm / 9" shallow cake tins)	**1 large rectangular sandwich cake (serves 30)** (2 x 38 x 23cm / 15" x 9" roasting tins)
175g (6oz / 1½ sticks) butter, softened	500g (1lb 2oz)
175g (6oz / 1 cup) golden granulated sugar + 1 tbsp extra for topping	500g (1lb 2oz) + 3 tbsp extra
110g (4oz / 1 scant cup) white flour	350g (12oz / 2½ cups)
2 tbsp polenta + 1 tbsp extra for topping	60g (2oz / ⅓ cup) + 3 tbsp extra
85g (3oz / ¾ cup) ground almonds	250g (9oz / 2½ cups)
3 eggs	9
2 tsp baking powder	2 tbsp
1 tsp ground cinnamon	1 tbsp
1 good pinch salt	¼ rounded tsp
approx. 2 tbsp milk	approx. 6 tbsp
approx. 3 tbsp flaked almonds	50g (2oz / ½ cup)
250g (9oz) fresh plums	750g (1lb 10oz)
100g (4oz / ½ cup) plum jam	340g (12oz / 1½ cups)
250ml (9fl oz / 1 cup) whipping or double cream	750ml (1½ pints / 3 cups)

1. Pre-heat the oven to 180°C (350°F / Gas Mark 4). Grease and line the tins with baking parchment.

2. Cream together the softened butter and sugar, then stir in the eggs, one or two at a time.

3. Mix together the flour, polenta, ground almonds, cinnamon, baking powder and salt. Fold this into the creamed mixture with a little milk to get a soft dropping consistency.

4. Spread half the mixture into one tin. Then spread *half* the remaining mixture into the other tin – leaving a quarter of the total mixture still in the bowl for later: this means that the batter in one of the tins will be half the thickness of the other. Bake in the oven for about 20 minutes.

5. While the cake is cooking, halve the plums lengthways and remove the stones. Cutting along the dimple of the plum allows you to find the stone lying flat and easier to remove, especially if using 'free stone' plums.

6. Remove the thinner cake from the oven when it is just set but scarcely browned at all (about 15-20 minutes, depending on the size). Spread the remaining cake mixture on top of this, then scatter with the flaked almonds and a little polenta before laying the halved plums on top, cut-side down. (The flaked almonds help to take the weight of the plums while the polenta absorbs juices.) Scatter meagrely with granulated sugar and return to the oven to finish baking. Your other cake may be done by now!

7. When the cakes are ready, they should be well risen and golden-brown – a knife or skewer should come out moist but clear of any cake mix.

8. Allow the cake with the plums on to cool in the tin. The other cake may be cooled on a wire cooling rack. Once the plummy cake is completely cool, loosen it around the edge, cover with either a clean cloth or bubble wrap (to cushion the plums) and invert it carefully on to a tray, rip off the baking parchment and then quickly turn the cake back again on to another board or cooling rack.

9. When the cakes are completely cool, place the plain one on a plate or chopping board. Spread liberally with plum jam, followed by a generous layer of whipped cream. Carefully lift the cake with the baked-in plums, and plant it gently on top of the cream. If making the larger version, ask someone to help you lift it using spatulas inserted under each end.

10. The plum and almond cake is now ready – though you may wish to streak a few iconoclastic jet-trails of melted chocolate over the top, as I often do – not local, but rather delicious and really puts into perspective where our cultural food journey has got to... !

Rich chocolate & hazelnut gateau

This lovely wheat-free 'gateau' is now one of my favourite chocolate cakes, and I am often asked for the recipe. It's not a child's chocolate cake: while dark and delicious, it is neither as dense nor as sweet as the now infamous American brownie.

I first came across the recipe when my friend Emma Hopkins asked me to bake it as her wedding cake. It comes from her friend Karen Austin, who runs the Lettercollum Kitchen Project in Ireland, and who, with some humour, manages to bring a bit of bodywork through into her cooking process, as you will see!

Having completed a Schumacher & Duchy Colleges diploma in horticulture with flying colours, Emma is now taking a part-time degree in Herbalism at London University – as well as caring for four sons, her husband and a dog called Buster. Good chocolate cake is just one of her well-deserved rewards.

1 medium cake (serves 8-12) (1 x 23cm / 9" loose-bottomed cake tin)	**3 bigger cakes (serves 40-50)** (3 x 28cm / 11" tins)
Cake	
300g (11oz) dark chocolate	1.2kg (2½lb)
150g (5½oz / 1½ sticks) butter, softened	600g (1lb 6oz)
150g (5½oz / ¾ cup) golden caster sugar	600g (1lb 6oz)
6 eggs	24
150g (5½oz / 1½ cups) hazelnuts	600g (1lb 6oz)
2 tsp baking powder* (optional – see Step 7)	2½ tbsp (optional – see Step 7)
1 small pinch salt	¼ tsp salt
Topping	
125g (4½oz) dark chocolate	500g (1lb 2oz)
75g (3oz / ¾ stick) butter	300g (11oz / 2¾ sticks)
100g (4oz / 1 cup) hazelnuts	400g (1lb)
100g (4oz / ¾ cup) natural glacé cherries	400g (1lb)

*If you want to keep this cake gluten-free, make sure you select GF baking powder.

1. Pre-heat the oven to 200°C (400°F / Gas Mark 6). Grease and line your cake tins with baking parchment.

2. *Nut preparation*: Spread both amounts of hazelnuts (for the cake and the topping) out on a metal baking tray one layer thick. Roast in the hot oven for 10 minutes until the skins are beginning to split open, revealing a creamy, lightly browning kernel. Next, rub off the skins by bundling the nuts together in a clean tea towel and rubbing them on someone's back . . . This is Karen Austin's "delicious patented hot nut massage". If there is no one around to enjoy your therapeutic offering, give yourself a hot thigh massage or rub the nuts between your hands. To brush away the skins, tip the nuts into a colander and go into the garden. Jump the nuts up and down so that some skins fly through the holes while others fly off in the wind. Don't worry if a few skins remain stuck on. Reduce the oven temperature to 180°C (350°F / Gas Mark 4).

3. Now weigh off the larger amount of nuts, for the cake, and leave the rest whole for the topping. Grind the amount for the cake in your food processor until they are as fine as you can get them (like coarse sand – or fine gravel!). Put aside.

4. Break and gently melt the chocolate for the cake (not the topping) in a heatproof bowl set over simmering water.

5. Beat the softened butter and sugar together until pale and creamy.

6. Separate the eggs, and stir the yolks into the creamed butter and sugar.

7. Whisk up the egg whites separately in a large bowl until snowy peaks are formed, adding a pinch of salt as you go. Once the whites are ready you will need to act quickly – bearing in mind that the swift and gentle incorporation of whipped whites into this cake is one of the secrets of its success. If making the large quantity, divide the cake mixture into two bowls, and the egg white into two more bowls, as this will greatly help you maintain a light operation with minimum beating. (If you feel unconfident about the process and wish to guarantee a good rise, the optional baking powder can be added, at the next stage.)

8. As soon as you are ready with the egg whites, add the melted chocolate to the butter/sugar/yolk mixture and fold in half the ground hazels. Now fold in half the whipped egg whites using a metal spoon, then the rest of the ground hazels (plus the baking powder, if using). Finally, add the rest of the egg whites, folding them in minimally. As soon as the mixture is fairly evenly speckled with white, stop mixing. Too much handling will burst the bubbles and lead to a deflated cake. Tip the mixture into your prepared cake tins and bake in the oven for 40-50 minutes. When ready, the cake will be well risen and a knife or skewer will come out clean. Leave to cool in the tin.

9. *Topping:* Gently melt together the chocolate for the topping with the butter in a bowl suspended over barely simmering water. Stir until smooth and set aside to cool. Halve the cherries, unless they are small, in which case you can keep them whole. When the chocolate mixture is beginning to thicken, 'sculpt' it over the sides of the cake, with a thinner layer on the top, using three-quarters or more of the icing. Gently re-warm the remaining chocolate icing until runny, then stir in the cherries and half of the reserved whole roasted hazels. Spoon these on to the cake. Finally, push the remaining whole hazels into the cracks between the lumps of chocolate-covered hazels and cherries. Leave to set.

Variations: The fruit-and-nut topping described here is my own addition, and chocolate lovers may wish to revert to Karen Austin's original recipe. For this, omit the cherries and just sculpt the chocolate topping over the whole cake in a plainer fashion, perhaps with just the whole roasted hazels scattered on top.

Pear & chocolate cake

Mother-of-pearl chunks of cooked pear bring a gentle fruity moistness to this bubbly chocolate cake. Making two shallow cakes, sandwiched together, allows for a good distribution of pears – overcoming the problem of all the pears collecting near the bottom of the cake, which can happen if you use a single deeper tin. Finish the cake with a dusting of icing sugar or, on special occasions, with the chocolate ganache given below, which contrasts subtly with dark chocolate bay leaves (see page 200). For a darker covering, the chocolate icing that goes with the Chocolate-courgette cake on page 190 can also be used. Keep refrigerated if not eaten straight away: like all cakes containing fresh fruit, this cake is best devoured within a couple of days.

This recipe is also the basis of the very simple Chocolate & pear topsy-turvy pudding, which we serve warm (see page 152).

1 small cake (serves 8-10) (2 x 23cm / 9" round sandwich tins)	**1 large rectangular cake (serves 30+)** (2 x 20 x 35cm / 8" x 14" tins)
3 medium pears (approx. 350g / 12 oz)	9 (approx. 1kg / 2lb 4oz)
100g (3½oz) dark chocolate	300g (11oz)
140g (5oz / 1¼ sticks) butter, softened	425g (15oz)
140g (5oz / ¾ cup) muscovado/granulated sugar mix	425g (15oz)
2 tbsp runny honey	6 tbsp (90ml / ⅓ cup)
3 eggs	9
200g (7oz / 1½ cups) plain or self-raising flour	600g (1lb 5oz)
1 tbsp baking powder (if using plain flour)	3 tbsp
1 tsp bicarbonate of soda	1 tbsp
25g (1oz / ¼ cup) cocoa powder	85g (3oz / ¾ cup)
¼ tsp mixed spice	¾ tsp
½ tsp organic orange zest	1½ tsp
2 tbsp fresh orange juice	90ml (3fl oz / ⅓ cup)
2 pinches salt	½ tsp
125ml (4fl oz / ½ cup) milk	375ml (12fl oz / 1½ cup)
100g (4oz / ½ cup) sticky jam (damson, apricot or plum)	340g (12oz / 1½ cups or 1 jar)

Ganache (for icing the cake)

125g (4oz) dark chocolate	350g (12oz)
125ml (4fl oz / ½ cup) whipping or double cream	350ml (12fl oz / 1½ cups)

1. Select pears that are ripe or firm – but avoid ones that are extremely hard and unripe, as the relatively short cooking time of the cake will not be enough to soften them. Very soft, mushy ones are also best avoided, as they will lose their shape when you stir them in. Peel, cut into four and core, then dice into chunks about 1cm (½") square. Set aside.

2. Chop up the dark chocolate into smallish chunky pieces – or use chocolate chips for speed (this will give a less interesting effect, as there will not be the same irregularity). Set aside.

3. Grease two small round or two large rectangular cake tins and line the bases with baking parchment. Pre-heat the oven to 180°C (350°F / Gas Mark 4).

4. Cream together the softened butter and sugar with the honey and orange zest. Blend in the orange juice too. Add the eggs, stirring in one or two at a time.

5. Measure together the flour, cocoa, salt, mixed spice and baking powder (if using). Sift this into the creamed mixture in two stages, stirring after the first addition and adding a little milk to ease the mixing in of the rest of the flour. Add the rest of the milk with the bicarbonate of soda so that the milk helps dissolve the soda (I normally spoon it into a puddle of milk on top of the mixture).

6. Tip in the pear chunks and chocolate pieces/chips and fold in gently until evenly incorporated.

7. Scoop the cake mixture into the prepared tins. Spread out a little and then bake for about 30 minutes until well risen, with a skewer inserted in the middle coming out clean but moist.

8. When the cakes are cool or almost cool, melt the jam gently in a saucepan. Move the base cake on to a plate or board, with the flatter bottom facing upwards. Spread the warm jam thinly over the surface and plant the second cake on top of it, so the bases are (literally!) jammed together. Allow to cool completely.

9. Now prepare the chocolate ganache (or see the next step). Chop up the chocolate and place in a heatproof bowl that fits snugly into a saucepan containing an inch or two of barely simmering water – ideally the bowl should not be actually touching the water. Cover with a lid. While the chocolate is gently melting, turn to whipping the cream until soft peaks form. Pour the hot melted chocolate on to the cream (not the other way round!), mixing as you go and whip until evenly blended. Spread the ganache over the top and sides of the cake using a palette knife. Before the icing sets, you can decorate simply by forking in a design, or decorate with chocolate bay leaves, crystallized flowers, nuts, etc. – the setting icing will hold your decorations in place.

10. Alternatively, use the simple dark chocolate icing that goes with the Chocolate-courgette cake on page 190, spreading it over the cake top and encouraging it to run temptingly down the edges (there will not be enough to completely cover the sides).

Cardamom cake

This deliciously moist, lightly spicy and modestly nutty cake is just the thing you need when you've invited a few (adult) friends around for coffee. It is gently rich, and the aroma of cardamom adds a subtle touch of the exotic. Anyone who wants to break free from the apron strings of a standard Victoria sandwich (while still secretly coveting that classic cakey texture) will deeply appreciate the blend. Leslie Glassmire introduced us to the original recipe, which she found in Mollie Katzen's *New Moosewood Cookbook*. She used to bake the cake often when she and her husband Bill ran a bakery in America. It soon became a firm favourite in our little patch of Devon too, when, after taking several short courses, Leslie joined Wayne's kitchen team as his most indispensable volunteer. Nowadays, we miss Leslie's gentle presence, and are reminded of her when we bake this cake. The honey and pistachios are my own additions, and can be left out when simplicity beckons.

1 small round cake (serves 8-10) (1 x 18cm / 7" round tin, 8cm / 3" deep)	**4 small or 2 large cakes (serves 40)** (4 x 18cm / 7" or 2 x 28cm / 11" round tins, all 8cm / 3" deep)
110g (4oz / 1 stick) butter, softened	500g (1lb 2oz)
100g (3½oz / packed ½ cup) light brown soft sugar	450g (1lb / 2⅔ cups)
140g (5oz / 1 cup) plain white flour (or self-raising)	600g (1lb 6oz / 4⅓ cups)
2 tsp baking powder (if using plain flour)	3 tbsp
2 tsp ground cardamom	3 tbsp
1 pinch salt	½ tsp
2 tsp honey	3 tbsp
2 eggs	9
½ tsp vanilla essence	2 tsp
125ml (4fl oz / ½ cup) sour cream or whole yoghurt	500ml (18fl oz / 2 cups)

Nut mixture

3 tbsp light brown sugar	50g (2oz / ⅓ cup)
½ tsp cinnamon	1 tbsp
25g (1oz / ¼ cup) walnuts	110g (4oz / 1 cup)
25g (1oz / ¼ cup) pistachios	110g (4oz / 1 cup)

(For my baked-in nut topping, you'll need half as much again of the nuts – see 'Fancy toppings', opposite.)

1. Begin by greasing the base of your cake tins and lining with baking parchment. Next, chop the nuts fairly finely and put each kind in a small bowl. Add half the sugar and cinnamon to each. Pre-heat the oven to 180°C (350°F / Gas Mark 4).

2. Measure and mix together the flour, ground cardamom, baking powder and salt. If you are preparing your own cardamom powder, first grind then sieve whole cardamom pods.

3. Cream the butter and (de-lumped) sugar together with the honey, then add the vanilla essence and the eggs, one or two at a time.

4. Now add some of the flour mix to the wet mix. Then add some of the sour cream, then more of the flour mixture, etc., until all is combined.

5. Tip one-third of the cake mixture into the cake tins and sprinkle either the chopped pistachio or the chopped walnut mixture over this. Spoon another third of the cake mix over this and then sprinkle over the other nut mix, followed by another layer of cake mix. Bake in the oven for 30-40 minutes (small tins) or 1-1¼ hours (large tins). When ready, allow to cool in the tins for 20 minutes, then invert on to a plate and back on to a wire rack. Mollie Katzen suggests you allow the cake to cool for at least 30 minutes before "wildly devouring"! Dust with icing sugar if you like

Fancy toppings:

Baked-in nut decoration: For special occasions, hold back a quarter of the cake mix and spread it on the cakes when they are just on the verge of being fully cooked. This acts as a layer of sweet 'cement' into which you can press concentric circles of (extra) pistachios and walnuts (chopped and halves). The decorating has to be done quickly, so the cake loses very little heat and can continue baking quickly once returned to the oven.

Iced-in nut decoration: I have sometimes topped this cake with a cardamom-lemon-vanilla butter icing pressed with nuts in a similar design. See lemon butter icing, page 179, but use less lemon juice and leave out the zest. Add a little ground cardamom and vanilla to taste.

Chocolate-courgette cake

This is a popular adaptation of the 'Julia's chocolate cake' recipe in *Gaia's Kitchen*. For anyone looking for a way to get their child to eat vegetables, hiding them in chocolate provides a lush way of achieving the goal! The peeled and finely grated courgettes (zucchini) add moisture to the cake – but you don't taste (or see) them at all. Recipes that involve adding vegetables to cake probably evolved when there were gluts of particular vegetables and people were tempted to put them into everything: soup, bread, stew – and cake. Sometimes the combinations would work – and sometimes they wouldn't. This one certainly does work. Indeed, it was one of my son's favourite cakes to share with his Park School classmates when they walked down through the woods and fields of Dartington with their teacher Alice Hoare to collect conkers from the famous Old Postern horse chestnut tree.

1 small 3-layered cake (serves 8-10)
(3 x 17cm / 7" round tins, 3cm / 1" deep)

85g (3oz / ¾ stick) butter, softened
85g (3oz / ½ cup) muscovado/granulated sugar mix
2 tbsp golden syrup or honey
2 eggs
2-3 drops vanilla essence (optional)
Half a medium courgette (100-140g / 4-5oz)
25g (1oz / ¼ cup) cocoa powder
115g (4oz / ¾ cup) plain or self-raising white flour
1½ tsp baking powder (if using plain flour)
1 tsp bicarbonate of soda
1 pinch salt
4 tbsp milk

Filling
85g (3oz / ¾ stick) butter
85g (3oz / ⅔ cup) icing sugar
1½ tbsp cocoa powder
2 tbsp golden syrup or honey
50g (2oz / ½ cup) ground roast hazelnuts (optional)

2 larger 3-layered cakes (serves 50-60)
(6 x 28cm / 11" round tins, 3cm / 1" deep)

500g (1lb 2oz)
500g (1lb 2oz)
150ml (5fl oz / ⅔ cup)
12
½ tsp (optional)
4 medium (600-800g / 1lb 4oz-1lb 12oz)
180g (6oz / 1½ cups)
700g (1lb 9oz)
3 tbsp
2 tbsp
½ tsp
350ml (12fl oz / 1⅓ cups)

500g (1lb 2oz)
500g (1lb 2oz)
6-8 tbsp (100g / 3½oz / ¾ cup)
150ml (5fl oz / ½ cup)
300g (12oz / 2 cups) (optional)

Dark chocolate icing (covers tops only – to cover the sides also, use a ganache: see Step 8)

70g (2½oz) 70% dark chocolate	200g (7oz)
20g (½oz) butter	50g (2oz / ½ stick)
1 tbsp water, coffee, orange juice or milk	3 tbsp

1. Grease the sandwich tins and line the bases with baking parchment. Pre-heat the oven to 180°C (350°F / Gas Mark 4).

2. Cream together the butter, sugar and golden syrup (or honey). Add the eggs, one or two at a time. Also add the vanilla essence, if using.

3. Peel the courgettes and then, ideally, grate on the fine side of your grater to produce gratings of courgette that are only 1-2mm (¹⁄₁₆") wide. If you don't have this option on your grater, the slightly thicker side will do.

4. Stir the grated courgette into the butter/sugar/egg mixture.

5. Measure together the flour, cocoa, salt and baking powder. Sift this into the courgette mixture in two stages, stirring well after the first addition. When it comes to the second addition, add some of the milk to ease the mixing. When you add the rest of the milk, add the bicarbonate of soda with it, so the milk helps dissolve the soda (I normally add it to a puddle of milk on top of the mixture).

6. Scoop the cake mixture into your prepared tins. As this is a three-layered cake, each layer should only be about 1cm / ½" (or less) thick before cooking. Spread out a little and then bake for 20-30 minutes until well risen: a skewer inserted in the middle will come out clean but moist. Leave in the tins for 5 minutes, then transfer to wire racks to cool thoroughly.

7. *Filling:* Cream together the softened butter, icing sugar, cocoa and golden syrup or honey until smooth and soft. Include the roast, skinned, ground hazels if you want to go for this more adult option (see page 185 for advice on how to prepare the nuts). Put the base cake, flatter side up (what was the top now becomes the bottom), on a plate that supports its curved shape well. Spread the filling on the top of the cake, about 0.5cm (¼") thick – only use half the filling if you've got three layers. Lift the other cake on to the filling so that the flat bases of the two cakes are now sandwiched together, with the filling peeping out between them. If you've got a third layer to put in place, use a bread knife to cut off the rounded top of the second cake, then spread the remaining filling over this, and finally put the third cake in place, flat side down.

8. *Icing:* Here are three options, with varying degrees of lavishness that will suit different occasions and tastes. a) Simply dust the cake with icing sugar. b) Make a dark chocolate icing, by combining the ingredients given above in a bowl suspended over hot water. Melt and stir until smooth (see tip on page 195), then spread over the top, encouraging the icing to dribble over the edges a bit. c) If you want to cover the top *and* sides, use the ganache on page 187 (as pictured in the photo opposite). Keep the quantities the same for icing the small cake, but for the two large chocolate-courgette cakes, *almost* double the large quantity given for the chocolate and pear cake (e.g. use 600g / 1lb 5oz dark chocolate and 600ml / 1 pint double cream) .

Dundee fruit cake

When it comes to cake – both eating and making – Sandy Lovelock is a bit of a devotee. Indeed, for over a decade she and Jim came to Schumacher College every year to discuss Gaia theory with the MSc Holistic Science students - and were introduced by Director Anne Phillips as *two people who unashamedly say that their favourite food is cake*! Being both so fit and slim, a merry twinkle would spread across their faces and you could tell they did not mind the reputation at all! On the occasion of Jim Lovelock's 90th birthday party at Blenheim Palace, in 2009, he listed his secrets for a long life as "a sound constitution, a daily walk, a good doctor and something to look forward to with each decade . . .". Once you have all these in place, life can not only *include* a regular piece of cake – it can *be* one!

This recipe from Sandy makes a lovely moist fruit cake: very traditional and wholesomely beautiful with its baked-in almond surface, reminiscent of cobblestones in a stable yard. Because the cake is fed with alcohol after baking, it keeps well and is useful to save for future occasions when there simply won't be time to cook everything fresh on the day.

1 smaller round cake or 2 loaf cakes (1 x 23cm / 9" or 2 x 1kg / 2lb loaf tins)	**2 larger round cakes or 6 loaves** (2 x 28cm / 11" tins or 6 x 1kg loaf tins)
175g (6oz / 1½ sticks) butter	500g (1lb 2oz)
175g (6oz / 1 cup) light muscovado sugar	500g (1lb 2oz)
Zest of 1 organic orange and 1 organic lemon	Zest of 3 and 3
1 squeeze lemon juice (approx. 1 tbsp)	3 tbsp
2 tsp molasses or black treacle	2 tbsp
1 tbsp brandy, rum or whisky	3 tbsp
3 eggs	9
225g (8oz / 1½ cups) plain flour	680g (1½lb)
2 tsp baking powder	2 tbsp
25g (1oz / ¼ cup) ground almonds	85g (3oz / ¾ cup)
1 tsp mixed spice	1 tbsp
1 pinch salt	¼ tsp
85g (3oz / ½ cup) natural glacé cherries, halved	250g (9oz / 1½ cups)
150g (5oz / 1 cup) currants	450g (1lb / 3 cups)
115g (4oz / ¾ cup) raisins	350g (12oz / 2½ cups)

100g (4oz / ¾ cup) sultanas	300g (12oz / 2 cups)
50g (2oz / ⅓ cup) candied citrus peel, chopped	150g (6oz /1 cup)
50g (2oz / ⅓ cup) dried apricots, chopped	150g (6oz / 1 cup)
85g (3oz / ⅔ cup) blanched almonds (for topping)	250g (9oz /2 cups)
approx. 6-8 tbsp (100ml / ½ cup) more brandy, rum or whisky for feeding with (i.e. the same spirit as used in the cake)	300ml (12fl oz / 1½ cups)

1. Combine the sugar with the chopped butter in a mixing bowl, and leave in a warm place to soften.

2. Grease your cake tins with butter and line them with baking parchment. It is very important to line both the base and the walls, as the cake is going to stay in the tin for some time and you don't want the metal of the tin to blacken it, as can happen with some older tins.

3. Weigh out all the dry ingredients (except the almonds for the top) and mix together. Set aside.

4. Blanch the almonds for the topping, if you are using whole almonds: place them in boiling water for two minutes, then scoop out with a perforated spoon and slip the skins off. If you are making the large quantity, avoid draining all the nuts in one go, as the skins tend to shrink back on as they dry – so skin them spoonful by spoonful. Set aside.

5. Pre-heat your oven to 170°C (325°F / Gas Mark 3).

6. Cream together the softened butter and sugar. When light and creamy, stir in the molasses or treacle, followed by the grated orange and lemon zest, then the lemon juice and your chosen alcohol. Next stir in the eggs, one or two at a time.

7. Add the dry ingredients (flour, fruit etc.), in two or three stages. Stir just enough after each addition to allow all the fruit to be evenly incorporated. Spoon the cake mixture into the prepared tins – ensuring it is no deeper than about 4cm (2") in any tin, as this will encourage faster and more even baking.

8. Smooth over the tops of the cakes and then arrange the blanched almonds over the surface in concentric circles, working from the outside inwards if you are making round cakes, and in short horizontal lines if you are decorating the loaf cakes. On the round cakes, place the nuts side-to-side with the tips pointing inwards; on the rectangular cakes, tip-to-tip: this minimizes the amount of nut you will have to cut through later – allowing you to cut, for the most part, between the almonds.

9. Bake for 1-2½ hours or until a skewer comes out clean. The larger round cakes will probably take the full 2 hours, whereas the loaves may only take one hour and the smaller round cake will be somewhere in between. Allow to cool in the tin.

10. When cool, make skewered holes between the nuts (about 2cm / 1" apart) then feed with brandy, rum or whisky – don't mix your spirits: use the same one you've used in the cake mix. Feed every day or two for up to a week (two or three feeds in total), keeping the cake covered in between. You can eat it a week or two after you've baked the cake – but it will keep and improve for a month at least.

Chocolate & almond sachertorte

This chocolate cake is amazingly delicious considering that it doesn't contain any butter. It is an absolute godsend when it comes to special-diet catering, because it appeals to both gluten-free and dairy-avoiding chocolate lovers – in fact it is one of the most popular cakes at the College, and often requested even by people who eat everything! Another great thing about *sachertorte* is that it improves over the course of a week and can therefore be made in advance with impunity and kept in an airtight tin, ready for last-minute icing.

For those adept at making real sponge cakes, the baking powder may be left out: it has been added as a security against over-zealous folding-in of whipped egg whites.

1 cake (serves 12-15) (1 x 25cm / 10" round tin)	3 cakes (serves 40-45) (3 x 25cm / 10" round tins)
Cake	
200g (7oz) dark chocolate	600g (1lb 5oz)
225g (8oz / 1 rounded cup) golden granulated sugar	675g (1½lb / 3⅓ cups)
50g (2oz / ⅓ cup) muscovado sugar	150g (6oz / 1 cup)
6 egg	18
1 tbsp strong fresh or instant coffee (use 1 tsp granules + 2 tsp boiling water)	3 tbsp (use 3 tsp + 2 tbsp water)
125g (5oz / 1¼ cup) ground almonds	375g (15oz)
1 heaped tsp baking powder* (optional)	3 tsp (optional)
1 pinch salt	3 pinches
Topping	
150g (5oz) dark chocolate	450g (1lb)
50g (2oz / 4 tbsp) butter**	150g (5oz / 1¼ sticks)
50g (2oz / ⅓ cup) whole or flaked almonds	150g (6oz / 1 cup)
5-6 tbsp apricot jam (double if sandwiching)	340g (12oz / 1½ cups) (double if sandwiching)

1. Use tins that are at least 6cm (2½") deep with detachable bases, and line with baking parchment. Pre-heat the oven to 180°C (350°F / Gas Mark 4).

2. Chop up the chocolate for the cake and place in a heatproof bowl set in a saucepan of simmering water (see tip below). Melt gently.

3. Separate the eggs and beat the egg yolks and sugar together until pale and creamy. Dissolve the instant coffee in boiling water and add to the creamed mixture – or add the strong, fresh coffee.

*If you want to keep this cake gluten-free, make sure you select GF baking powder. **For dairy-free diets, use margarine or coconut oil instead of butter.

4. Whisk up the egg whites in a large bowl with a rotary or electric whisk. Beat until gentle snowy peaks are formed, then add a pinch or two of salt and continue to whisk until stiff peaks are formed. Once the whites are ready you will need to act quickly, bearing in mind that the swift and gentle incorporation of whipped whites into this cake is one of the secrets of its success, as the bubbles contribute to the leavening of the cake.

5. As soon as you are ready with the egg whites, add the still-warm melted chocolate to the yolk/sugar mixture and fold in half the ground almonds (plus the baking powder, if using). Next fold in half of the whipped egg whites, using a metal spoon, then the rest of the ground almonds. Finally, add the rest of the egg whites, folding them in minimally. As soon as the mixture is fairly evenly coloured with egg white, stop mixing. Too much handling will burst the bubbles and the cake won't rise quite so much. Tip the mixture into your prepared tins. Bake for about 35-45 minutes (or just 20 minutes if you're subdividing the cakes and sandwiching them together – see variation below). For the deeper cakes, cover loosely with foil or baking parchment after 30 minutes to prevent the top burning. The cake is ready when it's well risen, shrinking slightly from the edges of the tin, and a knife or skewer inserted in the middle will come out clean. Leave to cool in the tin. Increase the oven temperature to 200°C (400°F / Gas Mark 6), if you will be toasting the almonds in the oven (see Step 7).

6. While the cake is still warm, spread the top with apricot jam using the back of a teaspoon. The heat of the cake will melt the jam, so it soaks into the top of the cake a little – and then sets as the cake cools, making a good surface for the chocolate to spread over. (If you forget to add the apricot jam at this stage, you'll need to melt it before spreading on to the cake later.)

7. Blanch the almonds by immersing in boiling water for 1 minute and then slipping off the skins. Pat dry and toast in the hot oven for 8-10 minutes. Alternatively, use toasted flaked almonds – which will take only 3-5 minutes in the oven or 1 minute under a grill.

8. *Chocolate icing:* Gently melt together the chocolate for the topping with the butter (see tip below). Stir together until smooth and remove from the heat. Remove the cooled cake from the tin and slide a large knife or spatula under it to remove the baking parchment. Pour the icing into the middle of the cake, on top of the apricot jam. Spread it out with a palette knife, carefully coaxing it over the edges and smoothing it over the sides – if it's very runny, leave to thicken for a few minutes before covering the edges. Decorate the top with the roasted blanched almonds (or toasted flaked almonds). Leave to set.

Variation: Make the cake in two sandwich tins and reduce the cooking time. Sandwich together with more apricot jam – our MA student Brigita Lajkovic tells me this is the traditional way of preparing *sachertorte* where she comes from, in the Czech Republic. I often now use this method (as pictured): the cakes cook more quickly and are less prone to sink in the middle. If using this method, you'll need double the amount of apricot jam – and, for a less sticky handling process, spread the top layer of (hot) jam only after you've sandwiched the layers together.

Tip: Chocolate can be temperamental stuff to melt. If it gets too hot or a cold liquid enters the pan, it can seize up and turn into a stiff 'truffle' mix, just when you least want it to! For foolproof melting, place the chocolate in a heatproof bowl suspended over a pan containing a few centimetres (or inches) of barely simmering water — the base of the bowl should be surrounded by steam, not touching the water. Never let the water go beyond simmering point — and, for small quantities, turn the flame right off. Use a lid to help focus the warmth evenly on the chocolate. Lastly, don't stir the chocolate until you can see that it is at least half or two-thirds melted.

Dartington apple cake

Every cook has their own favourite recipe for apple cake, and this is mine – evolved over the years of using the abundant Dartington apples from School Farm. I dedicate it to Voirrey and all the eager, tree-climbing course participants, students and helpers who have shinned the trunks, shaken the branches and dodged the fruity bombings. This cake can be made just as a loaf or slab cake, or as a sandwich cake. I prefer to use fairly tart apples, such as Coxs or even cookers, as these will keep a nice strong apple flavour when cooked, but almost any apple will work. Store the cake in the fridge – if not eaten up straight away!

1 small sandwich cake or 2 loaves (serves 10-12) (2 x 22cm / 9" round tins or 2 x 1kg / 2lb loaf tins)	**2 round layer cakes or 1 large slab cake (serves 45-50)** (4 x 28cm / 11" round tins or 1 x 47cm x 30cm / 19" x 12" roasting tin)
300g (10oz / 2 cups) apples	1kg (2lb 4oz / 7 cups)
110g (4oz / 1 stick) butter, softened	325g (12oz / 3 sticks)
110g (4oz / ⅔ cup) muscovado/granulated sugar mix	325g (12oz / 2 cups)
3 eggs	9
2 tsp molasses or malt extract	2 tbsp
2 tsp honey or golden syrup	2 tbsp
1 tbsp lemon juice and a little organic zest	Juice + zest of 1 lemon
1 tbsp orange juice and a little organic zest	Juice + zest of 1 orange
50g (2oz / ⅓ heaped cup) sultanas	150g (6oz / 1 heaped cup)
50g (2oz / ⅓ heaped cup) apricots, chopped	150g (6oz / 1 heaped cup)
180g (6oz / 1⅓ level cups) plain flour	550g (1lb 4oz / 4 level cups)
1 level tbsp baking powder	3 tbsp
½ tsp ground cinnamon	1½ tsp
½ tsp mixed spice	1½ tsp
1 pinch salt	½ tsp salt
25g (1oz / ¼ cup) sunflower seeds or chopped walnuts (optional)	75g (3oz / 1 cup) (optional)
1 red-skinned dessert apple for decoration	3
A little sunflower oil and/or butter	approx. 100ml (4fl oz / ½ cup)
5-6 tbsp apricot jam (if sandwiching)	1 jar – if making 4 small or 2 large sandwich cakes

1. Grease and line the tins with baking parchment and pre-heat the oven to 180°C (350°F / Gas Mark 4).

2. Measure together the butter, sugar, molasses/syrup and honey and put into a warm place to soften.

3. Peel, cut, core and further cut the apples until you have a bowl of roughly 1cm (½") chunky pieces. Check the weight of the prepared apples and adjust the amount if necessary. Also slice the red-skinned apple carefully into narrow half-moon slices with the core removed and the skin left on. Spread these out on a plate and paint on one side with sunflower oil and/or melted butter. Set aside.

4. Blend together the butter and sugar until creamy. Stir in the zest and juice of the lemon and orange. Add the eggs, one or two at a time.

5. Measure the flour, spices, baking powder and salt together and sift this into the butter/sugar/egg mixture in two or three stages. Mix enough to remove lumps and smoothly incorporate the flour, then mix in the apples, sultanas, apricots and chopped nuts / sunflower seeds (if using). Tip the mixture into the prepared tins.

6. Decorate the surface of the cake by laying the red sliced apple lightly on top, oiled side up to prevent drying out. If you are making a sandwich cake, only decorate one cake – with a ring of apples around the edge. Finally, sprinkle the decorative apple surface with a little granulated sugar and cinnamon – and more chopped walnuts or sunflower seeds if you like. The mixture in the sandwich tins should only be about 1.5-2cm (¾") thick.

7. Bake in the oven for 30/40/60 minutes (small loaf / round tin / roasting tin), until well risen and firmish to the touch. A knife inserted in the middle will come out clean and will also pierce through the cooked apples as easily as if they were butter!

8. Allow to cool in the tins. If making a sandwich cake, invert the base cake on to a suitable plate (so that what was its top is now its bottom), spread with the apricot jam, and carefully place the decorated cake on top.

Polish walnut-coffee cake

This is an excellent recipe to whisk up for people with wheat- and gluten-free diets. It comes to us from Sonia Hulejczuk, who attended several of the College's Roots of Learning courses – a series specially designed for teachers wanting to learn more about holistic education and happy to come on courses in deepest Devon during their half-term holidays.

The very existence of this walnut cake recipe, as a living formula in Sonia's family and community, is a lesson in the resilience of domestic culture in the face of political upheaval – and it is a lesson on what makes people feel whole. Being allowed to continue to make special food associated with happy times scores high up on the list! Sonia's grandmother and aunt memorized the recipe and brought it with them from a small village called Kuty in what was then Eastern Poland (and is now part of the Ukraine). With the recipe in their heads, they made a tortuous journey for freedom through Siberia, Asia, Persia and Kenya, to Liverpool and finally to London. Now, in times of peace, Sonia's Polish cousins have long since come down from the Siberian mountains – and when Sonia and her father made a return visit to their relations in Kuty, they were welcomed with this cake.

Because the wheat content was so minimal, Sonia found early on that she could successfully adapt it to her own wheat-free diet. She also reduced the sugar content to suit the modern palette, and this is how we serve it at Schumacher College. (In the version in this photo, an especially fancy decoration has been created for the birthday of Richenda Macregor, a local potter – when not facilitating courses at the College and elsewhere. Given Richenda's craft, some marzipan pottery seemed a fitting adornment for her cake. With thanks to Elizabeth Hawk for commissioning this surprise.)

1 small sandwich cake (serves 10-12)
(2 x 23cm / 9" round tins)

225g (8oz / 2 cups) + 50g (2oz / ½ cup) walnuts

160g (6oz) 50:50 caster / light muscovado sugar mix

7 medium eggs, separated

2 tsp whisky

1 tbsp coffee powder dissolved in 1 tbsp boiling water

3 tbsp gluten-free flour (or ordinary white, if preferred)

1 tbsp buckwheat flakes (or rolled oats or breadcrumbs)

2 tsp baking powder* and 1 pinch salt

3 small cakes, 2 medium or 1 larger (3-layer) cake (serves 30+)
(6 x 23cm / 9" or 4 x 28cm / 11" or 3 x 30cm / 12" tins)

675g (1½lb) + 150g (6oz)

500g (1lb 2oz)

21

2 tbsp

3 tbsp in 3 tbsp

70g (2½oz / ½ cup)

3 tbsp

2 tbsp and ½ tsp

If you want to keep this cake gluten-free, make sure you select GF baking powder.

Filling

140g (5oz / 1¼ sticks) butter, softened

225g (8oz / 1¾ cups) icing sugar, sifted

1 tbsp coffee powder dissolved in 1 tbsp boiling water

450g (1lb / 6 sticks)

680g (1½lb / 5¼ cups)

3 tbsp in 3 tbsp

Icing

Add to remaining filling:

85g (3oz / ¾ cup) more icing sugar

2 tsp coffee powder dissolved in 2 tsp water

250g (9oz / 2¼ cups)

2 tbsp in 2 tbsp

1. Begin by chopping up all the walnuts into quite small pieces – like coarse breadcrumbs. You don't want the pieces to be too large, or they will sink to the bottom of the cake – but nor do you want them as fine as sand, as you'll lose the interesting texture. A food processor is good for this job, though it can also be done with a knife or mezzaluna. Separate off the smaller amount of chopped nuts and put these aside for decorating the cake later.

2. Mix the larger amount of walnuts with the flour, baking powder and buckwheat flakes (or oats or breadcrumbs).

3. In a separate bowl, combine the egg yolks and sugar. Beat until light and creamy, then add the whisky and coffee essence.

4. Grease and line the base of the cake tins with baking parchment, then grease the parchment with butter/sunflower oil. Pre-heat the oven to 180°C (350°F / Gas Mark 4).

5. Fold half the combined dry ingredients into the creamed yolk and sugar, and then mix in the rest. The mixture will be quite stiff.

6. Whisk up the egg whites with a pinch of salt until snowy peaks are formed. Fold the whipped whites into the cake mix, adding a little at a time to begin with so that the mixture begins to loosen up. Once it begins to feel quite sloppy, gently fold in the rest of the whites, being careful not to beat them. You want the whites to remain as foamy as possible, as the trapped bubbles will contribute to the leavening of the cake.

7. Pour this marshmallow-like mixture into the tins so that it is about 2cm (1") deep. Place in the centre of the oven undisturbed for about 25 minutes. Test with a knife or skewer, inserting it in the middle. If it comes out clean, the cakes are cooked. Allow to cool for a few minutes. Then go around the edges with a knife and tip on to wire racks to continue to cool. Remove the baking parchment.

8. *Filling:* Blend together the softened butter, sifted icing sugar and coffee essence until creamy. Use some of this to sandwich the cakes together, making the filling about 0.5cm (¼") thick. Add the extra icing sugar and coffee essence to the remaining butter icing and spread this more thinly over the sides and top of the cake. Press the chopped walnuts into the butter icing on the edges of the cake, and decorate the top with a few whole walnuts.

Variation: A 'mocha' theme, can be achieved by substituting the buttercream icing with the dark chocolate icing used for the Rich chocolate & hazelnut gateau on page 184. Alternatively, add melted dark chocolate to the surplus filling instead of icing sugar (same weight).

For dairy-free diets: Use margarine instead of butter in the filling and icing.

Chocolate bay leaves

Chocolate leaves add a beautiful touch of natural decoration to special cakes and are very simple to make. Bay leaves are the ideal leaf to use, because they are strong enough to support melted chocolate and have a waxy surface. Also, you can rest assured in the knowledge that, because they are edible, they will not taint the chocolate.

1. Pick 6-12 bay leaves – choosing the best specimens. Rinse or wipe them clean, then dry them or leave them to dry.

2. Melt a minimum of 50g (2oz) of chopped dark chocolate in a bowl suspended over simmering water, initially with a lid on the bowl. The water should not touch the bottom of the bowl. Once the water is simmering, turn it off, so the chocolate melts at the lowest heat necessary – so as to preserve its sheen or 'tempering'. Don't stir it until you see that it is melting well, and then keep your stirring to a minimum, as chocolate can thicken if disturbed too much at this stage.

3. When the chocolate is evenly melted, take a teaspoon and spread a layer of chocolate over the underside of the leaves. This should be 2-3mm (⅛") thick. Don't worry about a few lumps or bumps. The important thing is to try to spread the chocolate right up to the edge of the leaf – but not over it. There's no need to cover the stalk. Lay the leaves uncoated side down on some non-stick baking parchment on a tray or plate. When you've coated all your leaves, put them to cool in the fridge.

4. When the chocolate has set thoroughly (10-15 minutes), the leaf can be very carefully peeled away from its chocolate coating. Don't worry if your first chocolate leaf breaks – you will soon get the knack of separating green from brown. If, as you are peeling away the green leaf, you notice the chocolate to be extremely thin in one spot, stop separating the two and instead gently press them together again, apply a few extra blobs of chocolate to the thin area, and leave to re-set in the fridge.

5. Once the chocolate leaves are ready, and free from any condensation that may have come from the fridge, you can varnish them with a vegetarian confectioner's glaze,* which gives chocolate leaves a nice shine that will contrast lusciously with whipped cream or a lighter brown ganache. They are also beautiful unvarnished. Store in a box, in a cool place or the fridge, avoiding anywhere very damp, as this can lead to the leaves discolouring.

*Corn-protein-based glazes should be available on the shelves of cake-decorating counters in certain specialist kitchen shops (and online) – avoid selecting 'edible shellac', which is not vegetarian: it is made from a resin produced by the laccifer lacca beetle, hundreds of thousands of which will die in the production process just to get 1kg of 'lac'.

Coconut cake

This light coconut cake was inspired by a Norwegian boat trip. Per Ingvar Haukeland, Schumacher College teacher and disciple of Arne Naess, invited us to board his family yacht and share some of his mum's delicious coconut cake. It was the first time I'd had coconut cake since being served it drowned in custard at primary school, so this came as a cakey revelation, and when I got home I found I could make my own version using the ingredients we already had in the College food store.

1 small slab cake
(or 2 x small round cakes) (serves 16-20)
(1 x 30 x 25cm / 12 x 10" tin or 2 x 20cm / 8" round tins)

200g (7oz) organic creamed coconut (block)	
150g (5oz / 1¼ sticks) butter	
300g (10oz / 1½ cups) granulated sugar	
5 eggs	
350g (12oz / 2½ cups) white plain or self-raising flour	
4 tsp baking powder (if using plain flour)	
½ tsp salt	
110g (4oz / 1⅓ cup) desiccated coconut	
3-4 tbsp milk	
100g (4oz / ½ heaped cup) raspberry jam (for topping)	
25g (1oz / ⅓ cup) more desiccated coconut, toasted (for topping)	

1 large slab cake
(serves 50-60)
(1 x 28 x 48cm / 11 x 19" tin)

400g (14oz)
300g (10oz / 2½ sticks)
600g (1lb 5oz)
10
700g (1½lb)
2 tbsp
1 tsp
225g (8oz / 2⅔ cups)
approx. 100ml (4fl oz / ½ cup)
225g (8oz / 1 heaped cup)
50g (2oz / 1 cup)

1. Roughly chop and then gently melt the creamed coconut in a saucepan on a low heat. Allow to cool a little. Pre-heat your oven to 180°C (350°F / Gas Mark 4). Grease and line the cake tins with baking parchment.

2. Cream together the softened butter and sugar. Once the lumps have gone from the butter, add the melted creamed coconut and blend some more. Add the eggs, one or two at a time.

3. Measure together the flour, baking powder, salt and desiccated coconut. Fold these dry ingredients into the wet mixture in two or three batches. Add a little milk – enough to give a soft dropping consistency.

4. Pour the cake mixture into the prepared tins. It should come to a depth of about 2cm (1"). Bake for about 30-45 minutes until well risen and golden-brown. A knife or skewer inserted in the middle should come out clean but moist. Leave the oven on and the cake in the tin.

5. Prepare the desiccated coconut by spreading it out thinly in a baking tray and toasting it in the oven until just beginning to brown – it will be speckled white-brown when mixed. This can also be done under a grill – but you have to be very vigilant as it will burn quickly! Set aside.

6. Melt the raspberry jam in a small saucepan and then spread it in a 1-2mm (¹⁄₁₆") thin layer over the top of the still-warm cake. Sprinkle the toasted desiccated coconut over this, tipping the tin from side to side to help spread the coconut evenly. Press the coconut down gently with your clean hand or a rolling pin to help it stick firmly. Allow to cool and then cut the cake into roughly 5cm (2") squares or wedges to serve.

Fruity bread pudding-cake

Bread puddings have a long history, and were probably eaten hundreds of years ago in Totnes. Indeed, it is thought that the first bread puddings may have originated back in the medieval era, when loaves of hollowed-out bread were used by cooks as a kind of edible bowl in which to serve a sweet dish. With the amount of bread crusts and abandoned half-slices our Schumacher bread bins accumulate, we now find ourselves freezing the scraps and making a version of bread pudding-cake on a regular basis. Served cold and sliced in squares, it's excellent and popular for both coffee breaks and field trips. Our pud-cakes typically include an assortment of various breads, from sourdough rye to white polenta loaves – adding greatly to the depth of flavour. In the apple season, chunks of apple can also be added, creating an alternative form of apple cake.

For approx. 12 slices (2 x 1kg / 2lb loaf tin or 19 x 19cm / 7½" x 7½" roasting tin)	For 1 large slab cake (serves 50-60) (1 x 28cm x 48cm / 11" x 19" tin)
225g (8oz) stale brown or white bread	1.25kg (2½lb)
275ml (10fl oz / 1¼ cups) whole milk	1.4l (2½ pints / 3 US pints)
85g (3oz / ½ cup) brown sugar (+ 2 tbsp for top)	425g (15oz / 2½ cups) (+ ¼ cup)
50g (2oz / ½ stick) butter, melted	250g (9oz / 2¼ sticks)
2 eggs	10
50g (2oz / ½ cup) sultanas	250g (10oz / 2 cups)
50g (2oz / ½ cup) raisins	250g (10oz / 2 cups)
Zest of 1 organic lemon or 1 organic orange	Zest of 4-5
1 tsp mixed spice + ¼ tsp nutmeg, grated	1½ tsp + 1 rounded tsp
3 tsp rolled oats	100g (4oz / 1 cup)
300g (12oz / 3 cups) apple, peeled & chopped (optional)	approx. 1.5kg (3lb) (optional)

1. Grease and line your tins with baking parchment, or just butter the tins, and pre-heat the oven to 180°C (350°F / Gas Mark 4).

2. Break up the old or abandoned (but definitely *not* mouldy) bread. If you want to speed up the preparation time, you can then whizz the torn bread into crumbs in your food processor. Set aside 3 tbsp (½ cup) of fine breadcrumbs to scatter on the top later. Put the rest of the bread in a bowl and cover it with the milk. Soak for 30-60 minutes – the longer time is suitable for broken, as opposed to crumbed, bread.

3. When all the milk has been absorbed by the bread, there should be a sloshy mix with no very hard nuggets of crust outstanding (if there are hard nuggets of crust, rub them through a sieve or pick them out and compost them). Next add the melted butter, eggs, sugar, oats and mixed spice, followed by a good stirring, then the dried fruit and citrus zest, followed by another stir. If using apple, add it too at this stage.

4. Pour the mixture into the prepared tins. Sprinkle the top of the mixture with nutmeg, the reserved fine breadcrumbs and a little brown or demerara sugar. Bake in the oven for 45-60 minutes. Serve warm or cold, cut into generous squares.

Variation: Flaked almonds, sunflower and sesame seeds can also be scattered under the sugar for the topping.

Date, walnut & carrot cake

A wholesome cake that you can slice into healthy chunks and take on a ramble in the countryside! If you are one of those people who maintain you can't make fruit cakes because the fruit always sinks to the bottom, you'll love this one, because the grated carrot holds the fruit in place.

1 large or two small loaves (serves 8) (1 x 1kg / 2lb loaf tin or 2 x 500g / 1lb tins)	6 medium loaves (serves 50) (6 x 1kg / 2lb loaf tins)
150g (5oz / 1¼ sticks) butter, softened	600g (1lb 4oz)
100g (4oz / ⅔ cup) soft brown sugar	450g (1lb)
2 tsp malt extract (optional)	3 tbsp (optional)
Zest and juice of 1 organic orange	Zest and juice of 4
3 eggs	12
150g (5oz / 1 cup) white flour	600g (1lb 5oz)
100g (4oz / ¾ cup) brown or spelt flour	400g (14oz)
1 level tbsp baking powder	4 level tbsp
1 pinch salt	½-1 tsp
1 tsp mixed spice or ground cinnamon	1 rounded tbsp
175g (6oz / 1 cup) carrot, grated	700g (1½lb)
85g (3oz / ⅔ cup) walnuts, rough-chopped	350g (12oz / 2½ cups)
175g (6oz /1 cup) stoned dates, chopped	700g (1½lb)

1. Cream together the butter, sugar and malt extract, if using. Stir in the orange zest and juice, then add the eggs, one or two at a time.

2. In another bowl, mix together the chopped dates, chopped walnuts and grated carrot.

3. In a third bowl, combine the flour, baking powder, salt and spices.

4. Pre-heat your oven to 180°C (350°F / Gas Mark 4) and grease and line the loaf tins with baking parchment.

5. Fold the flour into the butter/sugar/egg/orange mixture. Finally, stir in the date/walnut/carrot combination and mix just enough to ensure an even distribution of ingredients.

6. Spoon the cake mixture into the prepared loaf tins. The mixture should be about 4cm (1½-2") deep and there should be a good 2cm (1") of rim still exposed for the cake to rise into. Bake mid-oven for 35-40 minutes. When ready, a knife will come out clean but moist and the cake will be beginning to come away from the edges. Cool for 15 minutes or so in the tin and then turn on to a wire rack to cool completely.

Moist-as-moss ginger cake

The sunken garden in the abandoned swimming pool at the Old Postern was lovingly created by one of the College's first short-course participants, Angela Malyon-Bein, with her partner John Griffin. With the help of our earliest students and teachers, they lined it with stone and made benches, fern beds and a waterfall. They then returned to building their own mud-brick house in Tasmania, entirely without the use of power tools. When we explored Tasmania with them many years ago, a moist dark ginger cake came with us on every foray. I have been baking it ever since, for both home and College – adapted only by the addition of molasses. (The imperial quantities have been rounded for ease of use – giving a slightly bigger cake.)

1 loaf cake (serves 8)	**7-8 loaf cakes (serves 50-60)**
(1 x 1kg / 2lb loaf tins)	(6 x 1kg / 2lb loaf tins)
100g (4oz / 1 stick) butter	800g (2lb)
150g (2oz / 3 tbsp) molasses or black treacle	400g (1lb / 1⅓ cups)
50g (2oz / 3 tbsp) golden syrup	400g (1lb / 1⅓ cups)
100g (4oz / ⅔ cup) muscovado sugar	800g (2lb)
200g (7oz / 1½ scant cups) plain white flour	1.6kg (3½lb)
¼ tsp salt	2 tsp
1 tsp mixed spice or ground cinnamon	2-3 tbsp
4 tsp ground ginger	70g (2½oz / rounded ½ cup)
1 tsp bicarbonate of soda	2 level tbsp + 2 level tsp
1 egg	8-9
150ml (¼ pint / ½ cup + 2tbsp) milk	1l (2 pints / 2½ US pints)

1. Butter the loaf tins and line with baking parchment. Pre-heat the oven to 180°C (350°F / Gas Mark 4).

2. Combine the flour, salt, spices and bicarbonate of soda in a bowl.

3. Roughly chop the butter and gently melt it in a saucepan that will be large enough to take the total mix. (If making the large quantity, swap to a large mixing bowl after the melting stage if you don't have a big enough saucepan.) Add the molasses and golden syrup to the almost-melted butter – using a low heat to avoid making toffee! Remove from the heat when the butter is melted.

4. Stir in the sugar, then the eggs. Next add half the flour mixture, then half the milk. Follow this with the rest of the flour and the rest of the milk. Mix well to remove any floury lumps.

5. Pour into your prepared tins, allowing an edge of 2-3cm (1") for rising.

6. Bake on the central oven shelf for 30-45 minutes. A knife inserted in the middle should come out moist but clean. Allow to settle in the tins for 10-15 minutes before cooling fully on wire racks. Cut into generous slices to serve.

Crystallized flowers

Crystallized flowers, made simply using egg white and fine white caster sugar, make a stunning decoration for any celebration cake. They can be prepared when in season and stored in a box until you need them. Suitable flowers are the simple-shaped, non-waxy, edible ones, such as primroses, violets, and the cultivated members of those families – the primulas and violas. Primroses are normally abundant in the countryside from March to April. Violets come at about the same time but are rarer – so by preference you should use cultivated violas, which flower throughout the summer and are often added to salads. Never take more than your share of any wild flower: they may be protected by law and need the chance to reproduce.

1. Lightly beat the egg white with a fork to break down the membrane (otherwise it can dribble off your flower in globs).

2. Hold your flower by a short length of stalk and, using a soft paintbrush, carefully paint it back and front with the egg white (ideally, use a paintbrush reserved for edible uses – I use a 1cm (½") flat sable brush). Just dipping the flower in egg white won't lead to an even covering, because of the flower's natural waterproofing.

3. Dust the front of the painted flower evenly with fine white caster sugar, using a small sieve or teaspoon (avoid using your warm fingers as this will cause the sugar to stick in uneven crumbs). Shake off surplus sugar. Repeat on the back of the flower.

4. Leave the flower face down on a piece of non-stick silicone baking parchment to dry. An airy warmish place such as a drying cupboard or boiler room is ideal for this. In the right spot your flowers should be ready in 1-3 days. They will be dried out and brittle, so handle carefully.

5. *Dealing with the green bits:* You can pinch off the stalks and calyxes of flowers straight away, or you may like to leave them intact, as it gives you something to hold on to. You can then pinch them off next day, once the petals have stiffened. Once this is removed, remember to crystallize the exposed part of the flower and leave it to dry out. The green calyx of a primrose can also be left on and crystallized along with the flower.

6. Arrange crystallized flowers on top of your cake before the icing sets. As the surface of the icing or ganache dries, the flowers will be held in place.

7. *A note on colour:* The natural colour of violas and primroses seems to keep its brightness well. Other petals, though – from roses, cherry blossom, polyanthus, etc. – have been noticed to fade over time when crystallized.

Cookies

Basic cookie/biscuit method

Most of the recipes in this section are a sort of hybrid 'cooscuit' that can be cooked either bigger and fatter with a softer middle, like a classic American 'cookie', or thinner and snappier like a classic English 'biscuit'. Because we have so many American visitors coming to the College, for whom a 'biscuit' means something different (a kind of scone), the word 'cookie' often creeps on to our lips at coffee break – but then it creeps off again at tea time, to be replaced with "mmm, biscuits . . .". The simple truth is that we lump biscuits and cookies together here. Terminology aside, here is a basic method for making these tempting snacks.

Beginning: Measure together all the *fine*-textured dry ingredients in a roomy bowl – no nobbly nuts or dried fruit at this stage!

Incorporating the butter: This can be done in various ways – fingertips, a grater or a food processor. Every cook has their own preference.

If you are grating butter into the mix straight from the fridge, you will need to regularly lift the grater and dust the grated fat with flour that is already in the bowl , otherwise it can get pressed together into a large clump inside the grater. Once grated, the butter needs to be rubbed in further with the fingertips to achieve a finer crumb, which is quickly done.

If rubbing in the butter with your fingertips from the start, remember to take it out of the fridge a few hours earlier, or even the day before. Chop it into the finer dry ingredients. You can then use a hand-held metal shredder to cut the lumps into the flour, or do the whole job with your fingertips. You are aiming for a fine 'breadcrumby' texture – don't press together at this stage. In cold weather I often warm the cookie/biscuit mix in the oven briefly, so that the butter pieces melt slightly and become easier to work in.

Adding texture: Having made your fine crumb mix, it is time to add other ingredients, so stir in any chopped nuts, fruit or chocolate chips, etc. Break apart any sticky chopped fruit with your fingers, to ensure all ingredients are evenly distributed.

Binding the dough: Make a shallow well in the middle of the dry ingredients and put into this any wet ingredients, for example egg, tahini, molasses, syrup. Sometimes the wet ingredients can be mixed together separately first, to aid even distribution. Cover the puddle of wet ingredients with some of the dry mix, then use a flat wooden spatula (or wooden spoon) to mix everything together. Once most of the wetness has been absorbed, use your hands to press the mixture into a fairly firm dough – just pliable and not too crumbly.

Cookie logs: This is a method we often use for mass-producing cookies/biscuits at the College. It allows advance preparation to be done and followed up quickly another day. If using this method to shape your cookies, take your (just prepared) dough – or, if making a larger quantity, half / one-third of it, and roll on a chopping board into a round log, about 5cm (2") across. Other simple-shaped biscuits can also be made by forming the log into an elongated triangle, or standing a fairly short log on its end and cutting through it carefully with a simple cutter, such as for love-heart cookies on Valentine's day. Once you've got your basic log shape, you can coat it with small seeds or oats – sesame and poppy seeds work well. If the logs are fairly sticky, simply toss a length of seeds on to a clean work surface (a tray is very useful for this, as the edges will stop the seeds and crumbs going everywhere), then roll the logs in them, adding more seeds until the whole surface of the log is evenly covered. If the logs are quite dry on the surface, paint the top lightly with a little milk and sprinkle seeds on top of this. Press or roll to stick these down, then paint milk on the sides and base and repeat until completely coated. Finally, wrap the log in old butter papers, greaseproof paper or even a clean carrier bag. Refrigerate for 30-40 minutes or until needed, or freeze for future use.

When you are ready to use the cookie logs, take them out of the fridge and let them 'warm up' a bit – normally for 10-15 minutes. You are simply aiming to remove the brittle edge of coldness that can cause the cookie to crack when sliced; you are not aiming to bring the logs back to room temperature, or they will squash down when you slice them, and the advantage of the method will be lost!

Put the unwrapped logs on a chopping board and use a bread knife or other large sharp knife to cut them neatly into round disks of about 0.6cm (¼") wide. Use a sawing motion, as pressing a knife right through like a guillotine tends to misshape the cookie. Similarly, resist the temptation to slice up all the cookies in one go without transferring each one in turn to the baking tray, as this also results in some getting misshapen or incompletely cut. Most cookies/biscuits will spread slightly in the oven, so place them on the prepared baking tray a little apart – a finger's width (1cm / ½") is normally about right.

Hand-moulded cookies: These are perhaps the most tactile and fun cookies to make. Simply take a walnut-sized lump of dough in the palms of your hand, roll it into a ball, and then press down gently with your palms. Place on to the prepared baking tray and press down some more, with your fingers or a fork. Paint with milk for a sheen, or to stick on seeds or nuts. This hand-made method lends itself to making larger, fatter cookies, and ones with softer, 'chewier' middles – more 'cookies' than 'biscuits'!

Cut-out cookies: Some cookie/biscuit doughs, especially the smooth, malleable ones, lend themselves to the use of cutters. This is the best way to make interesting shapes. For this you will need to roll out a grapefruit-sized portion of the dough on a lightly floured board or tray and roll

it with a lightly floured rolling pin. Roll in one direction, then the other, turning the dough occasionally to make sure it does not stick. Once the dough measures an even 0.6cm (¼"), use the cutters to cut out shapes, one by one – lifting them with a spatula if necessary to loosen their bases. Transfer them on to a prepared baking tray and, as before, keep a finger's width apart. Press together remaining scraps of dough and incorporate with your next lump. Roll and cut more shapes until all the dough is used up – you may have to press the last little piece into the cutter to get your last cookie shape. If your cutter starts to stick, dip it in plain flour in between cuttings.

Preparing the baking tray: Your baking tray can be simply lined with siliconized baking parchment (which can be reused many times), or it can be lightly oiled or buttered and tossed with flour, which is then tapped down over the whole surface of the tin. This gives a very effective non-stick coating. The advantage of the silicone paper is more practical than ecological, since it is instant (if you have it!) and does not require washing up in warm soapy water after use. I am *not* advocating non-stick baking trays, as we don't use them at all at Schumacher College: they get scratched quickly and this releases possibly toxic and/or non-biodegradable particles into what is otherwise a wholesome, organic cooking routine, and into the environment.

Baking: Place in the centre of a pre-heated moderate oven (usually 180°C / 350°F / Gas Mark 4) and check regularly. Move tins around so that the cookies/biscuits are baked evenly – balancing out any uneven heat distribution spots in your oven. If necessary, remove some earlier than the rest, as soon as they are ready.

When ready? The cookies/biscuits should be golden-brown at the edges and no longer look doughy in the middle. The underneath will also have turned light brown at the edges, or across the whole base. Be very careful when trying to peer at the base, as cookies can easily break if they are not ready, especially if gluten- and egg-free. Use a metal spatula to lift and check the underneath if necessary. Although fatter, hand-formed cookies often remain softer or chewier in the middle, you may not notice this until you bite in!

Cooling and keeping: Remove the cooked cookies/biscuits from the oven, and after leaving them for 5 minutes to gain strength on the tray, transfer them to a wire rack to cool completely. When completely cold they can be stored and kept crisp in an airtight tin or plastic box. Never store cookies/biscuits in the same tin as cake or bread, as the moisture in these will be transferred to the cookies and soften them. If they are left out overnight, they may also become a little soft, but they can be re-crisped in a moderate oven for 5 minutes – until just hot through; no more.

A note on cup measurements: A number of the recipes in this section lead with cup measures, and were evolved after a stay in America. During this time I became increasingly happy with using this handy volume measuring system – so much so that I would advocate it as a regular method for use in the home – especially when making cookies (or biscuits!).

Fruity chocolate & coconut cookies

These cookies were first evolved as a gluten- and dairy-free option for special-diet course participants – but they proved so popular that I was soon making them for everyone, and found that they are just as good with or without dairy ingredients. When trying to make something really more-ishly tasty and vegan, it helps to have chocolate and nuts in the recipe! As to why I should want to use butter rather than margarine anyway, my answer is simply that it is locally produced and less highly processed.

For 30-plus cookies

1 cup (85g / 3oz) oats, gluten-free oats* or buckwheat flakes*

1 cup (140g / 5oz) spelt or barley or buckwheat flour*

½ cup (70g / 2½oz) white wheat flour or gluten-free plain flour*

¼ cup (30g / 1oz) white or maize flour or soya flour*

¼ cup (30g / 1oz) cocoa powder

1 cup (170g / 6oz) muscovado brown sugar

1 cup (85g / 3oz) desiccated coconut
(+ extra for rolling if making logs – see Step 4)

½ tsp salt

250g (9oz / 2¼ sticks) butter, margarine** or coconut oil**

½ cup (70g / 2½oz) raisins or figs, finely chopped

1 cup (140g / 5oz) chocolate chips

1 tsp mixed spice or ground cinnamon

2-3 tbsp tahini

1 egg yolk + a little white (omit for vegan option)

For approx. 60-80 cookies

2 cups (170g / 6oz)

2 cups (280g / 10oz)

1 cup (140g / 5oz)

½ cup (60g / 2¼oz)

½ cup (60g / 2¼oz)

2 cups (340g / 12oz)

2 cups (170g / 6oz)
(+ approx. 1 cup extra if required)

1 tsp

500g (1lb 2oz)

1 cup (140g / 5oz)

2 cups (280g / 10oz)

2 tsp

⅓ cup (80ml / 5-6 tbsp)

1 egg (omit for vegan option)

1. Pre-heat the oven to 180°C (350°F / Gas Mark 4). Rub the butter, margarine or coconut oil into the flours, oats, flakes, cocoa powder, spices, desiccated coconut, sugar and salt, as described in the basic cookie/biscuit method.

2. Chop up the raisins or figs into fairly small pieces, to prevent the cookies cracking.

3. Combine the dried fruit and chocolate chips with the butter and flour crumb mix and then add the binding ingredients – tahini, and also egg if using.

4. Either roll into cookie logs (which can be rolled in more desiccated coconut) and chill, or shape into individual cookies in the palm of your hand.

5. If using the log method, slice the cookies after chilling. Arrange cookies a finger's width apart on a prepared baking tray (see basic cookie/ biscuit method) and bake for 20-25 minutes.

*Gluten-free option **Vegan option

Florentines

These chewy, chocolate-slippered, almond-and-fruit delicacies are not just popular in Florence, or indeed Italy: they are among the treasures of elegant tea shops and patisseries everywhere. My first attempt at making florentines involved so much repeated coaxing back into shape as the mixture spread in the oven that I abandoned the attempt for several years. I've now discovered that a little extra pre-cooking on the hob makes them behave in a much more civilized way when in the oven.

For approx. 25 florentines

50g (2oz / ½ stick) butter, roughly chopped
125ml (4fl oz / ½ cup) double or whipping cream
100g (4oz / ⅔ cup) golden granulated sugar
50g (2oz / rounded ⅓ cup) plain flour (or rice flour for GF diets)
1 pinch salt
15g (½oz / 2 tbsp) sour cherries or cranberries (optional)
50g (2oz / ½ cup) ground almonds
50g (2oz / ½ cup) whole almonds, finely chopped
50g (2oz / rounded ½ cup) flaked or slivered almonds
15g (½oz / 2 tbsp) pine nuts (or more flaked almonds)
50g (2oz / ⅓ cup) dried apricots, finely chopped
75g (3oz / ½ cup) candied mixed peel, finely chopped
75g (3oz / ½ cup) natural glacé cherries, halved
Zest of 1 organic orange
A few drops vanilla essence
175g (7oz) dark chocolate

For approx. 75 florentines

150g (6oz / 1½ sticks)
375ml (12fl oz / 1½ cups)
300g (12oz / 2 cups)
150g (6oz / 1 heaped cup)
¼ tsp
50g (2oz / ⅓ cup) (optional)
150g (6oz / 1½ cups)
150g (6oz / 1½ heaped cups)
150g (6oz / 1¾ cups)
50g (2oz / rounded ½ cup)
150g (6oz / 1 cup)
250g (9oz / 1½ cups)
250g (9oz / 1½ cups)
Zest of 3
1 tsp
500g (1lb 2oz)

1. Begin by preparing the fruit and nuts. Combine the chopped whole almonds with the ground and flaked almonds, the chopped apricots, candied peel, orange zest, pine nuts and sour cherries / cranberries (if using) and halved or quartered glacé cherries. Mix. (Note: you can make the different textures of almond involved in this recipe yourself from whole nuts – or for convenience buy them as indicated above.)

2. Measure the flour and keep separately (so it doesn't stick to the candied fruit so much that lumps are caused). Pre-heat the oven to 180°C (350°F / Gas Mark 4).

3. Next, make the caramel cream. Combine the butter, cream, sugar and salt in a deep saucepan. Heat gently, stirring almost continuously to avoid burning. Once the butter has melted and the mixture has just come to the boil, cook vigorously for 2 minutes, stirring all the while. Turn off the heat. Test the caramel for setting in a saucer of cold water: it should hold together and not disperse. (Four minutes of boiling will give you a proper 'soft ball' and avoid any spreading in the oven – but I generally prefer to stick with just 2 minutes' boiling and accept a little spreading in the oven, as this gives a more authentic florentine look.)

4. Stir the vanilla essence into the hot caramel, followed by the fruit-and-nut mixture and the flour. Mix well.

5. Dollop heaped teaspoonsful of the florentine mixture on to a baking tray lined with baking parchment (or greased and floured). Each little mound of mix should be about 4cm (2") apart to allow for spreading. Press down very slightly.

6. Bake in the oven for 5-6 minutes. Check after 3 minutes and reshape with a 7cm (2¾") round pastry cutter – or a drinking glass. To do this, simply use the cutter to pull back in the straying caramel so that it again forms part of a unified, circular, mound of fruit and nut. It should not be necessary to do this more than once if you have followed the pre-cooking method, and sometimes not at all. Cook until lightly browned at the edges (and underneath). Allow to cool on the baking tray for 5 minutes and then shift to a wire cooling rack.

7. Rough-chop the dark chocolate and melt it gently in a bowl resting in a saucepan containing an inch of simmering water.

8. When the florentines are completely cold, dip their flat bases carefully into the melted chocolate, slightly submerging the edges to obtain a characteristic rim of visible chocolate at their base (or see the variation below). Gently rest the florentines with their bases up so that the chocolate begins to set. After you have dipped about 20, go back to the first one and draw a fork across the chocolate, making wavy lines (if you do this straight away the chocolate will still be too runny to hold an impression). When all the florentines are done and the chocolate completely set, they can be stored in airtight tins, preferably with greaseproof paper between the layers – if they're not eaten straight away!

Variation: The alternative to dipping the florentines in chocolate is to simply spread a teaspoon of melted chocolate across the base – considerably easier, if you are happy to sacrifice the 'chocolate-slippered'-edge effect.

Taralli

These simple ring-shaped cookies with a hint of lemon zest have the great virtue of being dairy-free because they use olive oil as the shortening agent and have no added egg, so are therefore suitable for vegans and those with a lactose intolerance. The recipe was gathered many years ago by my sister-in-law, Sarah Jackson, when she was staying with an Italian family at Easter. Sarah is not, and was not, a vegan – she wrote down the recipe simply because she liked it, and has a nose for good recipes! *Taralli* are also served in savoury form; in fact, our former volunteer Paola Umberti said she had never before eaten *taralli* that were *sweet* and was pleasantly surprised. They were *still* irresistible, she said! For a savoury version, leave out the sugar and add a few dried herbs to the dough – and perhaps (if you are not avoiding dairy) sprinkle some Parmesan-style cheese on top, as the Italians do.

For 20-25 *taralli*	For 80-100+ *taralli*
250g (9oz / 2 scant cups) plain white flour	1kg (2lb 2oz)
75g (2½oz / scant ½ cup) caster sugar	300g (10oz / 1½ cups)
1½ tsp baking powder	2 tbsp
1 pinch salt	½ tsp
4 tbsp + 1 tsp (¼ cup) olive oil	280ml (10fl oz / 1-1¼ cups)
4 tbsp + 1 tsp (¼ cup) white wine	280ml (10fl oz / 1-1¼ cups)
Zest of half an organic lemon, finely grated	Zest of 2
1½-2 tbsp lemon juice	6-8 tbsp
3 tbsp sesame or poppy seeds (optional)	approx. 50g (2oz / ½ cup) (optional)

1. Pre-heat the oven to 200°C (400°F / Gas Mark 6). Mix together the flour, sugar, baking powder and salt.

2. Measure together the oil, wine and lemon juice. Whisk the grated lemon zest into this, using a fork.

3. Make a well in the dry mixture and pour the liquids into this. Stir, then mix all together with your hands until you have a stiff dough. Knead in the bowl until glossy.

4. Pull off small pieces and roll into thin, 'pencil length and pencil thickness' (15-18cm / 6-7") sausages with tapering ends – you can roll these in sesame or poppy seeds if you like (though not part of the original recipe). Now form the dough sausages into rings by overlapping the tips and pressing them together: Paola tells me that sometimes the two ends will cross over slightly; sometimes they slide next to each other 'like a snake eating its tail' – so there's no need to worry about making the joint invisible. The desired appearance is more the rustic look of an artisan cookie produced quickly by a team of village ladies, or a family, for a festival.

5. Place the dough rings on baking parchment, or an ungreased baking tray, each a finger's width apart. Bake in the hot oven for 5-15 minutes until golden-brown.

Lemon & poppy-seed galactic swirls

These lusciously lemony cookies embrace a subtle swirl of poppy seeds – an inverted galaxy where tiny indigo stars unfurl in their own golden cookie universe . . . (But sometimes I feel a pang of guilt – what if I'd sown all those poppy seeds? The whole front lawn could have been colonized by gorgeous red flowers – a universe of petals billowing in the breeze!)

For 25-30 cookies

2 cups (280g / 10oz) white flour
1 cup (85g / 3oz) rolled oats
1 cup (175g / 6oz) caster sugar
Zest of 2 organic lemons and juice of 1
250g (9oz / 2¼ sticks) butter
½ tsp salt
1 tbsp honey
1 egg yolk
⅓ cup (40g / 1½ oz) poppy seeds

For 50-60 cookies

4 cups (560g / 1lb 4oz)
2 cups (175g / 6oz)
2 cups (350g / 12oz)
Zest of 4 and juice of 2
500g (1lb 2oz)
1 tsp
2 tbsp
2 yolks or 1 egg
approx. ⅔ cup (80g / 3oz)

1. Using a sharp peeler, skim off the yellow zest of the lemons in thin strips, avoiding the bitter white pith below. Chop this and combine with the oats, sugar and half the flour. Pulverize this mixture in batches in your (clean) coffee or spice grinder, until the zest is powdered. (Alternatively, if you don't have a grinder, grate off the zest on the finest side of your grater then mix with the oats, sugar and flour.)

2. Combine the lemony mixture with the rest of the flour and the salt. Rub in the butter.

3. Make a concentrated lemon syrup by placing the lemon juice in a small saucepan and boiling until reduced to about 25ml (1fl oz / 2 tbsp) (small quantity) or 50ml (2fl oz / ¼ cup) (large quantity). Keep a close eye on this and stir occasionally to avoid burning. Stir in the honey at the end.

4. Add the lemon reduction along with the egg yolk to the crumbed mixture, and mix until you can press the dough together into a malleable lump.

5. Divide the dough in two. On a very lightly floured board or piece of greaseproof paper, roll into a 1cm (½")-thick rectangle – the large quantity will give two rectangles about the size of a piece of A4 paper, whereas the small quantity will give two rectangles of half that size. Now brush the surface lightly with lemon juice and sprinkle with a single dense layer of poppy seeds, leaving the top 1cm (½") of the long edge free if possible. Turn this long edge over and roll up the dough. Roll and squeeze the log until you have the diameter you want for your cookies. Wrap in greaseproof paper and refrigerate for 40 minutes or longer, as convenient. Pre-heat the oven to 170°C (325°F / Gas Mark 3).

6. Allow the cookie logs to unchill slightly, then carefully slice into 0.5cm (¼")-thick disks with a bread knife. Arrange a little apart on the prepared baking trays (see basic cookie/biscuit method). Bake fairly slowly for 20-25 minutes, until crisped through and light golden-brown at the edges.

Chocolate & vanilla swirls

The dramatic swirling beauty of these cookies makes the additional effort of carefully rolling up a two-tone cookie log well worthwhile. Look upon the construction experience as an opportunity to re-enact a bit of geological fast-formation connecting us with the tensions and responses of different materials as they get stretched over one another, uplifted and occasionally cracked! These cookies will store well in an airtight tin – if well hidden.

For approx. 30 cookies	For approx. 60 cookies
Chocolate cookie dough	
¼ cup (35g / 1¼oz) brown flour	½ cup (70g / 2½oz)
½ cup (70g / 2½oz) white flour	1 cup (140g / 5oz)
½ cup (40g / 1½ oz) oats	1 cup (85g / 3oz)
¼ cup (30g / 1oz) cocoa powder	½ cup (60g / 2oz)
½ cup (85g / 3oz) muscovado brown sugar	1 cup (175g / 6oz)
125g (4½oz / 1¼ sticks) butter	250g (9oz / 2½ sticks)
½ cup (70g / 2½oz) dark chocolate chips	1 cup (140g / 5oz)
¼ tsp fine salt	½ tsp
1 egg yolk + a little white if necessary	1 egg
Vanilla cookie dough	
½ cup (70g / 2½oz) brown flour	1 cup (140g / 5oz)
½ cup (70g / 2½oz) white flour	1 cup (140g / 5oz)
½ cup (40g / 1½oz) oats	1 cup (85g / 3oz)
½ cup (85g / 3oz) golden caster sugar	1 cup (175g / 6oz)
125g (4½oz / 1¼ sticks) butter	250g (9oz / 2½ sticks)
½ tsp vanilla extract	1 tsp
¼ tsp fine salt	½ tsp
1 egg yolk + a little white if necessary	1 egg

1. Measure the dry ingredients (flours, oats, sugar, salt and cocoa for the chocolate mix) and butter into two separate bowls, one for the chocolate mixture and one for the vanilla mixture.

2. Rub the butter into the dry ingredients (see basic cookie/biscuit method). I normally start with the vanilla mix so I can move on to the chocolate without washing my hands. Stir the chocolate chips into the chocolate crumb mixture.

3. Add the egg to the crumb mixtures to bind them. Also add vanilla essence to the dough for the vanilla mixture. Mix well to distribute the egg evenly around, then press each mixture into a fairly soft, malleable dough.

4. If making the large quantity, first divide each piece of dough into two. On a clean, lightly floured work surface or tray, roll out each piece of dough into a rectangle about the size and shape of an A5 piece of paper (say 16 x 22cm / 6 x 9") and about 0.75-1cm (⅓") thick. Make sure they don't stick to the work surface – you can roll them out on baking parchment or greaseproof paper if you like.

5. Next, place a vanilla rectangle on top of a chocolate rectangle, with the longer edges slightly offset so that about 1-2cm (½") of the chocolate dough pokes out beyond the vanilla rectangle. The shorter edges should be level. If the surfaces of the dough are at all dry or floury, paint them thinly with milk to moisten them (otherwise don't bother, as it is helpful if the two surfaces can slide over each other when you roll them up).

6. Curve the exposed edge of chocolate dough over the vanilla dough, pressing it into shape. Once you have the first long twist in place, continue to roll the log up, pressing gently and moulding the log as you go. You will need to keep a fairly light touch – allowing the slightly larger chocolate dough to slide into place over the vanilla dough before pressing down and sticking the two doughs together firmly. When fissures appear in the chocolate dough, cut off some of the chocolate dough from the bottom edge and use this to fill in the cracks. Once the doughs are rolled up into a log, roll the whole thing back and forth a few times to make it nice and round, pressing firmly but gently together, and flatten the ends. The width of the log should be the width you want the eventual cookie to be – about 5cm (2") – or larger! Cover and chill for at least 20 minutes.

7. Pre-heat the oven to 180°C (350°F / Gas Mark 4). Remove the cookie logs from the fridge and cut carefully into 0.5cm (¼") disks. A thin painting of milk at this stage will give a nice sheen to these cookies.

8. Arrange a little apart on trays covered with baking parchment and bake for about 15 minutes, until the outer rings of vanilla cookie are beginning to turn golden-brown. When ready, allow to cool on the sheet for a minute or two before carefully transferring to a wire cooling rack.

Arizona cookies

These oaty fruit-&-nut cookies were invented after the discovery of an abundance of pecan nuts in a dusty outback grocery store in Arizona. We were staying in a bird-watcher's lodge, not far from the countryside where the young Aldo Leopold was inspired to see the world from nature's point of view, which later led to him to write his seminal work *A Sand County Almanac*.

This oft-requested recipe was designed to be easy to use (especially with cup measures) – and easy to remember. When I make these cookies for my own small family I halve the smaller quantity and use a half-cup of almost everything as my guide.

For 30 cookies	For 60 cookies
1 cup (140g / 5oz) brown flour	2 cups (280g / 10oz)
1 cup (140g / 5oz) white flour	2 cups (280g / 10oz)
1 cup (85g / 3oz) rolled oats	2 cups (170g / 6oz)
1 cup (175g / 6oz) soft brown sugar	2 cups (350g / 12oz)
2 tsp cinnamon or mixed spice	1 tbsp
½ tsp fine salt	1 tsp
250g (9oz / 2¼ sticks) butter	500g (1lb 2oz)
3 tbsp tahini	6 tbsp or ⅓ cup
1 small egg	2 eggs
1 cup (115g / 4oz) walnuts or pecans	2 cups (225g / 8oz)
1 cup (140g / 5oz) raisins (or sultanas or currants)	2 cups (280g / 10oz)
2 tbsp sesame seeds + more (25g / 1oz) for rolling	4 tbsp (+ ½ cup / 60g / 2oz)

1. Combine all the finer dry ingredients (flours, oats, sugar, spice, salt, sesame seeds).

2. Add the butter and rub in until you have a breadcrumby consistency (see basic cookie/biscuit method). Pre-heat the oven to 180°C (350°F / Gas Mark 4).

3. Chop the nuts and dried fruit fairly small. This can be done in a food processor with the knife attachment if the raisins are first mixed in with some of the butter, flour and nuts. (Dried fruit cannot be chopped in a food processor on its own – it just whizzes around remaining whole – whereas nuts will chop easily, and indeed can quickly become too fine. I sometimes use this rapid method to cut the nuts and raisins, and at other times prefer to use a mezzaluna, or a large sharp knife – plus a happy dose of time and patience!)

4. Add the nuts, dried fruit, egg and tahini to the crumb mix and mix/press the mixture into a dough.

5. Make logs and refrigerate before cutting (see basic method – logs are usually rolled in sesame seeds), or form individual cookies by hand.

6. Bake the shaped cookies mid-oven for 15-20 minutes. When ready they will be lightly browning at the edges, with no doughiness left on the base (if you dare look). Leave to firm up on the baking tray for a few minutes, then move to a wire cooling rack.

Fair Trade slice

This recipe was sent to me by Maya Richardson, a family therapist who has facilitated many courses at Schumacher College and who also happens to be the daughter of a great restaurateur and chef. With a nose for a good recipe, Maya sent me this one from her local organic cooperative in Roanoke, Virginia. It was originally cooked up by Christopher Ryding to celebrate cooperative heritage and Fair Trade ethics – using two of the most iconic ingredients of the Fair Trade movement, bananas and chocolate. It's a sort of cross between a flap jack, a cake and a cookie – deliciously moist and tasty, but not too crumbly.

For 20+ bars
(1 standard roasting tin)

140g (5oz /1¼ sticks / ¾ cup) butter, softened
100g (4oz / ⅔ cup) brown sugar
1 egg, beaten
1 tsp vanilla extract (optional)
3 peeled bananas (300g / 10oz / 1 rounded cup)
100g (4oz / ¾ cup) plain flour
100g (4oz / 1 rounded cup) rolled oats
2 tsp baking powder
1 pinch salt
100-150g (4-5oz / ⅔-1 cup) dark chocolate chips
50g (2oz / ½ cup) pecans or walnuts, chopped (optional)

For 80+ bars
(4 roasting tins)

560g (1lb 4oz)
400g (14oz / 2 packed cups)
4
3-4 tsp (optional)
1.2kg (2½lb)
400g (1lb / 3 cups)
400g (1lb / 4 rounded cups)
2 rounded tbsp
1 tsp
400-600g (1-1½lb / 3-4 cups)
225g (8oz / 2 cups)

1. Pre-heat the oven to 180°C (350°F / Gas Mark 4). Oil and line your baking tin.

2. Cream the butter and sugar together in a mixing bowl, then beat in the egg and vanilla extract (if using).

3. Mash the bananas with a fork and fold this into the mixture also.

4. Combine the flour, oats, baking powder, salt, roughly chopped nuts (if using) and chocolate chips.

5. Mix the dry ingredients into the wet ingredients and stir thoroughly. Spread the mixture into the prepared tin. It should be only about 1 cm (½") thick and will rise slightly.

6. Bake for about 25-35 minutes until set and golden-brown on top. Cool before cutting into squares or rectangles.

For gluten-free diets: This recipe converts easily to gluten-free, if you can get hold of certified GF oats and GF white flour to use instead of ordinary white wheat flour. And don't forget to select a GF baking powder as well!

For dairy-free diets: Just use margarine instead of butter.

Butter biscuits (with variations)

These are wonderfully short, melt-in-your-mouth cookies that are ideal for rolling and cutting into shapes, as well as for making into cookie logs – and dipping in dark chocolate! They are simple to make, nut-free and easily convert from vanilla to chocolate flavour. I designed this recipe to use with kids during a Dartington open day workshop for children. Although, officially, it was Sarah and I who were in charge, Oscar, aged 5, was under the impression he was running the show. It was a jolly good thing that the parents of his infant pupils knew what they were doing – and didn't listen too carefully to his enormously confident and inaccurate instructions!

This is also the cookie dough I use for making stained-glass window biscuits at Christmas and 'jammy dodgers'. We rarely, or never, serve these fanciful variations at College coffee breaks, but they are fun to do with, and for, children. Thanks must go to the parents at Park School for showing me how to 'jam' a dodger!

For 15 biscuits

160g (6oz / 1 level cup + 3 level tbsp) plain flour

25g (1oz / 3 tbsp) rice flour or gluten-free white flour

85g (3oz / ½ cup) caster sugar

¼ tsp fine salt

140g (5oz / 1¼ sticks) butter

1 egg yolk

½ tsp vanilla essence

For 60 biscuits

640g (1½lb / 5 level cups)

100g (4oz / ¾ cup)

340g (12oz / 2 cups)

1 tsp

560g (1lb 4oz)

1 egg + 1 yolk

2 tsp

Extra ingredients for variations:

Chocolate butter biscuits: Substitute 2 tbsp (small quantity) / 40g / 2oz / ½ cup (large quantity) of plain flour with the same amount of cocoa powder and add some chocolate chips if you like – about 50g (2oz / ¼ cup) for the small quantity and 200g (7oz / 1 cup) for the large.

Jammy dodgers: strawberry or raspberry jam: 125g / 4oz / ½ cup (small quantity); 500g / 1lb / 2 cups (large quantity)

Stained-glass biscuits: naturally fruity boiled sweets: 100g / 4oz / ½ cup (small); 400g / 14oz / 2 cups (large)

Chocolate-dipped or Chocolate-topped biscuits: dark chocolate or chocolate chips: 100g / 4oz / ⅔ cup (small); 400g / 14oz / 3 cups (large)

Ginger swirls:
ground ginger: 4-5 tsp (small); 6 tbsp (large)
crystallized ginger: 50g / 2oz / ⅓ cup (small); 200g / 7oz / 1 cup (large)
molasses or black treacle: 25g / 1oz / 1½ tbsp (small); 100g / 4oz / ⅓ cup (large)

1. Pre-heat the oven to 180°C (350°F / Gas Mark 4). As usual, begin by rubbing the butter into the dry ingredients until a breadcrumb-like consistency is obtained. Then add the egg and vanilla essence. Mix, then knead the dough gently until a soft round, malleable lump is formed.

2. Roll out the dough on a clean, lightly floured surface – taking only half (small quantity) or one-eighth (large quantity) of the mass at a time. Roll lightly, aiming to make the dough about 0.5cm (¼") thick – or perhaps a little less. Cut the cookies with your cutter. Line up the cookies on a prepared baking tray (see basic cookie/biscuit method), keeping them about 1cm (½") apart to allow for expansion.

3. Bake for about 15-20 minutes, until golden-brown at the edges. Allow to cool on the baking tray for 5 minutes before transferring to a wire cooling rack.

Jammy dodgers: Roll the dough out extra thin, and cut out matching pairs that will be sandwiched together with jam after cooking. These could be two rounds: leave one whole and cut a shape out of the other with a small decorative cutter – this could be a star shape, a love heart, an animal, or simply a smaller circle. After baking the biscuits and allowing them to cool until they are strong enough to handle, turn a whole biscuit over and place 1 tsp of strawberry jam in the middle of it – on top of what was its base. Spread it very slightly with the back of the spoon, but keep it well away from the edges. Press the biscuit with the centre cut out on top of the jam, so the two bases are facing. Press down gently so that the jam begins to fill the cut out shape. Return all the biscuits to the baking tray, jammy shape uppermost, for a final 5 minutes in the oven. During this time the jam will heat up and melt a bit and the surface of the jam inside the cut-out shape will dry out, forming a 'skin' which makes it less sticky when it cools. Take the biscuits out before the jam bubbles up or they start browning.

Stained-glass window biscuits: These pretty cookies are only one layer thick – so you can see the light through the reconstructed sweets in the middle when they harden, becoming like coloured glass. Alternative flavours can be added to the biscuit dough, such as cinnamon, ginger and lemon or orange zest. Roll out the dough to the thickness of a £1 coin. Typically use 7cm (3") cutters to cut out shapes and 4cm (1½") cutters to cut out holes in the middles. Re-roll leftover pieces. Carefully lift on to parchment-covered baking sheets, then use a skewer to make a small hole at the top of each biscuit. Crush the boiled sweets in their wrappers or in a bag using a rolling pin. Fill the centres of the biscuits with the crushed sweets until they are level with the top of the cookie dough. Bake for 15-20 minutes until the cookies are golden-brown and the sweets have melted. Leave to harden, then thread thin red satin ribbons through the holes, ready to hang on your Christmas tree. Will keep for a month in a tin, but best eaten within three days of being left to dangle!

Chocolate-dipped: Half-dip the vanilla butter biscuits in 200g / 8oz (small quantity) or 400g / 1lb (large quantity) of 70% dark chocolate that has been chopped and gently melted in a bowl over a pan of steaming water (with the burner off so the chocolate maintains its tempering). To maintain the depth of melted chocolate for easy dipping, pour the melted chocolate into a small cup that's wider than your biscuit (a measuring cup will do fine). After dipping half a biscuit (back and front), lay it, base down, on non-stick silicone baking parchment to cool and set. Leave the other half undipped!

Chocolate-topped: Alternatively, chocolate-topped biscuits are easily made by sprinkling *one teaspoonful* of chocolate chips on top of each cookie *as soon as* they come out of the oven, while still on the baking tray. The heat of the cookies will melt the chocolate chips, so that by the time you've finished distributing the chocolate chips over them, you can go back to the first biscuit and spread out the (now melted) chocolate chips with the back of a teaspoon. Go back to the first biscuit a third time with a fork and streak a little wavy path across the top. Chocolate lovers may like to try this covering with other cookies/biscuits too – ginger (page 227), orange-polenta (page 233), etc.

Ginger swirls: Use ground ginger instead of vanilla in the dough. Rinse the crystallized ginger in boiling water to remove excess sugar, before draining and chopping quite small. Roll out the ginger dough in rectangles as for Chocolate & vanilla swirls (page 216) then paint or streak with gently melted molasses. Sprinkle the chopped crystallized ginger over this and roll up into logs. Wrap and chill before slicing 0.5cm (¼") thick and baking until golden-brown.

Wild golden oaties

These golden, oaty cookies are so sweet and crunchy that many of our sweet-toothed students go wild for them at coffee break . . . indeed, they have quite a following!

Sarah found the original recipe in Mary Ford's classic step-by-step biscuit cookbook and finds these cookies brilliant for whisking up at the last moment. Since the butter is melted, no rubbing in is needed, so it's a very quick process. Sarah's secret of success is to be very generous with the golden syrup – now almost double what Mary Ford suggested, so measure carefully!

For approx. 30 cookies	For approx. 90 cookies
115g (4oz / rounded ¾ cup) plain or self-raising white flour	350g (12oz / 2 ½ cups)
2 tsp baking powder (if using plain flour)	2 tbsp
115g (4oz / 1⅓ cup) rolled oats	350g (12oz / 4 cups)
115g (4oz / ⅔ cup) light soft brown sugar	350g (12oz / 2 cups)
1 tsp ground ginger	1 tbsp
115g (4oz / 1 stick) butter	350g (12oz / 3 sticks)
50ml (2fl oz / 3 tbsp) golden syrup	150ml (5fl oz / ½ cup + 2 tbsp)
2 tsp water, orange or lemon juice	2 tbsp
¼ tsp salt	¾ tsp

1. Pre-heat your oven to 180°C (350°F / Gas Mark 4) and prepare your baking tray, greasing or lining with baking parchment.

2. Combine the flour, oats, salt, ground ginger and sugar in a mixing bowl. Break up any lumps in the brown sugar with your fingers.

3. Measure the butter into a saucepan and heat very gently until the butter is melted. Stir in the (carefully measured) golden syrup and turn off the heat.

4. Make a well in the middle of the dry ingredients and pour in the melted golden syrup, butter and water or juice. Scrape out the saucepan and stir the mixture together until all the dry ingredients are incorporated and a doughy lump is formed. Leave to cool for 5 minutes.

5. Now take walnut-sized portions of the oatie dough and roll into balls between your palms. Place these a good 'hand's-width' apart (8cm / 3") to allow for spreading. Bake for 15 minutes approximately on a middle shelf.

6. When the cookies are ready they should be golden-brown and tempting. Leave to stiffen on the tray for a few minutes before transferring to a wire rack to cool.

Variations: You can also make this recipe with other thick sugary syrups instead of golden syrup – for example rice syrup, honey and molasses (for a darker look) – these too require careful measuring!

Cheese, walnut & rosemary straws

The secret of a good cheese straw is to make them really cheesy and really 'short', so they melt in your mouth and you feel like you want another immediately! MSG eat your heart out!

My recipe has evolved over many years – since I was asked to make them for the cocktail-party-style launch of an upmarket kitchen showroom and my 'agent', Theo Woodham-Smith, said my straws weren't quite crisp enough and gave me her recipe, which contained far more butter. My current recipe is an amalgamation of Theo's long-lost recipe, Delia Smith's rich walnut pastry – and rosemary from the garden.

Cheese straw dough can be prepared in advance, cut to shape and frozen. When you want to serve the straws, all you need do is whisk them out of the freezer and bake until golden-brown.

Small batch (serves 6-10) – 50-70 straws	Large batch (for a party of 50!) – approx. 250 straws
75g (2½oz / ½ cup) brown flour	300g (10½oz / 2 full cups)
150g (5½oz / 1 rounded cup) white flour	600g (1lb 5oz)
50g (2oz / ½ cup) smoked cheese (or mature Cheddar), grated	200g (7oz / 1¾ cups)
50g (2oz / ½ cup) medium or mild Cheddar, or Leicester, grated	200g (7oz / 1¾ cups)
25g (1oz / ¼ cup) fresh Parmesan-style cheese, finely grated	100g (4oz / 1 cup)
125g (4½oz / 1 stick + 1 tbsp) butter	500g (1lb 2oz)
100g (4oz / 1 cup) walnuts, chopped quite finely	400g (14oz / 3½ cups)
1 egg yolk + a little white if necessary	1 egg + 1 yolk
1 rounded tsp smooth mustard	2 tbsp
1½ tsp olive oil	2 tbsp
1 tbsp cold water	4 tbsp
2 x 8cm (3") sprigs rosemary, leaves finely chopped (1-2 tsp)	8 x 8cm (3") sprigs (approx. 2 tbsp)
¼ tsp fine salt	1 tsp
⅛ tsp cayenne pepper (or black pepper)	½ tsp
approx. 4 tbsp sesame seeds (or sesame and poppy seeds) for coating (optional)	125g (4½oz / 1 cup) (optional)

1. Combine the brown and white flour in a bowl with the roughly chopped, room-temperature butter. Rub in the butter to obtain a breadcrumby consistency.

2. To this add the grated cheeses and the finely chopped walnuts (if preparing the walnuts in a food processor, be careful not to grind them completely into 'sand' – they should still have some texture, like coarse grit). Also add the salt, pepper and very finely chopped rosemary leaves (plucked from their stems before chopping). Mix these together.

3. Now add the wet ingredients to form a dough – egg, water, oil and mustard. Add a little (or a little more) egg white if the dough does not come together easily. Reserve the remaining egg white for later.

4. Once you have a stiff but malleable dough, take grapefruit-sized portions of it, knead briefly and roll out on a lightly floured surface until the dough is about 1cm (⅜") thick. Use a sharp knife to cut the dough into a rectangle and remove the outer edges. Paint thinly with beaten egg white and then sprinkle with sesame seeds, which you can press down gently with your rolling pin. Now cut the rectangle into smaller fingers (say, 6cm x 1cm / 2½" x ½"). You can also use a cutter to make round cheese biscuits. The sesame finish is, of course, optional, and some people may prefer to put the sesame seeds straight into the dough for simplicity (use only a quarter of the amount if doing this). Poppy seeds, mixed with the sesames, also give a nice finish.

5. Continue to roll out the dough and cut into straws until you have used all the dough up. If freezing or refrigerating to bake-off later, pack the cheese straws on some greaseproof paper in a box, putting further layers of greaseproof between each layer of cheese straws. This will make them easier to get out later. (You can also freeze rectangular slabs ready to be cut to size later.)

6. When it's time to bake the cheese straws, heat up your oven to 200°C (400°F / Gas Mark 6). Lay the cheese straws out on a baking tray lined with baking parchment (or a buttered/oiled and floured baking tray) – making sure each straw is about a finger's width apart. The frozen straws will defrost very quickly and can be spread out while still frozen, or when defrosted (either works well). Bake for 15-20 minutes, until the straws have turned a tempting golden-brown and are sizzling and smelling delicious. Cool and serve. Once cold, the cheese straws can be kept fresh in an airtight box or tin for at least a week.

Pão de queijo (Brazilian cheese snacks)

In Brazil, tapioca is used in a more varied way than in the UK, where our knowledge of it is often limited to pearled tapioca milk pudding (somewhat reminiscent of frogspawn). Tapioca is a refined starch that is produced when cassava roots are processed. As a flour, it is often now found in Western gluten-free cooking, and is delicious in these classic Brazilian snacks.

This recipe comes from Amelia Gregory, a creative designer and producer of *Amelia's Magazine*, who attended Lynne Hull's 'Creating Nature' course in 2008. With the steady flow of ecologically aware Brazilians coming to Schumacher College, it's not surprising that these temptingly puffed-up, golden-brown balls, with their gooey, moon-cratered middle, have been baked here on many festive occasions. My last accomplice in making these snacks was Clara Dos Santos (Economics for Transition 2013), who helped me iron out a few glitches in the recipe – with the help of her mother's recipe, emailed in from Brazil.

For 25-30 ('ping-pong-sized') balls	For 100-120 balls
150g (5oz / 2 cups) Parmesan-style cheese, grated	600g (1lb 4oz / 8 cups)
250g (9oz / 2 cups) tapioca flour	1kg (2lb 4oz / 8 cups)
100ml (4fl oz / scant ½ cup) milk	400ml (14fl oz / 1⅔ cups)
50g (2oz / ¼ cup) butter or olive oil	200g (8oz / 1 cup)
1 egg	4
¼ tsp salt	1 tsp

1. Pre-heat the oven to 200°C (400°F / Gas Mark 6). Grate the 'Parmesan' (or other local medium-fat hard cheese) using the finer side of your grater. Mix the tapioca flour and cheese lightly together in a bowl.

2. Combine the milk, chopped-up butter and salt in a large saucepan. Bring to the boil.

3. Stir the boiling hot liquids on to the dry ingredients. Mix well, adding the egg as you go. Knead into a smooth, soft dough.

4. Next, pull off small walnut-sized (2-3cm / 1") pieces that, Amelia says, "fit snug in your palm", and roll them into balls.

5. Arrange the cheese balls about 2cm (1") apart on an oiled or parchment-covered baking tray.

6. Bake for approximately 20-30 minutes. When ready, the *Pão de queijo* (literally 'bread of cheese') will have puffed up beautifully (to the size of a ping-pong ball) and they will be golden-brown on the top (and bottom). Serve right away, while still warm and gooey in the middle.

7. These cheesy treats are very more-ish – great for serving as a (warm) gluten-free appetizer or snack.

Ginger biscuits

"Run, run as fast as you can – you can't catch me, I'm the Gingerbread Man."

These dark spicy ginger biscuits have a nice snap to them. The dough is excellent for rolling out and cutting into 'gingerbread men' – or rather 'ginger biscuit people'. It also lends itself to making everyday ginger biscuits using the cookie log method – a safer bet, perhaps, when you consider the reputation that gingerbread men have for running straight out of the oven and into the fox's mouth!

For 30 biscuits / 10 big ginger people

1 cup (140g / 5oz) brown flour
2 cups (280g / 10oz) white flour
1 cup (175g / 6oz) muscovado brown sugar
250g (9oz / 2¼ sticks) butter
3 tbsp molasses or black treacle
1 small egg or 2 egg yolks
4-5 tsp ground ginger
2 tsp ground cinnamon or mixed spice
1 tsp baking powder
½ tsp salt

For approx. 60 biscuits

2 cups (280g / 10oz)
4 cups (550g / 1lb 4oz)
2 cups (350g / 12oz)
500g (1lb 2oz)
6 tbsp (90ml / ⅓ cup + 1 tbsp)
2 eggs
3-4 tbsp
4 tsp
2 tsp baking powder
1 tsp

1. Rub the butter into the flours, baking powder, sugar, spices and salt, until a fine breadcrumby consistency is obtained. The strength of ground ginger is quite variable, so taste your dough and add more if necessary.

2. Add the binding ingredients – molasses/treacle and egg. (If the molasses is very stiff, first warm it gently in a small bowl or jar placed in a saucepan of boiling water.) Mix everything together to form a soft malleable dough, with no streaks.

3. If you will be baking the biscuits straight away, pre-heat your oven to 180°C (350°F / Gas Mark 4). Dust your work surface lightly with flour and roll portions of the dough out 0.5cm (¼") thick. Cut into ginger biscuit shapes – people, animals, rounds, etc. (Alternatively, roll into cookie logs and chill – see basic cookie/biscuit method.) If you wish to decorate the ginger people, first place them a little apart on a prepared baking sheet. Paint thinly with milk and press on currants for eyes and buttons, and nuts, etc. You can add to the decoration by piping icing sugar details on after the ginger people have been cooked and thoroughly cooled. (Use egg white to mix the sifted icing sugar to a pipe-able paste, as this will give a firm set.)

4. Bake your ginger shapes for 15-25 minutes. The length of time needed will depend on how temptingly fat they are! When ready, the biscuits will be turning a slightly darker brown at the edges and will have become opaque, no longer doughy. Transfer to a wire cooling rack after 5 minutes' firming up – then guard carefully! When completely cool, the biscuits will keep well in an airtight tin for a week or two.

Laughing pistachio & cardamom cookies

These gently aromatic, green-flecked cookies contain two expensive non-local ingredients, which even used in tiny amounts make the result something very special – such that I am frequently asked for the recipe. Cardamom is a seed pod little bigger than a pea, and the third most expensive spice after saffron and vanilla. It originated in India and Sri Lanka and has been an item worthy of trading abroad for at least a thousand years.

Pistachio – the 'laughing nut' – is olive-sized, pleasingly green (from chlorophyll) and grows on a small tree native to parts of western Asia and the Levant. It is highly prized and usually costs three or four times as much as other nuts. Nowadays its cultivation has spread across southern Europe, North Africa and the Middle East, and it is also grown in California. When ripe, the shell gapes open at one end to expose the kernel – a feature known as khandan or 'laughing' in Iran.

To offset the cost of pistachios, some chopped almonds are included in this recipe. They can be used to entirely replace the pistachios if you like – or, if you are feeling flush, replace the almonds with more pistachios!

For approx. 20 cookies	For approx. 80 cookies
¾ cup (100g / 4oz) white flour	3 cups (425g / 15oz)
½ cup (70g / 2½oz) spelt or brown flour	2 cups (280g / 10oz)
¼ cup (40g / 1½oz) light muscovado sugar	1 cup (175g / 6oz)
¼ cup (45g / 1½oz) caster sugar	1 cup (175g / 6oz)
¼ cup (35g / 1¼oz) shelled (unsalted) pistachios	1 cup (150g / 5oz)
¼ cup (35g / 1¼oz) whole almonds (or use double quantity of either nut)	1 cup (150g / 5oz) (or double quantity of either nut)
¼ cup (25g / 1oz) ground almonds	1 cup (110g / 4oz)
125g (4½ oz / 1 stick + 1 tbsp) butter	500g (1lb 2oz)
1½ tsp honey	2 tbsp
1½ tsp tahini	2 tbsp
1 egg yolk	1 egg
3-4 tsp freshly ground, sieved cardamom	4-5 tbsp
2 tsp sesame seeds + extra for rolling	3 tbsp + extra for rolling
¼ tsp finest salt	1 tsp

1. Grind the cardamom pods finely in your coffee or spice grinder. Sift and then measure the amount you need into a bowl containing the flour, sugar, ground almonds and salt. If hand-forming the cookies or using cutters, pre-heat the oven now to 180°C (350°F / Gas Mark 4).

2. Rub the butter into these dry ingredients to achieve a fine 'breadcrumby' consistency.

3. Chop the pistachios and almonds into fairly small pieces and add them to the flour mix, along with the sesame seeds.

4. In a small bowl, measure together the honey, tahini and egg. Stir well and add these binding ingredients to the crumb mixture. Use first a wooden spoon, then your hands, to mix, then lightly knead everything together into a homogeneous cookie dough.

5. Remove from the bowl and form into one (small quantity) or 3-4 (large quantity) cookie logs. If the dough is fairly sticky on the outside, you can simply roll these logs straight into sprinkled sesame seeds and they will stick. Otherwise, paint with milk and then roll. Wrap in butter papers or baking parchment and chill for 40 minutes or until required. Alternatively, roll out the cookie dough and cut into shapes with cutters.

6. If the logs have been in the fridge overnight (see basic cookie/biscuit method), let them rest at room temperature for about 15 minutes before using, so they slice easily without cracking. Slice off cookie-disks with a bread knife, so each cookie measures about 0.5cm (¼") thick.

7. Arrange the cookies a finger's width apart on a baking tray that has been oiled or lined with parchment. Bake until golden brown in the centre of the pre-heated oven, turning as necessary. Cool the cookies on the baking tray for the first 5 minutes or so, then move to an wire cooling rack as they become stronger to handle.

Brutti ma buoni ('Ugly but good!')

These crunchy little Italian cookies are a favourite coffee-break snack that Tara makes. They are very easy to produce and can be served to anyone avoiding milk products and gluten. The ground almonds gives them a rich depth of flavour that makes up for the absence of butter. With a name that means 'ugly but good' you might think they'd look decidedly unappetizing – but when Tara makes them they're really quite cute. Everyone loves them, and no one has ever complained or said "Can't you make those warty little cookies look a bit prettier? They're putting me off my coffee . . ."

For 25-30 little cookies	For approx. 120 cookies
150g (5½oz / 1½ cups) ground almonds	600g (1lb 5oz / 6 cups)
115g (4oz / ⅔ cup) golden granulated sugar	450g (1lb / 2⅓ cups)
¼ tsp salt	1 tsp
2 egg whites (from fairly large eggs)	8
½ tsp vanilla essence	2 tsp

1. Mix the almonds, sugar and salt together in a large bowl.

2. Separate the eggs. (You will not need any yolks in this recipe, but they are excellent for using in many other cookie recipes, as you can substitute 3 yolks for each egg. They can also enrich a quiche or *sformato* – see pages 72 and 84 – or be used for making mayonnaise – see page 142).

3. Whip up the egg whites until stiff and foamy.

4. Add one-third of the whipped egg whites to the dry ingredients and stir. Then fold in the rest of them, along with the vanilla essence. You should have a soft dropping mixture that can be heaped up into uneven mounds without spreading out immediately – add an extra egg white if it seems too stiff.

5. Pre-heat the oven to 170°C (325°F / Gas Mark 3).

6. Prepare a baking tray by lining with parchment or oiling and dusting with cornflour or flour. With a couple of teaspoons – using one teaspoon to scrape the mixture off the other – drop small walnut-sized mounds of the mixture on to the tray. Place about 2cm (1") apart to allow for spreading in the oven. Bake for about 15 minutes, or until golden-brown. Leave to cool on the baking tray.

Crispy chocolate fruit 'n' nut slice

Really just a sophisticated version of a standard children's party treat, these crispy chocolate slices are very easy to stir up on the hob because of the pre-cooked cereal base. They're excellent for serving to people with wheat and dairy avoidances – and are popular with everyone else too.

For approx. 15 slices
(1 x 17cm x 25cm / 7" x 10" tin, or 2 bread tins)

200g (7oz) dark chocolate, chopped or 'chips'
100g (3½oz / 2⅓ cups) organic rice crispies*
1 tbsp butter, margarine or creamed coconut
1 tbsp honey or golden syrup
50g (2oz / ¼ cup) apricots or dates, finely chopped
50g (2oz / ½ cup) raisins, chopped
1 tbsp + 1 tbsp sesame seeds
70g (2½oz / rounded ½ cup) walnuts, chopped
1 pinch fine salt

For approx. 60 slices
(2 x 25cm x 33cm / 10" x 13" roasting tins)

800g (1lb 12oz)
400g (14oz / 10 cups)
60g (2oz / 4 tbsp)
4 tbsp
200g (7oz / 1 cup)
200g (7oz / 2 cups)
4 tbsp + 4 tbsp
280g (10oz / 2½ cups)
½ tsp

1. Put the chopped chocolate (or chips), butter/margarine/coconut, honey and salt in a heatproof bowl. Rest this in a saucepan containing a couple of inches of boiling water and simmer gently until melted.

2. Meanwhile chop the dried fruit and nuts into smallish pieces that will give a decent amount of texture. Set aside half the sesame seeds and just under one-third of the chopped walnuts, for scattering on the top later.

3. Combine the rice crispies in a bowl with the remaining dried fruit, seeds and nuts. Clean, dry hands are the best tool for mixing the two together, as you will need to break up any sticky dried fruit pieces without crushing the crisped rice.

4. Stir the melted chocolate until smooth, then mix with the dry ingredients, until all the rice crispies are uniformly coated with chocolate.

5. Tip into tins that have been lightly oiled and, preferably, lined with baking parchment. Spread out in a fairly general way and then scatter immediately with the chopped walnuts and sesame seeds you have set aside. Now get a flat-bottomed tumbler or a cup measure and use it to lightly press down the mixture so the top is flattened (but not crushed). Leave to set for an hour in a cool place.

6. When the slice is set, use a sharp serrated knife to carve into neat rectangular slices measuring 3cm x 6cm (1" x 2") – or try 3cm x 3cm (1" x 1") squares if you want to double your yield! The crispy slices will keep well in an airtight container.

*Important: if you're catering for anyone with a serious gluten intolerance, be aware that standard non-organic Rice Krispies (and Corn Flakes) are flavoured with barley malt, which is not gluten-free.

Squidgy choc-chip cookies

Typically 'Sarah Bayley', these cookies are squidgy and sweet – like a brownie in cookie's clothing. Chocaholics go crazy for them. Because of the high proportion of fat and sugar to flour, they spread wickedly in the oven, so make sure you space them well apart on your baking tray.

For 20-25 cookies	For 80-100 cookies
125g (4½oz / 1¼ sticks) butter or margarine, softened	500g (1lb 2oz / 4½ sticks)
1 cup (170g / 6oz) golden granulated sugar	4 cups (680g / 1½lb)
1 egg	4
1 tsp vanilla essence	4
1 cup (140g / 5oz) plain flour	4 cups (560g / 1lb 4oz)
⅓ cup (35g / 1¼oz 6 tbsp) cocoa powder	1⅓ cups (140g / 5oz)
½ tsp bicarbonate of soda	2 tsp
¼ tsp salt	1 tsp
½ cup (75g / 2½oz) chocolate chips	2 cups (280g / 10oz)
1 tbsp water (or coffee or orange juice) if using butter*	4 tbsp if using butter*

1. If you are planning to bake the cookies straight away, pre-heat the oven to 200°C (400°F / Gas Mark 6).

2. Cream together the softened butter or margarine with the sugar.

3. Add the vanilla essence and then the eggs, one by one. Also add the water / coffee / orange juice, if using butter.

4. Measure the flour and mix with the salt, bicarb and sifted cocoa powder.

5. Mix the dry ingredients into the wet mixture, along with the chocolate chips, until thoroughly combined. If you wish, you can chill the mixture at this stage for baking later.

6. Scoop out walnut-sized portions of the cookie dough with a teaspoon. Place these little chocolatey mountains well apart (about 8cm / 3") on a baking tray that has been oiled or lined with baking parchment – they will melt down and spread out. If the mix has been made in advance and chilled, the cookies can be rolled between the palms of your hands and then flattened a bit – otherwise the mixture is too sticky to hand-roll.

7. Cook for a mere 10 minutes in the hot oven until the crazed surface begins to dull and is no longer sticky. Once cooked, the cookies will stiffen as they cool but should still remain bendable and chewy: if they are brittle, try cooking them a bit less next time. Leave to cool on the baking tray for the first 10-15 minutes before shifting to a wire cooling rack.

In case you're wondering why liquid is added only if using butter, this is because Sarah always bakes these cookies with margarine, because her husband avoids dairy products. Margarine has a greater water content than butter, so you need to make up for this if you're using butter, to get the same squidgy effect.

Orange-polenta triangles

The crunch of polenta in these rustically sophisticated cookies really makes a pleasant change! Slice them as thinly as you can and cook them for half the time that most cookies take. Delicious with fresh coffee or a herbal tea . . .

For 30-40 cookies	For 60-80 cookies
1½ cups (250g / 9oz) fine yellow polenta	3 cups (500g / 1lb 2oz)
1 cup (140g / 5oz) white flour	2 cups (280g / 10oz)
1 cup (140g / 5oz) brown flour	2 cups (280g / 10oz)
1 cup (170g / 6oz) light brown / golden caster sugar mix	1 cup (175g / 6oz)
280g (10oz / 2½ sticks) butter	550g (1lb 4oz)
Zest of 2 organic oranges	Zest of 3
Zest of half an organic lemon	Zest of 1
Juice of 1 orange and half a lemon	Juice of 2 oranges and 1 lemon
1 egg yolk + a little white	1 egg + 1 yolk
½ cup (50g / 2oz) pine nuts (optional)	1 cup (100g / 4oz) (optional)
1 tsp ground cinnamon	2 tsp
½ rounded tsp salt	1 rounded tsp
approx. ½ cup (50g / 2oz) sesame seeds to coat	approx. 1 cup (125g / 4 oz)

1. Peel the zest thinly from the oranges and lemons with a potato peeler. Chop it up fairly coarsely, then mix it with approximately half the sugar and flour, then grind this, a bit at a time, in a clean coffee grinder until powdery.

2. Place this mixture in a large bowl and combine with the polenta, the rest of the flour, and the cinnamon and salt. Add the butter and rub in until a breadcrumby consistency is obtained.

3. Heat the lemon and orange juice in a smallish saucepan and simmer vigorously to reduce to 25ml / 1fl oz (small quantity), 50ml / 2fl oz (large quantity).

4. Add the egg, pine nuts (if using) and reduced orange/lemon juice to the crumb mixture. Mix with a wooden spoon then press together with your hands to form a malleable dough.

5. Divide the mixture into two or four pieces (depending on the quantity you're making) and shape into triangular logs with each side 5cm (2") wide. Improve the angles of the log by pressing each side of the triangle against the flat work surface and pinching along the corners. Paint with milk and coat with sesame seeds. Wrap and chill the logs for 30 minutes (or more). Pre-heat the oven to 180°C (350°F / Gas Mark 4).

6. Remove the logs from the fridge and allow to sit for a bit to lose their chill, then slice carefully into triangular cookies, only about 3mm (⅛") thick. Arrange on a prepared baking sheet and bake for a mere 10 minutes. The finished cookies should be a lovely orangey shade of golden-brown at the edges; lighter in the middle. Cool on the tray for 10 minutes before moving to a wire cooling rack.

Bread

Irish potato soda bread
Sunny spelt bread
Walnut & fig (or cranberry or apricot) bread
Introducing Borodinsky bread
Creating a sourdough leaven or starter
Borodinsky rye bread
Fruity Borodinsky variations
Gluten-free golden bread
Giant squash & sun-dried tomato baguette
Potato parathas
Oat & apple bread
Poppy, pitta & polenta breads
Pot bread

Irish potato soda bread

Soda bread is easy to make and provides a useful alternative to yeasted bread. As with scones, its character can be varied by the addition or deletion of sweet and savoury ingredients. So, for example, you can create another distinctive Irish soda bread taste by adding raisins, caraway seeds and a little sugar, while leaving out the cheese, potato and herbs. Or try adding lemon, poppy seeds and chopped almonds for a Czech flavour! The original recipe was sent to me by Zemfira Inogamova, who came from Kyrgyzstan on a scholarship awarded by the Christensen Fund to attend the MSc in Holistic Science 2008-9.

For 1 round loaf	For 6 round loaves
300g (10oz / 2 cups) flour (all white or 50:50 white/wholewheat)	1.8kg (4lb)
½ tsp salt	1 tbsp
1½ tsp baking powder (or use self-raising flour)	3 tbsp
½ tsp bicarbonate of soda	1 tbsp
1-2 tsp dried herbs (thyme, marjoram, mixed herbs, etc.)	2-4 tbsp
1 tbsp fresh parsley, chopped (optional)	4-6 tbsp (optional)
3-4 spring onions, chopped (optional)	2 bunches (optional)
1 medium potato, peeled and grated (approx. 150g / 6oz)	6 (about 1kg / 2lb)
85g (3oz / ¾ cup) Cheddar, grated (or feta / goat's cheese, crumbled)	500g (1lb 2oz)
1 large egg, beaten	6 large / 8 medium
75-100ml (3fl oz / ⅓ cup) whole milk	550-600ml (1 pint / 2¼- 2½ cups)
1 tsp grainy mustard	2-3 tbsp
1 tbsp olive oil or melted butter	100ml (3fl oz / ⅓ cup)

1. Mix together the dry ingredients – flour, salt, baking powder, bicarbonate of soda and herbs – with the spring onions and the fresh parsley, if using. Grate, crumble or chop the cheese and add to this mixture too.

2. Pre-heat the oven to 180°C (350°F / Gas Mark 4) and prepare a metal baking tray by oiling or lining it with baking parchment.

3. In a separate bowl, mix together the egg, milk, mustard and melted butter or oil.

4. Peel and grate the potato. Stir this into the egg mixture, then tip the lot into the dry ingredients. Mix well and form a dough with your hands. If the dough is too sticky to handle lightly, add a little flour. Knead lightly with your hands and shape into either one (small quantity) or six (large quantity) plump, flour-dusted 'frisbees'. Place on your prepared tray. If making more than one, the breads need to be 5cm (2") apart on the baking tray to allow for rising. Cut a cross on top with a sharp knife.

5. Bake straight away for 35-45 minutes, until the bread is turning brown, feeling fairly firm, and sounding hollow when the base is tapped. Cool on a wire rack for 10-15 minutes. Cut in thin slices or wedges and serve warm with butter.

Sunny spelt bread

Spelt is an ancient form of wheat, with roots that go back some 9,000 years to the 'Fertile Crescent' in the Middle East. In modern times it was almost forgotten, because the expensive equipment needed to remove its tight outer hulls made it uneconomical to produce. However, in the 1980s people suffering from health problems associated with modern hybridized wheat began to notice that they could eat spelt without negative effects. Although spelt contains more protein than other wheat, this protein forms less gluten when made into bread. Spelt also has higher levels of vitamins B and E than modern wheat, as well as more fatty acids, which are important for regenerating nerve cells.

Spelt flour absorbs more water than ordinary wheat, so the most successful spelt bread is made using a moist dough that requires little (or no) kneading. This loaf will rise faster than an ordinary wheat dough, and still be well aerated and full of flavour. You can also make it as a sourdough, by substituting rye with spelt flour in the Borodinsky recipe (see page 242).

For 1 loaf or 8-10 rolls
(1 x 1kg / 2lb loaf tin or 1 baking tray)

300g (10oz / 3 cups) spelt flour
100g (4oz / 1 cup) white spelt flour or plain flour
1 tsp dried yeast or ½oz (10g / 2 tsp) fresh yeast
300ml (11fl oz / 1¼ cups) warm water
1 tsp honey, or agave or date syrup
1 tsp salt
2 tbsp sunflower seeds + 1 tbsp for topping
A little milk or egg wash to glue seeds on top

For 6 loaves or 50-60 rolls
(6 x 1kg / 2lb loaf tins or 1 baking tray)

1.8kg (3lb 12oz)
600g (1½lb)
2 tbsp dried or 75g (2½oz) fresh
1.8l (3¼ pints / 4 US pints)
2 tbsp
2 level tbsp
150ml / ½ cup + 50ml / ¼ cup
1 egg / 2 tbsp milk or soya milk

1. Measure the warm water into a jug and stir in the sweetener and dried yeast or crumbled fresh yeast, stirring until dissolved. In a large bowl, combine the flour, sunflower seeds and salt. Traditional dried yeast can be left to froth up merrily if you wish, but this isn't a total necessity.

2. Stir the yeasty water into the flour. Mix until you have a soft dough that is sticky to touch, but not runny or lumpy. Turn out on to a floured tabletop and cut into portions for rolls or loaves, as required. Flour your hands and knead each piece briefly just to give it shape. For loaves, you are aiming at cocoon-shaped ovals that can be popped into an oiled and floured tin. For the rolls, go for tangerine-sized balls. Because this is a wet mixture, do not attempt the normal amount of kneading. Paint with beaten egg / milk / soya milk and sprinkle with sunflower seeds.

3. Leave to rise in a warm place for 30-50 minutes to double in size. The rolls will need only about 15 minutes.

4. Pre-heat the oven to 180°C (350°F / Gas Mark 4) about 10 minutes before your bread is ready to go in. Bake loaves for about 45 minutes: when ready, they should fall out of the tin easily and sound hollow when knocked on the base. Remove from the tins and cool on a wire rack. Rolls will be ready after 20-25 minutes: when ready, they too will sound hollow when knocked, and their sides will feel soft but not doughy when pinched.

Walnut & fig (or cranberry or apricot) bread

Ruth Rae's light brown, fruit-and-nut dappled bread is delicious with cheese and can also be served at teatime with jam and honey. It also provides the opportunity to experiment with a little decorative knife work – which is something Ruth is well practised at! Simply cut through the floured surface of the rising bread using a sharp knife (which could be serrated or just very sharp – some people use a scalpel). You'll also need swift, confident strokes – and a clear, simple concept.

For 1 loaf

300g (10oz / 2 cups) strong white flour
150g (6oz / 1¼ cups) wholewheat flour
55g (2oz / ½ cup) golden walnuts
85g (3oz / ½ cup) dried figs (or dried cranberries or apricots)
1 tsp dried yeast or 10g (⅓-½oz / 2 tsp) fresh yeast
300ml (10fl oz / 1 cup + 2 tsp) warm water
1-2 tbsp olive or sunflower oil
1 tsp molasses
1 tsp salt

For 6 round loaves

1.8kg (4lb)
900g (2lb)
350g (12oz / 3 cups)
500g (1lb / 3 cups)
2 tbsp dried or 75g (2½oz) fresh
1.5l (2¾ pints / 3½ US pints)
100ml (3-4fl oz / ½ cup)
2 tbsp
2 tbsp

1. *Preparing the fruit and nuts:* Just cover the dried fruit with hot water and soak for 30 minutes (figs or apricots) or 10 minutes (cranberries). Meanwhile, chop the walnuts roughly with a knife – each walnut half will go into about 4-6 pieces. After soaking, drain the softened fruit, reserving the water to go into the dough. Chop the figs or apricots) into small chunky pieces (about 1cm / ½" wide). Remove the woody stalk part of the figs if it's tough.

2. Measure 250ml (9fl oz / 1 cup) of warm water into a jug and stir in the molasses and the dried or crumbled fresh yeast. If using dried yeast, leave to froth up; with the fresh yeast, simply stir until dissolved. Easy-bake or fast-acting yeast can go in with the flour or with the water.

3. In a large bowl, combine the flours, salt, and chopped fruit and nuts.

4. Stir in the yeasty water, the rest of the warm water and the oil. Mix until you have a soft dough and all the ingredients are evenly distributed. Knead gently on a floured surface or in the bowl for a few minutes until fairly smooth, then return to the bowl to rise. Using a (dedicated) plant mister, spray the top with water to prevent it drying out, or cover the bowl loosely with a lid or tea towel. Leave to rise in a warm place for an hour.

5. When the dough has doubled in size, tip it on to a lightly floured surface and 'knock back'. Knead lightly and then divide into 6 if you are making the large quantity, then knead each ball again. Shape into rounds or ovals. Keep the joints at the bottom and make sure the top skin has not been over-stretched: if there is any sign of surface splitting, loosen it with a little gentle rocking, or let it rest and then knead again in a few minutes, being careful not to shape it too tightly.

6. Place the round cushions of dough on a baking tray, either floured or lined with baking parchment. If you're making more than one loaf, they should be placed about the width of your hand apart, to allow for spreading as they rise. Spray (or paint) with water and dredge with flour for a dusty finish. Use a sharp knife to cut a few criss-crossed lines at 2-3cm (1") intervals and about 2-3mm (⅛") deep – these will open up as the bread rises, creating an attractive textural contrast. Ruth also likes to cut a simple leaf-vein or 'winter tree' design into her loaves – a real classic for artisan bakers. Leave the bread to rise in a warm place for about 40 minutes.

7. Pre-heat the oven to 180°C (350°F / Gas Mark 4), 10 minutes before the bread is ready to go in.

8. When ready to go in the oven, the bread will have doubled in size. If you press it with a finger, the dough will be slow to spring back. Any sign of dimpling on the surface means it has over-risen, so rush it into the oven. It is better to put it in the oven when still – just – on the rise, so that its last burst of rising is stimulated by the heat of the oven. Bake mid-oven for about 45 minutes. Test by turning over and knocking: the loaf should sound hollow. Cool on a wire rack.

Introducing Borodinsky bread

"If Britons took their bread as seriously as Russians, it might be Waterloo or Trafalgar bread that adorned our shelves instead of . . . 'Mother's Pride'." **Andrew Whitley**

If anyone is going to put *real bread* back on the British map it will be Andrew Whitley, founder of the Real Bread Campaign (with Sustain) as well as The Village Bakery – and a teacher at Schumacher College (and elsewhere). Bread baking, it seems, is a pursuit that attracts all sorts of highly intelligent individuals, often men. Although they may be initially drawn to it as a recuperative leisure activity, bread gradually seems to take over their lives, opening the door to a whole realm of health, cultural and consumer issues that simply call out for articulate and dedicated champions.

Here at Schumacher College it is Voirrey Watterson, a small, vibrant and passionate woman who flies the flag for *slow* bread, and bakes the wholesome, tempting substance with great fervour several times a week. Voirrey first arrived as a volunteer at Schumacher College in time for a bread festival organized by Eva Bakkeslett. This was also Andrew Whitley's first visit as a teacher, and we can thank not only Eva but also Fritz Schumacher for drawing him here. As a young man, Andrew had been enormously inspired by meeting E. F. Schumacher and reading his seminal works, *Small Is Beautiful* and *A Guide for the Perplexed*, and was thus intrigued to discover what was going on at a place named after the great man. Before Andrew departed, Justin West, founder of our forest garden, begged a little pot of leaven from him containing a trace of the original leaven Andrew had brought back from Russia, 17 years earlier. Now, several years later, this rye leaven has spread all over Totnes, fermenting, expanding and returning the possibility of real, battle-winning, Russian-style Borodinsky bread to its recipients.

Voirrey quickly acquired the job of baking the Borodinsky bread spawned by Andrew's leaven every week, and upped its production levels to such an extent that people quickly began to call it 'Vorodinsky'. But it didn't stop at that. Voirrey's bread has now become the mainstay of the College snack area, and includes several different varieties of slow bread. (Andrew's book *Bread Matters* is so well thumbed by Voirrey's leaven-drenched fingers that it almost looks as if it's turning into a loaf of bread itself!)

Back now to Borodinsky: the recipe – and the history. The story goes that this bread was first baked on the eve of the decisive battle of Borodino in 1812, when Russian forces confronted Napoleon in a small village just outside Moscow. The General's wife wanted to encourage the troops, and when she found coriander seeds ripening in the early September sun, she decided to crush some and include them in the mix, along with a rye malt called 'suslo', which Andrew has substituted with malt extract and molasses to obtain a similar taste – and the same "old-engine-oil texture"!

This bread is really very easy and satisfying to make. Because of the sweetness that the molasses and malt feed to the natural rye yeasts, it rises quite quickly for a *slow* bread (only a few hours!), so is a very encouraging sourdough bread to begin with.

When making Borodinsky bread, you will normally need to allow two days to complete the process, as well as one day to allow the bread to dry out. The sourdough method is particularly suited to making rye breads, as they need to be made with a sloppy dough and given a single long proving time. As rye doughs do not develop the same elasticity as wheat, there is no point in aiming for a kneadable dough, which will result in a bread that is too dry and, as Andrew says, "close to concrete".

Creating a sourdough leaven or starter

If you don't have a leaven, or access to one, you'll need to make your own, starting a week before you make your bread. After that, you can keep your leaven in your fridge, replenishing it every time you bake. The wild yeasts in rye flour make it the ideal flour to use for creating a leaven. To this you need only add water, air and time. Some bakers advise adding raisins or yoghurt to boost the process; others suggest making your leaven in the open air, so wild yeasts arrive in the mix – but I like the simplicity of this recipe, which is based on the one used by Andrew Whitley in *Bread Matters* and *Do Sourdough:* (see Bibliography), in which all liquid measurements are weighed for precision and convenience.

Find a warm spot to ferment your starter – 28-30°C (82-86°F) is optimum, and will encourage natural yeasts to operate at their maximum level of reproductivity. Below or above this temperature the process will take longer. A spot on a shelf near a radiator or cooker is often ideal.

Day 1. Combine:

25g (1oz / ¼ cup) organic wholemeal (dark) rye flour

4 tbsp (50g) warm water (at 40°C / 104°F)

Mix the rye flour and warm water to a sloppy paste. A bowl with a plate on top, or Kilner-style jar (not clipped down) can be used for this.

Day 2. Add:

25g (1oz / ¼ cup) wholemeal (dark) rye flour

50g (4 tbsp) warm water (at 40°C)

Starter from Day 1

Stir the fresh flour and water into the starter, cover and return to a warm place.

Day 3. Add:

25g (1oz / ¼ cup) wholemeal (dark) rye flour

50g (4 tbsp) warm water (at 40°C)

Starter from Days 1 and 2

Stir the fresh flour and water into the starter, which may now show signs of frothing. Cover and return to a warm place.

Day 4. Add:

25g (1oz / ¼ cup) wholemeal (dark) rye flour

4 tbsp (50g) warm water (at 40°C)

Starter from Days 1, 2 and 3 (300g / 10½oz total weight)

Once again, mix the fresh flour and water into the starter. By the following day you should have a sour mixture that has bubbled up and subsided. It should smell fruity and taste mildly acidic. If your starter shows no signs of life after Day 5, repeat the additions of Day 4 – it probably just needs a little longer to get going. (More detailed instructions in both *Bread Matters* and *Do Sourdough*). Store your starter in a plastic tub, small lidded crock or glass jar – with the lid closed to keep out stray bacteria, but not too tightly, as leavens can get very lively and swell up. Never fill your containers more than three-quarters of the way to the top.

Borodinsky rye bread

Day 1: Creating your refreshed starter

For 1 small loaf

50g (2oz / ⅓ cup) rye sourdough starter
150g (6oz / 1 rounded cup) dark rye flour
300ml (11fl oz / 1¼ cup) warm water

For 6-8 standard loaves

300g (10½ oz / 1 cup)
900g (2lb / 6 cups)
1.8l (3 pints / 4 US pints)

Mix everything together into a very sloppy dough, in a bowl that allows plenty of room for the leaven to rise and fall. Cover and leave in a warm place for 10-18 hours.

Day 2: Final dough and baking

For 1 small loaf
(1 x 500g / 1lb loaf tin)

270g (10oz / 1 cup) refreshed starter (see above)
230g (8oz / 1⅔ cups) light or wholemeal rye flour
1 tsp fine sea salt
100ml / (3½fl oz / just under ½ cup) warm water
20g (¾oz / 1 heaped tbsp) blackstrap molasses
15g (¾oz / 2 tsp) barley malt extract
2-3 tbsp coriander, caraway, sesame or sunflower seeds

For 6-8 standard loaves
(6-8 x 1kg / 2lb loaf tins)

2.25kg (5lb)
2kg (4½lb)
3 tbsp
900ml (1½ pints / 2 US pints)
180g (6oz / heaped ½ cup)
150g (5oz / ½ cup)
Up to 200g (7oz / 1-1½ cups)

1. Oil your loaf tins and sprinkle half your chosen seeds over the base. The oil will stop them rolling around. (If you don't want to use seeds, line the tin with baking parchment or a sprinkling of rye flour on top of the oil to ease the turning out.)

2. 10-18 hours after refreshing the sourdough starter, stir it well and measure off the correct amount for the recipe, putting the excess carefully away in the fridge for next time (while the refreshed starter is still young, recombine it with the rest of your unused starter to continue to develop potency. Later, if not used regularly, acidity will build up. This has the advantage of keeping away harmful bacteria, but to get a 6-week or older leaven back in good condition you may need to do a double refreshment, using just half the starter, then half again, over two days,).

3. Mix all the bread ingredients thoroughly into the measured-off starter. Most of the seeds can go in whole – keep a few back for the top. However, if you want to include coriander, Andrew suggests using it ground. Therefore grind the second half of the coriander seeds using an electric coffee/spice grinder or pestle and mortar, and include 1½ tsp (small quantity) or 4-5 tbsp (large quantity) in the mix, leaving a little remaining for the top. (Admittedly, there are so many people at Schumacher College who say that the taste of coriander seed does not go with their breakfast marmalade that we rarely put the ground seed in the bread, and only occasionally on the base and top.) The mixture will be too sloppy to mould, so, as Andrew says, "enjoy the slippery, mud-pie feeling and the fragrance of this wonderful dough" as you scoop it into the prepared bread tin, filling it just over half-full.

4. Leave for 2-6 hours, depending on the warmth of your kitchen and the vigour of your sourdough. It should reach the top of your tin when fully proven, and a few tiny burst bubbles may have appeared (as if to proclaim that the Borodinsky is alive, breathing and fit for battle!). Paint the top with a little of the leftover starter and sprinkle with the remaining seeds. Pre-heat the oven to 220°C (425°F / Gas Mark 7).

5. Put the loaf into the hot oven immediately. After 10 minutes, turn the heat down to 200°C (400°F / Gas Mark 6). Bake for about 50-60 minutes. When ready, the loaf should shrink away from the sides and come out of the tin easily. If not, return it to the oven for a few more minutes and try again. Slide a knife down the edges to release any sticking points if necessary. Voirrey says that in her experience the bread is ready when it comes out easily. As with other breads, it will feel fairly hollow when tapped on the base – though perhaps not quite so drum-like as with ordinary bread, because of the high moisture content. (If you pinch its sides they will feel firm, but with a hint of underlying wobble.)

6. Leave the bread to cool completely before wrapping and resting it for a day, as the crumb can be quite gummy in consistency when first baked. Voirrey likes to leave her bread unwrapped and drying in the open for a day or two before it is eaten. For some mysterious reason the crumb usually goes darker as the days pass.

Variations: One of the very photogenic variations of the Borodinsky rye sourdough is pictured above. Spot the glacé cherries and the nuts, and you'll know its Voirrey's Luxury fruit Borodinky (see overleaf) that has stolen the limelight from its plainer cousin – who really should have been shown here, posing with cheese!

Fruity Borodinsky variations

Voirrey and I have been so inspired by Andrew's recipe that we have produced a couple of fruity variations. My own is a malt-loaf-style bread that can be buttered and served at coffee break. Voirrey's recipe (pictured on page 243) is much more luxurious, and definitely requires no buttering. You can also make these breads using half rye and half spelt flour, for a more wheaty taste.

Everyday fruit Borodinsky

For 1 small loaf
(1 x 500g / 1lb loaf tin)

270g (10oz / 1 cup) refreshed starter (see page 242)
230g (8oz / 1⅔ cups) rye flour
1 tsp fine sea salt
100ml (3½fl oz / ½ cup) warm water
40g (2oz / 2 heaped tbsp) blackstrap molasses
30g (1½oz / 2 tbsp) barley malt extract
1 tsp mixed spice
1 pinch ground cinnamon
100g (4oz / ¾ cup) sultanas
100g (4oz / ¾ cup) raisins

For 7-8 standard loaves
(7-8 x 1kg / 2lb loaf tins)

1.6kg (3½lb)
1.4kg (3lb 2oz)
30g (2 tbsp)
550ml / 1 pint / 2¼ cups)
360g (12oz / 1¼ cup)
300g (10oz / 1cup)
2 tbsp
2 tsp
600g (1lb 12oz / 4½ cups)
600g (1lb 12oz / 4½ cups)

Simply follow the Borodinksy recipe on page 242, but double the molasses and malt extract (as indicated) and add the fruit and spices at Step 3.

Luxury fruit Borodinsky

(Ingredients as above, but with the following larger and more varied combination of fruit)

85g (3oz / rounded ½ cup) sultanas
85g (3oz / rounded ½ cup) raisins
50g (2oz / ⅓ cup) natural glacé cherries, used whole
50g (2oz / ½ cup) dried figs, apricots or mixed peel
115g (4oz / 1 cup) blanched almonds or cashews
approx. 300ml (½ pint / 1¼ cups) apple / orange juice (for soaking)

500g (1lb 2oz / 3 cups)
500g (1lb 2oz / 3 cups)
350g (12oz / 2 cups)
340g (12oz / 3 cups)
680g (1½lb / 6 cups)
approx. 1½l (2¾ pints / 3½ US pints)

Soak the dried fruit and *half* the nuts in the apple or orange juice overnight. Next day, drain the fruit (include the surplus juice as part of the recipe's liquid), then follow the plain Borodinsky recipe (page 242), adding the soaked fruit and nuts to the mix at Step 3. (Andrew Whitley says that pre-soaking the nuts gives them a lovely 'buttery' consistency.) Once the dough has risen, rough-chop and sprinkle the unsoaked half of the nuts on top, painting first with water or egg wash to help stick them down. Bake as for the plain Borodinsky bread.

Gluten-free golden bread

More and more people seem to be developing an intolerance to gluten – which is a natural, very elastic protein found in wheat, rye, barley and sometimes oats. Our wonderful post-grad liaison volunteer, Alex Lagaisse (Toombes), inspired this full-flavoured, well-aerated gluten-free bread, which doesn't rely on pre-mixes, and is now our number-one favourite in the 'GF' bread bin.

1 medium loaf of bread (1 x 1kg / 2lb loaf tin)	**3 medium loaves** (3 x 1kg / 2lb loaf tins)
140g (5oz / 1 cup) maize flour	400g (14oz / 3 scant cups)
140g (5oz / 1 cup) rice flour	400g (14oz / 3 scant cups)
100g (4oz / ¾ cup) buckwheat or GF oat flour	300g (11oz / 2 cups)
50g (2oz / ⅓ cup) sunflower seeds	150g (5oz / 1 cup)
2 tsp xanthan gum (if available)	2 tbsp
1 tsp salt	1 tbsp
1 tbsp sugar or honey	3 tbsp
1½ tsp dried yeast	4 tsp
1 egg	3
1 tsp white wine or cider vinegar	1 tbsp
370ml (13fl oz / 1½ cups) warm water	1.1l (2 pints / 4½ cups)

1. Combine the flours, xanthan gum and salt in the bowl of an electric food mixer (or ordinary mixing bowl). Dissolve the dried yeast and sugar or honey in the warm water, and leave in a warm place for the yeast to become foamy. Meanwhile, beat together the eggs and vinegar.

2. Add the yeasty mixture and the egg mixture to the dry ingredients. Mix well on a medium speed for 10 minutes using the mixer's paddle. You are aiming for a thick, free-flowing consistency – a bit like a cake mixture. If you don't have a mixing machine, beat well with a wooden spoon – we've found that the mixing stage really makes a difference to the eventual rise of this bread, so the workout is worth it!

3. Line the tin with baking parchment or brush with sunflower oil and dust with maize flour. Pour in the batter. Lightly dab the top with oil to prevent a skin forming, and leave in a warm, draught-free place to rise.

4. Allow the dough to rise until the dough is *almost* at the top of the tin. This will take 20-40 minutes, depending on the warmth of the kitchen. Pre-heat the oven to 190°C (375°F / Gas Mark 5).

5. Bake the bread for approximately 45 minutes. Turn out of tin and then return it to the oven for a further 10 minutes until the bread is golden-brown and sounds hollow when tapped. Leave to cool on a wire rack.

Variations: Enhance the savoury potential of this bread by adding finely chopped chillies, chilli powder or flakes – or include chopped herbs such as rosemary. For a sweet option, add cinnamon, a handful of currants and some mixed peel (not too much, or the rising will be inhibited).

Giant squash & sun-dried tomato baguette

I originally made this giant baguette for the first birthday celebration of the yurt village at Embercombe in Devon. It was one of those happy Sunday inventions constrained by what you have in the cupboard and garden, and is delicious served warm from the oven with butter. Choose a good flavoursome butternut or other orange-fleshed squash, such as Hubbard or Crown Prince.

For one large baguette (10 slices)	For 5 large or 8 smaller baguettes (serves 60+)
Filling	
225g (8oz / 1½-2 cups) squash, peeled and cubed to 1.5cm (½")	1.15kg (2½lb)
50g (2oz / ½ cup) sun-dried tomatoes	250g (10oz / 2½ cups)
5-6 cloves garlic, finely sliced	2 heads
225g (8oz / 1½ cups) medium Cheddar, cubed to 1.5cm (½")	1.15kg (2½lb)
1 tbsp olive oil (for drizzling)	5-6 tbsp
Dough	
550g (1lb 4oz / 4 cups) white unbleached flour	2.75kg (6lb 4oz)
100g (4oz / ¾ cup) rye flour	500g (1lb 2oz)
1 heaped tsp salt	2 tbsp
4-5 sprigs garden-fresh rosemary, approx. 5cm (2") long	18-24
1 tsp dried yeast or 10g (½oz) fresh yeast	5 tsp dried or 50g (2oz) fresh
1 tsp sugar or honey	2 tbsp
350ml (12fl oz / 1½ cups) warm water / tomato-soaking liquid	1.75l (3 pints / 3¾ US pints)
1 tbsp olive oil + 1-2 tsp for top	6 tbsp + 3 tbsp
approx. 1 tbsp pumpkin seeds and a little milk or egg for top	6 tbsp seeds and 1 egg

1. Cover the sun-dried tomatoes with water and leave to rehydrate for an hour. When ready, drain and keep the liquid to use in the dough. Chop into small pieces and set aside.

2. Make up the tomato liquid with warm water to the correct volume for the dough. If making the small quantity, add the sugar or honey, then stir in the yeast until dissolved. For the large quantity, separate off about a quarter of the warm liquid and dissolve the yeast and sugar into this.

3. Measure the flours and salt into a large bowl. Pull the lower leaves off the rosemary sprigs, chop these finely and add to the flour. Set aside the remaining tufty-sprigs (now with a bare 'trunk').

4. Once the dried yeast has frothed up (or fresh yeast dissolved), stir it into the flour along with olive oil (and, for the large quantity, the remaining liquid). When the liquid has been absorbed, knead together with your hands. You are aiming for a soft, pliable, but not too sticky dough. Only minimal kneading is required at this stage. Leave the dough in a warm, non-draughty place to rise in the bowl for 40-60 minutes. Either spray with water or cover loosely with a cloth or lid. Pre-heat the oven to 190°C (375°F / Gas Mark 5).

5. Meanwhile, prepare the squash. Spread it out one layer thick on a metal baking tray, drizzle with olive oil, season with salt, mix and spread out again. Roast in the hot oven for 20-25 minutes. After the first 10-15 minutes, stir in the garlic also. When ready, the squash should still be al dente and holding its shape well. Tip into a flattish ceramic baking dish to cool, and reduce the oven temperature to 180°C (350°F / Gas Mark 4).

6. When the squash is cool enough not to melt the cheese cubes, add these and the sun-dried tomatoes, and mix all together in the baking dish.

7. The dough should by now be well risen, so punch it down and turn on to a lightly floured surface. For the large quantity, divide into 5 pieces (or make 8 smaller loaves if you prefer). Knead each portion into a smooth ball, then roll out until the dough begins to resist. Leave it to relax while you move on to the next, then go back to rolling each portion again, by which time they will have less resistance. Shape each piece of dough into a large square-ish rectangle about 1cm (½") thick, and place on baking trays or on a floured work surface.

8. Spread the filling evenly over the dough, leaving 2-3cm (1") at the edges. Wet the edges, then, bending one of the longer edges over the mix, roll up into a sausage, pressing together as you go. Pinch the ends together, and make sure the joint line is underneath, so it doesn't open up.

9. Move the dough to a parchment-lined or flour-dusted metal baking tray, and poke a skewer deeply into it at 3cm (1") intervals, making sure it touches the bottom. This will allow some of the trapped air to escape during baking, without inflating the baguette. Paint with a mixture of milk and olive oil or egg and oil, and sprinkle with pumpkin seeds. Lastly, insert the reserved sprigs of rosemary into several of the skewered holes, so only the tufty top sticks out of the baguette. (Or just scatter rosemary over the top among the pumpkin seeds.) Set aside to rise for about 20 minutes.

10. Bake for 45-60 minutes. When ready, the baguette will be well risen and golden-brown, and sound hollow if tapped lightly on the base.

Potato parathas

I tasted my first potato paratha warm from a 'silver' tiffin tin some 20 years ago in Rajasthan. We were staying at Tarun Baharat Sangh, an ecological ashram founded by Rajendra Singh. This courageous man had dedicated himself to rooting out the illegal mining of dolomite for cosmetics in Sariska wildlife reserve, and was also committed to heading off the decline of tigers – but that's another story! Suffice to say, on a rather more mundane note, that I discovered at that time that potato parathas make great picnic food and are delicious served cold, as well as (even more delicious) hot.

Aman Singh, younger brother of Rajendra, and our guide on this occasion, subsequently came on two courses at Schumacher College and now runs his own NGO in Rajasthan with his wife Prathiba, who has also attended a course here.

This paratha recipe comes from Minni Jain, who lives in Dartington – but cooks 'in Indian' – and whose NGO, Earthlinks, straddles both these worlds, connecting Minni with Schumacher College and Rajendra Singh.

For approx. 6 parathas	**For approx. 50**
Potato filling	
250g (9oz) 'new' or waxy potatoes	2kg (4½lb)
½ tsp salt to taste	approx. 1½ tbsp to taste
1 pinch chilli powder (or to taste)	1-2 tsp to taste
Half a fresh green chilli, finely chopped (optional)	4 (to taste) (optional)
1 pinch asafoetida (if available)	1½ tsp
1-1½ tsp ground coriander	3 tbsp
1 tbsp coriander leaf, finely chopped (optional)	30g (1oz / ½ cup) (optional)
Dough	
150g (5oz / 1 cup) brown flour	1.2kg (2½lb)
75g (3oz / rounded ½ cup) white flour	600g (1½lb)
½ tsp sea salt	4 tsp
150ml (5fl oz / ⅔ cup) lukewarm water	1.2l (2 pints / 2½ US pints)
A little oil for frying (e.g. sunflower oil)	approx. 100ml (4fl oz / ½ cup)

1. Select your potatoes carefully: go for 'new' or waxy varieties, the sort that will produce a sticky mashed potato. Avoid the more 'floury' baked-potato varieties.

2. Several hours before you plan to cook and serve your parathas, wash the potatoes and cook them whole (unpeeled) until just tender. Turn off the burner and leave them to cool in the water – which may take a few hours if making the large quantity.

3. When the potatoes have cooled, begin making the dough. Mix the warm water into the flours and salt until you have a smooth, flexible dough-lump that resembles a fairly loose bread dough. Cover and leave aside.

4. Next, peel the potatoes – the skins should slip off easily with the use of your fingers and a little scraping knife – then mash.

5. Add the salt, herbs, spices and fresh chilli (if using) to the mash and taste.

6. If making the smaller quantity you can now begin heating your (empty) frying pan on the burner. Use a strong, cast-iron frying pan if possible. If making the larger quantity, wait until you have accumulated several parathas on a plate before warming your pan.

7. Get ready a small plate of flour and keep this close at hand. Next, take a portion of dough the size of a small tangerine and roll it into a ball with your hands. Dip the ball in the flour, covering it all over.

8. Roll out the dough ball with a rolling pin. Halfway through – when the dough is no more than 0.5cm (¼") thick, roundish, and about the size of your hand with the fingers outstretched, put a heaped tablespoon of potato mash into the centre. Now draw the dough together from all sides and bring it up and over the mash, gathering it together like bunched-up curtains. Pinch off the knob of surplus dough at the top, above the joining place. Roll the ball gently in your hands once more, so the joints become smoothed together.

9. Once again, dip and cover both sides of the ball with flour. Start rolling it out gently, jointed side down, and again using the rolling pin. Minni rolls the parathas out with a slight jilt of the rolling pin that spins the expanding circle of dough gently around – it looks very skilled, but she insists it's easy! When the round is again about 0.5cm thick and roughly the size of your hand, the paratha is ready to be fried. (Note: Minni's hands are not enormous – we're thinking smallish side-plate size here!)

10. Place the parathas, one at a time on the hot, flat, dry pan. Wait for 1 minute and then turn them and cook the other side. Wait for half a minute more and then add a teaspoonful of sunflower oil on top of the paratha and turn it over quickly so that it can fry on its oiled side. After a few seconds turn again and fry on the other side once more – no need to add more oil, unless you feel they are a little too dry. When golden-brown, remove from the heat.

11. If making a large quantity, keep your parathas warm in a low oven under some foil, or in a lidded casserole; if cooking for only a small group, serve them as soon as they are ready. They are delicious served with a dollop of melting butter, plain yoghurt and pickle. (For vegan diets, serve with margarine or virgin olive oil – and pickle.)

Oat & apple bread

Oat & apple bread is one of my favourite breads to serve with cheese, and it's a great way to use up some of the local apples that we have in abundance between September and February. The recipe is a kind of hybrid between a sourdough and a yeasted bread, with Andrew Whitley's starter (see page 241) introducing a delicious note of rye to the blend. The advantage of this morph (which has been inspired by one of Dan Lepard's recipes in *The Handmade Loaf* – see Bibliography) is that you get sourdough flavour without any slow-dough worry that your bread may not have risen in time for lunch.

Adding oats to wheat flour helps to lower the Glycaemic Index (GI) of the bread, making it healthier because the rise in blood sugar levels is slow and steady, reducing food cravings and making you feel full for longer. Oats also give bread a moist tenderness that lasts well – in fact, it's so nice that we frequently include leftover breakfast porridge in our 'toaster' bread.

For 1-2 loaves or 8-10 rolls	For 6-7 loaves or 50+ rolls
100g (4oz / ⅔ cup) refreshed rye sourdough (see below)	500g (1lb 4oz / 3⅓ cups)
50g (2oz / ⅔ cup) rolled oats	250g (9oz / 3 cups)
100ml (4fl oz / ½ cup) boiling water	500ml (18fl oz / 2 cups)
200g (7oz / 1 cup) apple, peeled	1kg (2lb 4oz)
½ tsp dried yeast or 2 tsp (10g / ⅓oz) fresh yeast, crumbled	1 tbsp dried or 2 tbsp (40g / 1½oz) fresh
3 tbsp warm water	250ml (9fl oz / 1 cup)
1 tbsp honey	6 tbsp (⅓ cup)
350g (10oz / 2 cups) strong white flour	1.75kg (3lb 2oz)
100g (3oz / ⅔ cup) rye, barley or brown flour	500g (1lb 2oz)
1 tsp caraway seeds (optional)	2 tbsp (optional)
1 tsp fine sea salt	1 tbsp
A little olive oil for kneading	A drizzle or two!
A little beaten egg (from 1 egg)*	1 egg, beaten (3-4 tbsp)*
Oats and a few apple slices for finishing	A handful of oats and 1 good apple

Refreshed sourdough starter (leaven)

50g (2oz / ⅓ cup) rye sourdough starter	100g (4oz / ⅔ cup)
150g (6oz / 1 rounded cup) dark rye flour	300g (12oz / 2 cups)
300ml (10fl oz / 1¼ cup) warm water	600ml (1 pint / 2½ cups)

*For vegan diets, substitute the egg with soya cream, or soya milk or other vegan 'milk'.

1. The day before you intend to make the bread, make sure you have enough leaven, by refreshing the rye sourdough starter as for the Borodinsky rye bread recipe (see page 242). You will need to double the quantity given there for the small loaf if you are making the large batch of oat & apple bread (as shown opposite).

2. On the day of baking, begin by measuring the rolled oats into a heatproof bowl or saucepan and covering with the boiling water. Set aside.

3. While the oats are swelling, grate the whole, peeled, apples down to the core on the coarse side of your grater. Measure the required amount of leaven into a large mixing bowl and stir the grated apple into it.

4. Measure out the warm water and stir the dried or crumbled fresh yeast into it, along with the honey, until dissolved. Mix this into the leaven, then add the soaked oats (which should by now have cooled from boiling to warm).

5. Weigh and mix the dry ingredients – flours, caraway seed (if using) and salt. Tip these into the wet mixture and stir well until you have a soft, sticky (but not runny) dough. (If the dough turns out very sloppy, as opposed to sticky, this is probably because the apples are very watery, and the leaven runnier than expected. Add a little more flour.) Leave to rest for 20 minutes.

6. Sprinkle the dough with a little flour and then knead it lightly on a work surface that has also been dusted with more flour. After a mere 10-20 strokes of kneading, return the lump of dough to an olive-oiled bowl. Allow to rise for an hour.

7. Once more, lightly knead the dough. Shape into one or two (small quantity) or six or seven (large quantity) smooth, oval loaves, with the seam downwards – or into individual tangerine-sized rolls. Place on an oiled and floured (or parchment-covered) baking tray, and brush with beaten egg. (For vegan diets, soya cream is best as a substitute for the egg, but soya milk works too.)

8. *Decoration:* Choose an apple with a nice, unblemished skin and cut into small neat slices. Arrange these decoratively on top of the dough – making some cuts with a knife to press the apple slices part-way into the dough to help prevent them popping off. Smooth a little oil on the uppermost surface of the apple to prevent it drying out. Scatter oats over the rest of the dough surface.

9. Leave in a warm place to rise. Allow 1-2 hours for the loaves, while the rolls will only need about 35-60 minutes, depending on the ambient temperature. Pre-heat the oven to 180°C (350°F / Gas Mark 4).

10. When the dough has almost doubled in size, the bread is ready. Bake mid-oven for about 40-50 minutes for loaves; about 25 minutes for rolls. When ready, the bread should be golden-brown and sound hollow when tapped on the base. Leave to cool on a wire rack.

Variations: A pleasant tea-time variation that is well worth trying is to add a little cinnamon and some sultanas to the dough – they go deliciously with both the oats and the apple.

Tip: If you don't have a leaven on the go and can't wait to make this loaf, simply mix some rye flour and water to a sloppy paste and substitute this for the starter – and double the quantity of yeast.

ppy, pitta & polenta breads

nether it's braided white loaves flecked with poppy seeds, or polenta bread with its gritty yellow crust and creamy interior, ight airy breads – made principally with strong, unbleached, organic white flour – make a refreshing change from the high-fibre, deep-brown loaves that colonize the College bread bins. Flat pitta breads, white or light brown, give further variety and are surprisingly easy to make. These can be served as 'food pockets' at meals that involve stuffable dishes such as fine leafy salads, alfalfa, houmous or grated cheese. All three breads use the same basic dough and basic method. The slight variations in ingredients are given below, with further baking details and shaping techniques on the following pages.

Basic white bread recipe

1 medium loaf or 10 rolls

450g (1lb / 3 rounded cups) strong white flour
1 tsp dried yeast or 2 tsp (10g / ⅓-½oz) fresh yeast, crumbled
250-300ml (9fl oz / 1 cup+) warm water
1 tsp sugar or honey
1-1½ tsp salt
1-2 tbsp olive or sunflower oil

6 loaves or 60 rolls

2.7kg (6lb)
2 tbsp dried or 75g (2½oz) fresh
1.5l (2¾ pints / 3½ US pints)
2 tbsp
2-3 tbsp
100ml (3-4fl oz / ½ cup)

Poppy-seed bread

Add to the basic recipe:

approx. 3-4 tbsp poppy seeds (+ 1-2 tsp for topping)
A little beaten egg (from 1 egg) for glazing*

approx. 150g (5oz / 1 cup) (+ 2-3 tbsp for topping)
1 egg, beaten*

Polenta bread

Substitute approximately one-sixth of the flour in the basic recipe with fine yellow polenta, e.g. use:

400g (14oz / 2½ rounded cups) white flour
50g (2oz / ½ cup) fine yellow polenta

2.25kg (5lb)
450g (1lb)

Pitta bread

Use the basic recipe just as it is, or substitute up to a quarter of the white flour with wholewheat flour. Don't be tempted to add malted-grain flour or large seeds, as these will impede the opening of the pitta pocket. A few sesame seeds are fine – but you need to keep the dough smooth and simple, with no intermeshing pieces holding the hot air back as it expands and blows up the bread pocket like a balloon.

*For vegan diets, substitute the egg with soya cream, or soya milk or other vegan 'milk'.

Basic method (loaves)

1. Measure the warm water into a jug and stir in the sugar or honey and the yeast (if using fresh or traditional dried yeast). Leave to froth up – or, with the fresh yeast, simply stir until dissolved. (In both cases it is the dissolving that really counts, not the froth, which is merely a happy indicator that the yeast is alive and well.)

2. In a large bowl, combine the flour, salt and other dry ingredients (e.g. polenta, poppy seeds, sesame seeds), including the yeast if using superfine dried yeast (which also goes by the names of 'easy bake' or 'fast acting' dried yeast and is often sold in sachets).

3. Make a well in the middle of the dry ingredients and pour in the warm water and the oil. Mix until you have a soft, elasticky dough that holds together in one big dollop and does not spread out like a batter. Knead briefly and gently on a floured surface or (for the small quantity) in the bowl. When fairly smooth, with no crusty edges, return it to (or leave in) the bowl to rise. Spray the top with water (using a dedicated plant mister) to prevent it drying out – or cover the bowl loosely with a large lid or tea towel. Leave to rise in a warm place for an hour. (If you have an electric dough hook, knead the dough for 5-10 minutes at this first stage, until the dough forms a smooth, tacky dough around the hook. If using your hands, the dough will be easier to knead after it has done its first rise.)

4. When the dough has doubled in size, tip it on to a lightly floured surface and 'knock back'. Knead lightly and then divide into 6 if you are making the large quantity. Knead each ball again, and shape into an oval the appropriate size for your tin. Keep the joints at the bottom so the

...mooth. Note: try to minimize the amount of extra flour you incorporate when kneading – if the dough is right, hardly any extra flour will ...uired to prevent it sticking to the surface.

...ace the dough 'cocoons' in the lightly oiled bread tins. Spray with water and/or brush with egg wash and scatter with seeds or polenta. ...e to rise in a warm place for about 40 minutes – until doubled in size. The time required will vary with the ambient temperature and thus with the season. Pre-heat the oven to 180°C (350°F / Gas Mark 4) about 10 minutes before the bread is ready to bake.

6. When ready to go in the oven, the bread will usually have completely filled the bread tins and be poking out of them by an inch or so (in the middle). Any sign of dimpling on the surface means it has over-risen, so rush it into the oven. It is better for bread to go in the oven when still (just) on the rise, so that its last burst of rising is stimulated by the heat of the oven. Bake mid-oven for about 45 minutes. When ready, a loaf will normally fall easily out of its tin and sound hollow when tapped on its base. Tip out and cool on a wire rack.

Pitta bread

1. To create individual pitta breads, you will need plenty of metal baking trays. If using heavy baking trays, it is best to get them really hot in the oven first, as they will take longer to heat up to the critical dough-splitting temperature. Thinner baking trays (such as aluminium ones) can go into the oven cold. There's no need to oil the trays, as the pitta bread dough should be dry and slightly floury – not sticky.

2. Make either white or light brown (part-wholewheat) dough as described in the basic method, and cut or tear off tangerine-sized portions of it. Knead each into a smooth ball, pushing the outer edges to the middle and then placing seam-side down. Finish with a circular rotation under your palm, if you like. Use a tiny bit of flour to stop the dough sticking to you and/or the table top, if necessary. Put aside for 5-10 minutes or so. Pre-heat your oven to 200°C (400°F / Gas Mark 6).

3. Take your first shaped dough ball. Press down on it with your rolling pin and roll out, upwards and downwards, to form an oval shape (don't roll sideways). Normally one rolling is enough, but if the dough seems very elastic and reluctant to stay stretched, you may need to go back and roll it a second time. The pitta bread will be about 18-20cm (7-8") long and possibly only about 0.25cm (⅛") thick at its thinnest middle point.

4. Line the pitta breads up on the baking trays. Only a slight gap between them is necessary, as they won't stick to each other. As soon as one tray is full, put it in the oven and bake for 10 minutes. By this time, 90 per cent of the pittas should have inflated like hot air balloons. Turn them over and cook for a further 10 minutes, until lightly browned in places, but still mainly pale. Remove from the oven and cool on wire racks or eat warm: some people like to cover the pitta breads with a damp tea towel as soon as they emerge from the oven, to ensure a soft crust. While the pittas are cooking you can roll out another batch and put this into the oven too, production-line style. Keep a good gap between each tray, so that the hot air circulates evenly throughout the oven. Don't worry if one or two pittas don't separate in the middle (they will still puff up, but not puff open) – it is all part of the mystery of bread-making!

Braiding & breadsticks

1. Follow the basic method up to the end of Step 4, keeping the dough plain for breadsticks. Divide each loaf into three. Knead each piece of dough and begin to roll it into a sausage with your outstretched fingers and palms. When the dough resists any more stretching, leave it to relax and move on to the next piece. Once you have all three (or 18 for the large quantity) pieces lined up like giant dough-grubs, go back to the first and roll some more. The dough will now stretch more easily, into small fat snakes, about 30cm / 12" long).

2. With 18 small fat snakes in front of you, you are ready to begin plaiting. I usually re-plait the end I begin with, so there's no need for the first few cross-overs to be perfectly neat. When you get to the bottom of your plait, pinch the three ends together, securing with a little water if necessary, then go back and plait the beginning again! Move the loaf to a parchment-lined or floured baking tray, spraying it with water to keep it moist as the plait begins to rise. Line the plaited bread up on the baking trays, a hand's-width apart. Paint with beaten egg (or soya cream or soya milk) and sprinkle with poppy or sesame seeds if you like. Leave to rise for about 20-30 minutes in a warm place.

3. Bake in the middle of a moderate oven for 35-40 minutes, until well risen and golden-brown, with a hollow-sounding base. As this bread is fairly shallow, it will cook more quickly than the deep loaves. Leave to cool on wire racks as usual.

Breadsticks: Cut each 'snake' in four and continue to roll until only about 1cm (½") wide. Spray with water and roll in seeds or sea salt as desired. Bake for 20 minutes only – plus a further hour at 140°C (275°F / Gas Mark 1) to dry out.

Rolls

Make shaped dough balls as described for pitta bread, Step 2. Place the balls on a baking tray a good three-fingers'-width apart, spray with water, and allow to rise for about 20 minutes. (If you want to make rolls-in-a-clutch, as pictured on page 253 – there glazed with melted honey and sprinkled with polenta – place them just touching in an oiled round cake tin.) For a glossy finish, paint with beaten egg. Sprinkle with polenta, poppy seeds, sunflower seeds, or any other seeds of your choice. Bake for 25 minutes at 180°C (350°F / Gas Mark 4). If in a hurry, you can put them straight in the oven without waiting for them to rise – because they are small, they will still rise well, but in a slightly more ungainly fashion.

ot bread

ge, round, flour-dusted loaves of bread generously await our College community at breakfast, each enormous slice serving two people, at least. Made at midnight by our resident night owl and sourdough baker, Voirrey, it is really Moon Bread – voluminous, light and full of craters for cradling butter and jam.

This very popular recipe has been brought to us by both former MSc student Rebeh Furze and our Vegetarian Chef Tara Vaughan-Hughes. Explaining the concept, Tara said that there was a New York baker (Jim Lahey of the Sullivan Street Bakery) who set out to find a way anyone could easily create a well-risen, crusty loaf of the kind he most enjoyed – using a domestic oven. He found that using a heavy iron stew pan (such as a Le Creuset) to cook a slow-rising and barely kneaded white dough gave the best results, moderating the oven temperature and simulating the confined, steamy space of a professional bread oven – or indeed a traditional brick oven. Children will love to eat this bread – but should definitely not be involved in the actual baking of it, because of the high temperatures and heavy pots involved.

For 1 large round loaf	**For 2 very large loaves**
(1 x 22-25cm / 9-10") enamelled iron casserole with lid	(2 x 28-30cm / 11-12" iron pots with lids)
500g (1lb / 3 heaped cups) unbleached white flour	2kg (4lb 4oz)
¼ tsp dried yeast or 1 tsp fresh yeast, crumbled	1 tsp dried or 15g (½ oz) fresh
1¼ tsp salt	1½ tbsp
450ml (15fl oz / 2 scant cups) warm water	1.75l (3 pints / 3¾ US pints)

1. The day before you want to bake your bread, mix together all the ingredients in a big mixing bowl, with room for rising (no need to dissolve the dried yeast separately in this case). A fairly elastic, wet, dough will result – don't knead, just cover with cling film (or a damp tea towel, or a large lid) and leave overnight. The dough can be left for 12 to 24 hours.

2. On the day of baking, turn the sticky mass of dough out on to a floured surface, dividing into two mounds if you're making the large loaves. Sprinkle with more flour and turn it 'in on itself' by scooping up its edges and folding them back over its floury middle, pushing them down into the dough just a fraction off-centre. Do this four to six times: right side over left, left over right, top over bottom and bottom over top, etc. – in a loose kind of semi-kneading action. Pockets of flour and potholes, which you would normally want to knead away, will later turn into delicious aerated bubbles using this method, so resist the need to knead! Again, cover with cling film, etc. and leave for 15 minutes.

3. Get ready a tea towel and a large square of baking parchment.* Put the parchment on a tray to allow for easy manoeuvrability, and sprinkle it heavily with flour. Then, after the dough has rested for 15 minutes, gather its edges together and flip it over so it rests on its seam on the

Alternatively, a second tea towel – also heavily floured – can be used underneath the dough as it rises. This makes turning the dough into the hot pot a bit more tricky, but saves on perishable resources. When ready, remove the top towel, revealing the heavily dusted top of the dough, then slide your hand under the bottom towel, and flip the dough over into the hot pan – as pictured opposite. The seam will open up attractively as the bread cooks, and the flour will prevent the base from sticking.

floured sheet of parchment. Dust the top with flour, gather the corners of the parchment up loosely around the dough, and cover all with the tea towel, tucking it cosily around the dough – closely but not really tightly, as there needs to be some 'give' to allow for the dough's expansion. Put in a warm spot and leave for about 2 hours. (Summertime room temperature is ideal, but the bread will also double at a cooler ambient temperature, given time.)

4. Thirty minutes before the time is up, pre-heat your oven with your pot in it (with the lid on) to 220-240°C (425-475°F / Gas Mark 7-9) – whatever is your highest temperature. Your pot will be piping hot when the bread is ready for baking.

5. Remove the tea towel and use the corners of the parchment to lift the dough and place it in the hot pan, with the parchment still underneath. Cover with the lid and bake for 30 minutes (small quantity) or 40 minutes (large quantity).

6. Take the lid off and bake for another 5-10 minutes (or 15-20 minutes for the larger loaves), until the top is lightly browned. Remove the bread from the pot, discard the parchment and cool on a wire rack. The parchment can be reused until it gets too brown.

Bibliography

Use this list as a springboard to discover more inspiring books by the same authors.

Vegetarian cooking

The Accidental Vegetarian: Delicious food without meat
Simon Rimmer
Mitchell Beazley (2010)

The Cranks Recipe Book
David Canter, Kay Canter
& Daphne Swann
Orion Books (1982, 15th edn 2004)

The Moosewood Cookbook
Mollie Katzen
Ten Speed Press (1992)

Paradiso Seasons
Dennis Cotter
Atrium Press (2003)

Plenty
Yotam Ottolenghi
Chronicle Books (2011)

River Cottage Veg Every Day!
Hugh Fearnley-Whittingstall
Bloomsbury Publishing (2011)

General cookbooks

(not vegetarian, but including some great veggie recipes)

The Biodynamic Food and Cookbook: Real nutrition that doesn't cost the Earth
Wendy Cook
Cygnus Books (2006)

Real Fast Food
Nigel Slater
Penguin Books (1993, re-set edition 2006)

The Riverford Farm Cookbook
Guy Watson & Jane Baxter
Fourth Estate (2008)

Vegan and gluten-free cookbooks

Gluten-free and Vegan Bread: Artisanal recipes to make at home
Jennifer Katzinger
Sasquatch Books (2012)

Healthy Gluten-free Eating
Darina Allen & Rosemary Kearney
Coeliac UK (2009)

Vegan Pie in the Sky
Isa Chandra Moskowitz
& Terry Hope Romero
Lifelong Books (2011)

Bread

Bread Matters: Why and how to make your own
Andrew Whitley
Fourth Estate Ltd (2009)

Do Sourdough: Slow bread for busy lives
Andrew Whitley
Do Books (2014)

The Handmade Loaf: The best European and artisan recipes for homemade bread
Dan Lepard
Mitchell Beazley (2008)

Food, lifestyle & ecology

These books give a context to our discussions about food that goes beyond the realm of cooking, entering the domain of politics, philosophy and social history.

Coming Home to Eat: The pleasures and politics of local food
Gary Paul Nabham
W. W. Norton & Co (2002, re-issued 2009)

Local Food: How to make it happen in your community
Tamzin Pinkerton & Rob Hopkins
Green Books (2009)

The Omnivore's Dilemma: The search for a perfect meal in a fast-food world
Michael Pollan
Bloomsbury Publishing (2006)

Small Is Beautiful: A study of economics as if people mattered
E. F. Schumacher
Abacus (1973), Random House (2011)

The Transition Handbook: From oil dependency to local resilience
Rob Hopkins
Green Books (2008)

Resources

The organizations listed below, many of which are mentioned in this book, are each working towards a more ecologically sustainable and fairer future. For all of them, a focus on food is central.

Fairtrade Foundation, London, UK
www.fairtrade.org.uk
Tel: +44 (0)20 7405 5942
Independent non-profit organization that licenses use of the Fairtrade mark on products in the UK in accordance with internationally agreed standards.

Institute for Food and Development Policy (Food First), California, USA
www.foodfirst.org
Tel: (+1) 510 654 4400
Shapes how people think by analyzing the root causes of global hunger, poverty and ecological degradation. Develops solutions in partnership with movements working for social change.

International Society for Ecology & Culture (ISEC)
www.localfutures.org
Tel: (+44) (0)1392 581175
Non-profit organization working to resist global-ization, educate for action and promote the renewal of local communities and economies.

National Farmers' Retail & Markets Association (FARMA), Winchester, UK
www.farma.org.uk
Tel: +44 (0)845 4588420
Cooperative of farmers and producers selling on a local scale. Organizes farmers' markets and provides links to them and farm shop news, etc.

Real Bread Campaign
Tel: (+44) (0)20 7837 1228
www.sustainweb.org/realbread
National organization championing community bakeries. Helps you search for real bread and baking lessons in your area. Part of Sustain: the alliance for better food and farming.

Roots of Change, San Francisco, USA
www.rootsofchange.org
Tel: (+1) 510 285 5639
Works to develop and support a collaborative network of leaders and institutions in California with interest in establishing a sustainable food system in the state by 2030.

Schumacher College, Devon, UK
www.schumachercollege.org.uk
Tel: +44 (0)1803 865934
Postgraduate and short courses that offer transformative learning for a sustainable future.

Slow Food International, Bra, Italy
www.slowfood.com
Tel: (+39) 017/2 419611
Global grassroots association, linking good food to a commitment to community and environment.

Slow Food UK, London, UK
www.slowfood.org.uk
Tel: +44 (0)20 7099 1132

Slow Food USA, Brooklyn, USA
www.slowfoodusa.org
Tel: (+1) 718 260 8000

Soil Association, Bristol, UK
www.soilassociation.org
Tel: (+44) (0)117 314 5000
Charity campaigning for planet-friendly organic food and farming. Organic certification in the UK.

Transition Network, Devon, UK
www.transitionnetwork.org
Tel: (+44) (0)1803 865669
Charity that links and supports practical, community-led responses to climate change and diminishing supplies of cheap energy.

Picture credits: All photographs are © Joanna Brown except as follows:
Izabella Ceccato: page 23, bottom left. Julia Ponsonby: page 9, centre; page 11, centre and far right; page 16, right; page 18, right of centre; page 19, left; page 23, top left and bottom right; page 99; page 181; page 218; page 222; page 226. Ruth Rae: page 180 (photo and lemon cake decoration!). Delia Spatareanu: pages 4–5. Bethan Stagg: page 9, bottom left and left of centre. William Thomas: page 9, right; page 11, right of centre; page 12, far left and far right; page 18, far left, far right and left of centre; page 19, right; page 23, top right. Tara Vaughan-Hughes: page 22, bottom left; page 230.

Index

Also by Green Books

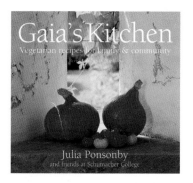

Gaia's Kitchen: Vegetarian recipes for family and community
Julia Ponsonby

Winner of the Gourmand World Cookbook 'Best Vegetarian Cookbook' Award, *Gaia's Kitchen* is filled with a sumptuous selection of healthy recipes that calls upon the best of Mediterranean, Californian, Indian and Mexican vegetarian cooking. As well as old favourites, rich in cheese and eggs, *Gaia's Kitchen* offers a variety of tempting new vegan dishes using ingredients such as pulses, tofu and tempeh. Alongside family-size quantities, the book includes community-size recipes, making it invaluable for teaching centres, caterers and anyone who wants to prepare a vegetarian banquet for thirty or forty friends.

Food from your Forest Garden: How to harvest, cook and preserve your forest garden produce
Martin Crawford and Caroline Aitken

How do you cook heartnuts, hawthorn fruits or hostas? What's the best way to preserve autumn olives or to dry chestnuts? Forest gardening gives you a novel way of growing edible crops in vertical layers – and this book offers creative and imaginative ways to enjoy the fruits of your labour. With over 100 recipes for over 50 different species, as well as details of preserving methods, this beautiful book is the perfect companion for the experienced forest gardener and will provide inspiration for anyone thinking of growing their own crops.

About Green Books

Environmental publishers for 25 years.

For our full range of titles and to order direct from our website, see **www.greenbooks.co.uk**

Join our mailing list for new titles, special offers, reviews, author appearances and events:
www.greenbooks.co.uk/subscribe

For bulk orders (50+ copies) we offer discount terms. Contact **sales@greenbooks.co.uk** for details.

Send us a book proposal on eco-building, science, gardening, etc.: see **www.greenbooks.co.uk/for-authors**

 @Green_Books   /GreenBooks